Counselling

The Skills of Finding Solutions to Problems

Robert Manthei

London and New York

First published 1997 by Addison Wesley Longman
46 Hillside Road
Glenfield, Auckland
New Zealand

Published in the UK by Routledge
11 New Fetter Lane, London EC4P 4EE

Simultaneously published in the USA and Canada by Routledge
29 West 35th Street, New York, NY 10001

Printed in Malaysia through Longman Malaysia

British Library Cataloguing in Publication Data
A catalogue record for this book is available from the British Library

Library of Congress Cataloguing in Publication Data
A catalogue record for this book has been requested

ISBN 0-415-16206-8

Preface

What is this book about?

This book describes counselling as the intentional use of skills in the process of helping others to identify and implement solutions to their problems. The approach taken is primarily practical rather than theoretical and has been designed to give readers numerous opportunities to practise skills, consider and reflect on ideas and concepts, and to integrate new learning into their previous knowledge about counselling. Numerous exercises have been provided to aid this process.

Counselling: the skills of finding solutions to problems combines micro-counselling skills and two models of counselling (problem-solving and solution-focused) in a way that will enable counsellors to know, understand and clearly describe what they are doing with clients. The result is a generic model of counselling that tends to accelerate the process of client change; is respectful of clients' abilities and wishes; is optimistic in its orientation, and is reality-based in that it seeks solutions to client problems that enable them to cope better in their daily lives rather than 'self-actualise' to a higher level, though that too may occur.

The material in the book is presented as a sound and broadly-based orientation to the practice of professional counselling. It represents *one* phase of a professional counsellor's learning and development.

Whom is it for?

The book has been written for people in a variety of roles and work settings: those new to counselling and seeking basic or initial training, experienced counsellors wanting to extend their learning, social workers, community workers, social service volunteers, rehabilitation workers, medical personnel, speech and language therapists, and counsellor educators. The book has been written in simple, straightforward language that makes the process of counselling accessible and understandable to experienced and inexperienced helpers alike.

How the book was developed

The book was derived from the author's more than twenty years' experience as a counsellor educator, the last six of which have been spent teaching the approach described in this book, a model which integrates problem-solving and solution-finding. It has always been my belief that the process of counselling should be demystified and that the skills should be shared widely with people both inside and outside of the profession. Therefore, I have made every effort to present a model of helping that is clear, easy to teach and learn, encouraging of critical reflection and analysis, effective with and respectful of clients, and one that produces results with clients that are readily assessible. The result, I think, provides counsellors with a clear 'road map' to guide their work and a solid foundation upon which to build future learning and self-development as a counsellor.

Students trained in this model have reported the following sequence of development:

- at first they are reluctant to give up focusing on client problems and working in ways that are largely intuitive and feel right;
- initially they find that learning discrete skills feels awkward and disruptive to their natural, intuitive styles;
- however, as they learn more about the skills of problem solving and finding solutions to problems and start to apply this new learning with their clients, they quickly begin to see the enhanced effectiveness of their counselling and become confident in the model;
- as their confidence and expertise grow they attend less to client problems and more quickly guide clients into identifying abilities and new possibilities for change, and searching for solutions that work;
- finally, after they have developed competence in applying the finding-solutions-to-problems model, some then begin to evaluate other models of helping and incorporate appropriate aspects of those models into their work.

This sequence of development is not the same for every student; nevertheless, it represents a general pattern that has been observed over six years of teaching the model. In that time, the finding-solutions-to-problems model has proved to be an effective approach that has enabled students safely and quickly to increase their confidence and counselling competence. I hope that in reading this book you will experience the same thing!

Acknowledgements

I am especially indebted to John Small and Anne Munro with whom I authored three versions of a book on counselling skills, the most recent being *Counselling: the skills of problem-solving* (1988). Some of the material from that book appears, albeit extensively altered and rearranged, in this one. My two co-authors have retired from counsellor training and school counselling respectively, and while neither was interested in contributing to *Counselling: the skills of finding solutions to problems*, they were encouraging and willing to have appropriate material from the 1988 book used in this one. I thank them for their generosity and support. Also, John's careful proofreading of the manuscript was invaluable.

I am also greatly indebted to Judi Miller with whom I have taught, researched and published since 1988. She has been a creative teacher, insightful critic and willing collaborator in helping to develop a counsellor education programme that integrates problem-solving with solution-focused counselling. Her many insightful suggestions on the manuscript were greatly appreciated.

Perhaps the most important person in helping me decide to write this book has been my wife, Marjorie. From the beginning she has been an enthusiastic supporter and persistent motivator. And, being a trained counsellor and a former vocational counsellor herself, her many comments on the manuscript have been incisive and unfailingly helpful.

Two other people have played key roles in my thinking and development as a counsellor educator. Distinguished Professor Allen Ivey has for many years been a role model, supporter and friend. His positive comments on chapter 2 came at just the right time. Insoo Kim Berg (of the Brief Family Therapy Center, Milwaukee, Wisconsin, USA) first introduced solution-focused counselling to me in 1991. Her competent and clear exposition on the model radically altered my thinking about counselling, and for that, I thank her.

Thanks also to Rosemary Stagg, Managing Director of Addison Wesley Longman Publishers, for planting the seed for this book by suggesting that a revision of the 1988 book be written. Finally, my heartfelt thanks to all of the students who over the years have contributed to and helped refine my ideas on the practice and teaching of counselling. They have all been willing and able students, counsellors, critics and supporters.

Robert J. Manthei
December 1996

Contents

Introduction

 ounselling is becoming increasingly professionalised. As this happens, there is a need to show how, with training and practice, it can be performed more effectively. This is a challenging task, and this book does not claim to cover all aspects of counselling. Its main contribution is to show how people can be helped by the ethical use of certain practical skills within the finding-solutions-to-problems model of counselling.

The focus of the book: finding solutions to problems

The purpose of this book is to describe how people seeking counselling can be helped to solve their problems. For clients, this process of **finding successful solutions to problems** should also lead to enhanced self-understanding and an increased ability to find solutions to other problems in the future. The term *counselling* is employed here to cover the various skills and principles of helping used in this process. Although the skills and principles that follow are described within a face-to-face relationship between two or more people (counsellor and client(s)), it is recognised that the essentials of individual counselling are directly applicable to other settings as well.

The approach presented assumes that it is imperative for counsellors to work within a framework or model that ensures that their counselling is a planned, intentional activity. Counselling should never be a wholly subjective process that is guided by whim, hunches and the random use of techniques. While the intuitive side of counselling is acknowledged, more emphasis is placed in this book on the thoughtful application of observable skills guided by sound principles of helping.

The focus is on giving counsellors a structure for dealing with client problems that is neither too loose nor too restrictive and one which allows a variety of skills to be used, depending on the counsellor's purpose and the client's needs at any particular time. The central features, described in chapters 5, 6 and 7, include a range of verbal skills that can be used at each stage of the finding-solutions-to-problems model of helping. This is preceded, in chapters 2, 3 and 4 by a discussion of cross-cultural competence, counsellors' self-awareness and their role in the counselling relationship, and the process of finding solutions to problems.

Throughout the book there is an emphasis on values, attitudes, skills, and ideas that can be readily learnt and put into practice by counsellors working in a wide variety of settings. There are several assumptions in this book about counselling which should be made explicit. Firstly, the counselling skills described focus on influencing people through talking. Other techniques (such as the use of specialised tests, equipment or medication) or the specialised knowledge that is required to work effectively in particular settings (e.g., hospitals, substance abuse clinics, child-care centres), raise complex issues about the rights of clients and the qualifications of counsellors and are considered beyond the scope of this book.

Secondly, the model of helping and the interpersonal skills described are not presumed to be neutral or value-free. Rather, counselling, whatever the approach used, is taken to represent a set of beliefs and assumptions about people, about interpersonal relationships, and about ways of influencing others. For example, when a counsellor and client represent different cultures, genders, life experiences, world views, ages, religions and income levels, such differences will very often have important effects on counselling. Thirdly, since such differences are present in every counselling relationship, counsellors must also learn to be comfortable with diversity and competent to deal with it (see chapter 2).

Another basic issue concerning values is whether, in any particular case, face-to-face counselling is in fact the most appropriate way of helping. Instead of encouraging clients to keep making appointments to discuss their problems, the counsellor may be well advised to suggest other means of improvement such as participation in drama, music, physical activity, a change of diet, meditation, or one of the many other forms of helping described in chapter 9. Broadly construed, counselling encompasses a wide variety of helping roles besides the traditional face-to-face relationship with an individual client. It is important that counsellors be knowledgeable about such alternatives, and when they seem appropriate, encourage clients to try them.

Effective counselling requires much more than the practice of particular verbal skills. Counsellors need to know themselves well. They need to know and understand other people. They need to know about and be able to work effectively with cultural differences. They need to know a good deal about social institutions and their influences, and they need realistic knowledge about the forces in society which create advantages and disadvantages: the market-place, politics, racism, sexism, and similar forms of prejudice. Power and status issues underlie many of society's problems, and as discussed later in this chapter, they are also present within counselling relationships, no matter how much counsellors would like to minimise them or deny their importance. This book does not deal directly with all of these important topics, but no one should claim competence as a counsellor without some knowledge of them.

The finding-solutions-to-problems model for counselling is a skills-based, problem-solving model that emphasises solutions rather than difficulties and client strengths and abilities rather than deficits. The model is flexible and robust enough for counsellors to incorporate aspects of other approaches. There are, however, several important themes and assumptions about counselling and counsellors that underlay the specific model presented in this book:

- All counselling can be thought of as a process of problem-solving, a commonly used, meta-theoretical approach identified by Dixon and Glover (1984). Within this meta-model, however, there are different approaches to and perspectives of problems. One such perspective, *solution-focused counselling*, will be presented as a preferred form of brief, client-respectful counselling (see chapter 3).

- Many people need help in coping with their difficulties. In general, counselling seeks to help people manage their affairs more effectively in daily life, not to find a cure for some diagnosed personality deficit.

- Because positive outcomes are usually achieved in five to ten sessions (Lambert & Cattani-Thompson, 1996), counselling should be planned to be as brief and simple as possible.

- Most people who seek counselling have within themselves most of the resources for coping which counsellors can help them to identify and strengthen.

- While counsellors offer a variety of counselling skills within a relationship of caring, respect and optimism, ultimately it is the client who determines the nature of the problem, the goals to be achieved and the success of counselling.

- People usually respond better to counselling when they feel some degree of sincerity, warmth, acceptance and empathy towards them, and their counsellor's optimism and confidence about the resolution of their problems.

- The activity of counselling is usefully described as the appropriate use of specific, definable skills at each stage of the helping process (see chapters 5, 6 and 7).

- The definition of counselling should not be restricted to face-to-face work with clients. It is much more broadly based than that and includes a variety of other change agent roles, activities and skills, including consultation and training, family counselling, group work, social work, teaching, supervision, and administration (see chapter 9).

- All counselling involves cultural differences (Pedersen & Ivey, 1993). Since counselling cannot be divorced from these considerations, it is essential that all counsellors develop competence in cross-cultural interactions (see chapter 2).

- Counsellors must be self-aware – of their values, beliefs, biases, cultural capital, motivation and desire to help others. An attitude of critical self-reflection – of oneself and one's work – must be central to every counsellor's work (see chapter 3).

- Counsellors have responsibilities as professionals to their clients, their colleagues and to the wider community (see chapter 8).

- Counsellors have an ethical duty to maintain and develop themselves professionally by undergoing supervision and continuing their education.

Learning the material presented in this book should be seen as the beginning of your training as a counsellor. It will give you a sound model for conceptualising your work with clients, teach you the necessary skills to implement the model, and encourage you to practise cultural sensitivity and critical self-reflection in your work. However, your on-going training and development should continue for as long as you counsel (see chapter 10).

What is counselling?

It is useful to consider at the outset some of the ways in which counselling relationships differ from ordinary social interaction between friends, acquaintances, and colleagues. There are, of course, many similarities, but in counselling certain features are evident to a greater degree. People start to become clients when they seek help or begin to express their concerns to another person who is willing to listen, clarify what is heard, and help them find solutions using interpersonal skills of the kinds described in this book. Many of these skills are not unique to counselling, but the relationship in which they occur approximates counselling when the relationship is voluntary; when it provides hope, healing and comfort (Peavy, 1996); when it is based on the understanding that there will exist a high degree of confidentiality and when it includes agreement on the personal responsibility of the client. In addition, counsellors do not allow their counselling relationships to be compromised by any other relationships they might have with their clients (called boundary violations (Sheppard, 1994)), for example, as friends or business associates. The more clearly these features are apparent, the more appropriate it is to regard the relationship as counselling.

Like related activities such as teaching, administering, or leading others, counselling can seem somewhat mysterious. But it should not be regarded as a mystique or special gift bestowed on only a few individuals. While it may be true that some people seem to be effective as counsellors without having studied counselling systematically, enough progress has been made in studying and teaching the counselling process to justify confidence in describing it as observable skills used in a planned and intentional way, within a certain kind of relationship and for the purpose of helping clients find solutions to their problems.

A skills-based approach to training

If counselling is to be demystified and made more widely available to clients, the first step is to describe the process and its component skills in language that is both clear and non-technical. There are many possible views of the counselling process, but for learning and teaching purposes it is particularly useful to view it as a series of purposeful, goal-oriented interactions within an authentic relationship, consisting of certain behaviours by one person which partly influence the way the other person responds. What the counsellor says usually has some effect on what the client says, and vice versa. This perspective is not intended to diminish the importance of qualitative factors such as the degree of empathy shown by the counsellor. These factors can be extremely important in counselling and it is essential that counsellors are knowledgeable about them. This book, however, deals with these matters only briefly; its main focus is on explicating specific interactions and their effects within a finding-solutions-to-problems model.

A skills-based approach has been used for several reasons:

- Skills-based training approaches have been shown to be more effective in training counsellors than alternatives (Pedersen & Ivey, 1993, p. 2). By teaching identifiable skills that are embedded within a sound model or framework of helping, trainees can more quickly develop competency, confidence and greater clarity about the structure and aims of the process.

- A skills-based approach helps to demystify counselling and makes its practices and techniques more accessible to students and the public. Skills-based training also reduces the likelihood of the trainer being seen or portrayed as a guru – one whose skill and insight is unfathomable and therefore unattainable by others.

- A skills approach will increase a counsellor's range of options and possibilities in working with clients, a notion described by Ivey et al. (1993) as *counsellor intentionality*.

- The teaching, supervision, assessment and monitoring of counselling practices can be based on specific, observable behaviours using a common terminology and a language that is relatively objective, neutral and one that clarifies the process rather than obscures what takes place. Skills training can still allow for less easily identifiable factors such as personal qualities, attitudes and processes of decision-making to be taught, discussed and evaluated.

In practice, the use of specific skills and techniques is common to virtually every model of counselling. Effective counsellors, whatever model they follow, use different skills at different times according to what seems to be most helpful. For example, in the early stages of counselling when one is trying to get a clear view both of what is working well for the client and what is not (the problem), it is usually best to listen carefully and to take note of the client's overt behaviours, abilities and concerns. At other times, influencing clients by encouraging them to do something may be much more appropriate. For example, sometimes a counsellor will purposely ignore obvious signs of anxiety in a client. At other times the signs may be commented on openly but neutrally, but nothing more is done, thus indicating an acceptance of the behaviour.

Alternatively, a counsellor may decide to try to reduce the anxiety level so a freer discussion can take place. Whatever is decided, counsellors must not only be aware of the likely consequences of such variations but also have the skill to carry out their intentions. Exactly what the counsellor decides to do is, of course, both a personal and professional decision – a function of training, experience, knowledge and the approach to counselling being used.

There are limitations to skills-based training, of course, and these need to be borne in mind when using this book. First, skills are not in and of themselves therapeutic – they are merely verbal techniques that may prompt, provoke or promote solution-finding thought, self-assessment, and/or action, but to do so they must still be used with care, good judgement and theoretical intention. Second, skills themselves are not culturally neutral. This cannot be stressed enough. They need to be tested, modified and adapted to fit particular cultures and contexts (Pedersen & Ivey, 1993).

Third, there can be a period early in skills-based counsellor training when counsellors report feeling less natural and increasingly awkward in their counselling styles. They almost invariably report, however, that as their familiarity with the skills and their competence in using them increase, so too do their feelings of fluency and naturalness. Because of this, it is useful to forewarn counsellors at the beginning of their training and to reassure them that their initial awkwardness will gradually evolve into greater confidence and self-assurance with the skills.

Research and theory in counselling

In spite of clear evidence that counselling is effective when compared with no-treatment and placebo controls, it is important to emphasise, that so far, years of careful comparative studies have failed to show consistently that any one theory or approach is generally superior to any other (Lambert & Cattani-Thompson, 1996; Seligman, 1996). In fact, there is a growing belief that no single approach is adequate for use with all client problems (Norcross & Grencavage, 1989). There are a number of reasons for this belief. The main ones are:

- It is extremely difficult and expensive to design controlled studies which satisfactorily compare even just two theories, and even more difficult to generalise empirically-derived results from such studies to actual counselling settings (Seligman, 1996).

- The hope that sophisticated, comparative methods such as meta-analysis would show which theories were best has not yet been realised either (Ivey et al., 1987; Lambert & Cattani-Thompson, 1996). It should be noted, however, that this does not mean that counselling, generally speaking, is ineffective – only that it is very difficult to show that one particular approach is best. Nevertheless, it is now widely accepted that counselling is indeed effective, that client gains are made in a relatively short period of time and that those gains are maintained over time (Lambert & Cattani-Thompson, 1996; Seligman, 1996).

- Because of the cross-fertilisation of ideas through journals, training programmes and professional organisations, it is most unlikely that any theory is now distinctly different from all others in the way it is practised. In fact, it is currently accepted that common factors across approaches, rather than specific differences, account for a sizeable proportion of the improvement in clients due to counselling (Lambert & Cattani-Thompson, 1996).

- Individual differences between clients require different approaches, so that unless a counsellor has the means, ability and the desire to match every client to a distinct theory and set of techniques, some sort of eclecticism seems inevitable.

- Finally, research has shown that the best predictors of counselling outcome are not specific approaches, but client variables and relationship factors – in that order (Lambert & Cattani-Thompson, 1996).

Using research on counselling to inform and guide one's work should be every counsellor's aim. Unfortunately, using research in this way is not at all common, as evidenced by Sexton and Whiston's (1996) findings that most counsellors neither read research nor conduct it. With increasing calls for accountability in counselling and greater regulation of the profession by insurers (called third-party payers), counsellors can no longer afford to ignore current research findings (Sexton & Whiston, 1996). Although keeping up to date with current research is not easy, it can be done by:

- subscribing to and reading journals that publish outcome research (see, for example, the list provided by Sexton (1996));

- reading reviews and meta-analyses of large numbers of studies which are published in journals (some journals now publish regular reviews of research every two or three years);

- reading books that publish reviews of research and counselling practices, e.g., the *Handbook of psychotherapy and behaviour change* (Bergin & Garfield, 1994);

- attending seminars, workshops and discussion groups where there is regular discussion of current research and best practices.

exercise **1.1**

1   In order to begin familiarising yourself with the counselling research literature and how to access it, think of a question or concern you have about counselling. Next, go to a library to search what the literature has to say about that topic. To do this you may have to learn how to search *Psychological Abstracts* or *Sociological Abstracts*, use computer-assisted searching tools (CD-ROM data bases like *ERIC*, *Psychlit*), and, finally,

integrate in a sensible way the results of the studies you are able to access. After you have finished your search, share your findings and experience with others by discussing the following:

  i   how and why you selected your original question or topic;
  ii   the process which you used to search for relevant literature;
  iii a brief summary of what you discovered about your topic;
  iv a summary of what you learned about the whole process by doing this exercise.

2   Repeat this exercise at various points during your training. Very quickly you should become familiar with the resources that are available to you and how best to access them.

Although this book presents a specific model of counselling (finding solutions to concerns within a problem-solving framework), it is recognised that there are many other theories and approaches to counselling – by one count over 400 (Karasu, 1986). Counsellors are urged to acquaint themselves with the major ones and to integrate features of those that seem most useful into their own work in an informed, purposeful way. Learning different theories can provide new perspectives on clients' problems and suggest alternative ways for counsellors to help. This approach fits in with the growing integration movement that stresses the common aspects rather than the differences among the many approaches (Norcross & Grencavage, 1989).

Theorising about counselling is presented in this book from a very practical point of view: as providing a rationale for whatever model of counselling is adopted, and for guiding the counsellor's thinking and behaviour about practical issues as they arise in the counselling relationship. However, the specific theory or model outlined is that of an overarching model of problem-solving (see chapter 3). Briefly, it is recommended that counsellors accept as meaningful the problems and complaints that clients present, and to assume that clients can be helped to understand themselves and their situations better, can identify and implement their own solutions, and can use their existing strengths and competencies to implement these solutions. The model does not require extensive investigations into causes and factors from the past, although these may be useful in some circumstances. Nor does it depend upon counsellors being expert at psychiatric diagnoses and interpretations, although such skills may also be useful to have. The approach described does assume that counsellors will be constantly considering possible reasons and explanations for things they find puzzling and regularly reflecting critically on their work.

Self-reflection in counselling

When talking to clients, counsellors are often processing many different kinds of information at once and considering the relevance of that information to the particular case. Counsellors may wonder, for example, how well they are communicating with their clients and vice versa; what sorts of approaches might be best to try first; their subjective reactions to clients and what they are saying, and the possible impact on clients of various life crises that have been mentioned. Counsellors deal with these issues simultaneously, and some counsellors may find the pressure of doing so difficult and stressful. But effective counselling demands constant analysis of the process and questioning oneself. Acquiring the habit of self-reflective thinking about their counselling and talking difficulties over with supervisors (see chapter 8) are ways counsellors can monitor their work, confirm their preferred theories and practices, and develop further their own personal theories of counselling. This sort of self-critical and self-reflective theorising is every bit as important, in fact usually more important, than the theoretical knowledge that is gained only from reading.

exercise 1.2

One of the aims of this book is to encourage you to articulate your own theory of helping by describing the values, attitudes and beliefs that shape and influence your work as a counsellor, the goals you have for clients and the techniques you use in helping others. It is accepted that counsellors' preferences for particular approaches to counselling reflect their personal experiences, culture and personality (Ahia, 1991; McConnaughy, 1987). Therefore, their theoretical preferences can be read as a form of personal and professional autobiography. That is, the choice of theory will reveal as much or more about the counsellor as it does the current standing of that theory as a method of helping. As a counsellor, you should recognise this subjective element in your preferred way of working, understand it and be able to use it in your counselling.

1   Write down in some detail the values, attitudes and beliefs that presently shape your view of counselling and how it should be conducted. Where did these views originate? How do they translate into practices with clients? How do they govern your aims or goals for clients?

Complete this exercise before proceeding further.

2   Save the notes you made in #1. Update them at the end of your training by amending or adding to your personal theory of counselling. What aspects of your theory have changed and why? How does this information add to your autobiography as a counsellor?

3   Save these first two versions of your personal theory. Update them a second time, at least a year after you have completed your formal counsellor training. When you have done so, note the modifications you made and the reasons for them.

NOTE: You may find writing a personal theory to be a difficult and challenging exercise. Be assured that others who have written one have attested to its value over time.

Ethical practice in counselling

The primary role of a counsellor is not that of merely using certain techniques with warmth and sympathy and guided by an acceptable theory or model of counselling. Counselling is essentially an ethical task: its purpose is to serve the client's best interests. These may be difficult to determine, but the roles of servant and ally are central to counselling, for the counsellor's ultimate responsibility is to empower people, to help them to get what they want, provided that this does not endanger the client or others or seriously conflict with the counsellor's personal or professional values. Professional codes of ethics are usually instructive in these matters by laying down guidelines for best practice (see, for example, the codes of ethics in appendices A and B).

However, if clients show clearly that they do not want help and do not wish to change – for whatever reason – then counsellors have no right to use their skills to impose their views, regardless of their expertise, insights, or their ability to predict outcomes. Behind this assertion lies an awareness that sometimes the counsellor's desire to give help may be as strong as, or even stronger than, the client's need to receive it. As will be discussed in chapters 2 and 3, counsellors must be knowledgeable not only about others, their values, beliefs and culture, but also about their own values, beliefs and culture.

Values

Values can be thought of as the 'oughts' or ideals on which decisions are based. They are an indispensable part of counselling. All individuals behave in accordance with a set of values, whether these have been thought out and made explicit or not. Therefore, it is impossible for a counsellor to maintain a position of neutrality.

Counsellors will be concerned with four types of values: moral, social, legal, and spiritual. Moral values are concerned with concepts of good and evil and often find expression in social values. We may subscribe to the idea that love is good and express this socially in upholding the institutions of marriage and the family. The law may then support these values by regarding marriage as a legal contract, and by protecting children through laws relating to custody and maintenance. When these values are placed in a larger context, such as consideration of the meaning and purpose of life, the spiritual dimension exists.

Since counsellors will be involved in value questions of varying levels of importance, are there any basic values to which society can expect counsellors to subscribe? In chapter 3, a number of desirable counsellor characteristics are described, among them acceptance of others, open-mindedness, respect for others, self-awareness and objectivity. It is reasonable to assume that underlying such personal qualities are the basic values of tolerance, concern for others, recognition of the worth of each individual, honesty, truthfulness, goodwill, and caring. These values are widely accepted as essential to constructive community life. Because of the nature of the counselling relationship, society expects that counsellors will also hold these values. In fact, many counselling codes of ethics list similar principles that are meant to guide counsellors' ethical decision-making and practice: doing clients no harm, keeping one's promises, promoting the welfare of clients, and exercising professional integrity and social responsibility (Schulz, 1994).

Inevitably, counsellors will find themselves at variance in values and lifestyle with some of their clients and with sections of the community, particularly on controversial issues such as sexual preferences, contraception, abortion, euthanasia, drug use, and attitudes towards racial and gender differences. Differences in age, race, sex, and socio-economic status increase the likelihood of these sorts of value conflicts. For example, a counsellor may believe that open sharing of feelings, respecting the rights of others, and talking through disagreements are the best ways of working through a conflict. The client, however, may live in a setting where physical violence is an acceptable method of settling arguments and anything else is regarded as soft or ineffective. When social workers investigate adoption or fostering placements, they may be convinced of the personal qualities of the prospective parents but the home may not meet the physical criteria. Schools often expect guidance counsellors to persuade academically able pupils who resist attending university to change their minds. How counsellors resolve and act on these differences will determine their acceptance by and effectiveness with those clients. The starting point is for counsellors to be aware of their own values (review exercise 1.2).

In cases where a particular client's values are inconsistent, counsellors are faced with a choice. They could choose to confront the client with the inconsistencies, hoping to help the client clarify these values, or they could choose not to confront the client and focus instead on another aspect of the client's situation. Whatever is done, the outcome can still be difficult. Very aggressive clients may appear to value their children's well-being by seeking help with parental management skills, but may then refuse to compromise at all, revealing their real position which is one of rejection. It takes courage to confront such clients, and skill and sensitivity to search for and focus on their abilities and successes. This choice – whether to focus on solutions and client strengths or on problems and client deficits – is central to the approach outlined in chapter 4 and discussed in more detail in chapters 5, 6 and 7.

Counsellors usually work within institutional limitations. Each agency, preferably explicitly but sometimes only implicitly, has boundaries within which counsellors are expected to function. A church counselling agency may insist that its counsellors be committed Christians and that the spiritual dimension be an essential part of any counselling. A school may insist on the right of parents to know that their children are receiving counselling and may place age limits on certain types of counselling.

Society's expectations of the counsellor's role, especially in the counselling of juveniles, may cause value conflicts for counsellors. Consider, for example, the position of the counsellor counselling a 16-year-old schoolgirl who is living with a 32-year-old separated father of two. The girl's concern may be to cope with the stresses associated with this situation while choosing to remain in it, but the parents', the school's and society's expectation would probably be that the counsellor should attempt to persuade the girl and her partner to terminate the relationship. Counsellors may also meet clients who have contravened society's standards or broken the law. There might then be a conflict between the counsellors' duty to their clients and their duty to society, especially where serious crimes are revealed, e.g., serious drug offences, extensive theft, hit-and-run driving or even murder.

It is not possible to give specific directions to resolve all of these types of value conflicts, but the following general guidelines may help.

- Everyone has the right to follow his/her own conscience.

- To remain true to their own values, counsellors cannot divorce themselves from their own social, moral, and spiritual beliefs. They have a right to them. But they must know themselves, recognise the cultural origins of their values, be honest about them and still act in a professionally ethical manner.

- Their task is to help clients clearly examine their own values, establish their own identity, make their own decisions (preferably avoiding harmful extremes) and implement them.

- Most clients are quick to see through phoney values and to challenge double standards. Counsellors should recognise the justice of some allegations clients make rather than automatically defending the institution and their colleagues. Instead, it may be possible and more productive to teach clients appropriate ways of challenging the system.

- Counsellors do not have the right to impose their own values on clients or pursue their own needs in counselling.

- Their position is not that of judge: their function is not to assign guilt or innocence but to engage in and encourage objective evaluation of attitudes, standards and actions through the use of a procedure for ethical decision-making. This matter is discussed in greater detail in chapter 8 (in the section *Commitment to a Code of Ethics*).

- Many clients have an expectation and fear of being judged. They already feel guilty because of having contravened their own, their family's, or society's moral code. They are seldom helped by denying the reality of this conflict and minimising their behaviour or its consequences.

- Counsellors do not operate in isolation. They are usually a type of social agent, expected to work within the law and basic values of society. Their boundaries may be reasonably narrow and defined by statute as in the case of social workers in a government department, or they may be wide as in the case of detached youth workers. However, at some stage all counsellors will have to decide how much latitude they will want and/or will accept.

- Counsellors have a responsibility for deciding how and when to inform clients of these boundaries and restrictions on their work.

- If there is any place for judgement, it should be actions rather than persons that are judged.

Confidentiality

The client's right to confidentiality generally is regarded as a basic right because the counselling relationship is an intimate one based on trust. Most clients, it is assumed, divulge information to the counsellor about their situations, their past, and their innermost feelings precisely because they believe that they are sharing confidences. They trust the counsellor with such information, assuming it will remain confidential. However, unlike the counsellor, clients are not in any way bound by confidentiality and may share with anyone matters that have been discussed in counselling. Counsellors need to remember this and accept it as every client's right. For counsellors, however, confidences must be respected – within limits.

In practice, confidentiality means not disclosing any information concerning clients which they have revealed in the course of counselling. Absolute confidentiality is probably rare because of human fallibility, staff discussions, inter-agency sharing, times when confidentiality is regarded as unethical, or when clients give permission for information to be divulged (informed consent). Bond (in Winslade, 1996), for example, suggests that there are at least four occasions when counsellors might disclose information given to them by clients:

1 in discussions with third parties (e.g., parents, employers, other family members)

2 in discussions with other professionals (e.g., counsellors, medical personnel)

3 in times of emergency (e.g., when clients or others are thought to be in danger)

4 in situations of conflicting ethical principles (e.g., when the principle of justice supersedes the requirement to maintain confidentiality).

Clearly, then, the principle of confidentiality is not inviolate. On the other hand, any decision to break confidentiality must be carefully considered in relation to other ethical requirements, such as client safety or social justice.

The following general guidelines for maintaining confidentiality are suggested:

• Clients should know where they stand in relation to confidentiality. For example, if case discussion is routine within an agency, clients should be told this.

• Where referral to another agency or consultation with another family member seems appropriate, the client's prior permission should be obtained.

• Where confidentiality has to be broken because of the law or because of danger to the client's or another person's life, the client should be informed as soon as possible.

• Records of interviews should be factual, noting only what is essential within the particular agency setting. Records should be kept locked away, shared only with authorised personnel who would also be bound by confidentiality rules, and stored in a secure place for several years following termination (see *Note-taking*, chapter 8).

- An atmosphere of confidentiality is even more important than any verbal assurances of it. If, for example, notes are taken during interviews, counsellors could offer to let their clients see what is being written or even suggest that clients write or amend the notes themselves.

- Confidentiality, when part of the counsellor's professional code of ethics, should be upheld (see appendices A and B).

Physical contact

Another ethical question relates to physical contact between counsellor and client. Some counsellors say that they sometimes hold a client's hand, or put an arm around a client's shoulder, or even embrace a client. The question is whether such behaviour is ethically and professionally justified as a means of helping clients.

Physical contact between counsellor and client is more acceptable in some institutions, such as hospitals, than in others, such as welfare agencies. Even within an institution it is more justified in some situations than in others, for example an interview resulting in much emotional upset compared with one involving only calm, rational discussion. Finally, in some counsellor-client pairings physical contact seems to be more accepted than others, for example a female counsellor with a female client compared with an older male counsellor with a younger female client. Although norms are changing, female counsellors may still be seen more naturally and effectively to initiate contacts involving touch with both males and females.

The following may be the crucial question: when the issue of physical contact arises, how will the client's needs be served by such contact? As a rule of thumb, if you cannot answer that question positively, do not touch.

Power in counselling

The term *power* as used here refers to the ways and the extent to which one person gains and maintains influence or ascendancy over another. Some interpersonal power is sanctioned by law (e.g., parents over children, teachers over students); some is a consequence of social conventions and conditioning (e.g., older people over younger people); and some is achieved by psychological or social means (e.g., asking questions in certain ways, acquiring status symbols). It is possible to see interpersonal power as a factor or at least a potential issue in virtually every social relationship, including counselling.

Relationships in counselling are unequal from the outset. Merely asking another to help confers power on the person asked. Clients, in confessing their needs and/or weaknesses, make themselves vulnerable. It is the counsellor's task to empower clients so that they can overcome the feelings of being stuck and unable to change. By the same token, counsellors need to appreciate that they are also empowered by clients when the latter take the risk of opening themselves to counselling.

This inherent inequality in the relationship is usually enlarged when there are ethnic, gender, or other important differences between the counsellor and the client. The differences in power between the sexes and between ethnic groups are often so great that some have argued that counselling should take place only between people of the same sex and the same race. Desirable though that may seem, it is not always possible, and in any case, inequality exists in every counselling relationship.

What does this mean for counsellors? Mainly, it means that counsellors should stay in their role of empowering clients and resist temptations to use their power to force clients to accept advice, adopt values, and make decisions that they might not want. They should also resist a temptation to proceed at a pace that may be inappropriate for a client. To truly empower clients, counsellors must first recognise that they cannot give help: they can only offer it. They must accept that if power is to remain with the client, the client must be left free to choose whether or not to change. True helping depends on choice and the freedom to exercise that choice.

Counsellors may work as part of a team that includes psychologists, social workers, medical personnel, teachers, or managers. It is important that roles within the team are defined clearly, and that people work within their roles, respecting the work and the rights of colleagues. Conflicts over power are likely to occur if this is not the case.

Some relationships within an organisation will be hierarchical, and counsellors may be subject to the authority of a person, such as a section manager, who is not trained in counselling and who does not accept typical counsellor values. Acceptance of a position within the organisation presumes acceptance of its authority structure. However, it is not necessary for counsellors to accept all directives if these are not in accordance with their personal or professional values, or if their authority as a counsellor is threatened. Counsellors have the right, and indeed the duty, to state their point of view and to assert themselves in defence of it. They should be equipped in their training with the skills which enable them to reduce or resolve disagreements and conflicts (see chapter 9).

To be seen as honest and trustworthy within their organisation, counsellors should model desirable counselling qualities in their relationships with colleagues. That is, they should show warmth, empathy and respect for others; they should be prepared to disclose themselves as persons with both strengths and weaknesses; and they should be prepared to listen to other points of view, face conflicts honestly and where necessary accept workable compromises.

The environment in which counselling takes place often affects the power relationship. Much counsellor training appears to assume that individual counsellor-client contact will occur in an office that is soundproof, private, and pleasantly decorated, and that the time available will be free from interruptions. However, the reality may be very different.

Counsellors from inner-city, walk-in welfare agencies may work in noisy, publicly situated, poorly furnished offices and be subject to frequent interruptions from the telephone and from other staff. These factors underline their comparatively low status in the institution, and because their clients are usually not people of high standing, their status as counsellors often is lower than, for instance, that of colleagues from private medical practice.

School social workers will often interview people in their homes, perhaps to the accompaniment of the television, or the distractions caused by pre-school children. Being on someone else's territory, counsellors may need to be more circumspect in their counselling because they could be asked to leave at any time. In the case of telephone counselling, there is no face-to-face contact, and this greatly limits counsellors' interpersonal power.

At times, counselling takes place in a vehicle en route home, to the court, or to a hospital. In such settings, some otherwise quiet clients will open up. By contrast, young people in particular may confide in a counsellor during a game of table tennis or some other recreational activity. On the other hand, what might appeal to a counsellor as an ideal office with colourful artwork and tasteful, soft decor may be inhibiting to clients accustomed to less affluent surroundings. Such a setting may serve to emphasise differences in status, and thus make it more difficult for the counsellor to help.

exercise 1.3

Try to see your office and work surroundings through the eyes of your clients. What messages are conveyed to them by the decor, the physical set-up, the reception and waiting facilities? How welcoming is the environment? What can be done to improve things?

The mere fact of requiring a client to come to the counsellor's territory confers further power on the latter, no matter how well the surroundings may accord with the client's background and values. It is almost always the client who has to adjust to a strange setting which conveys some powerful messages, especially about relative status. On the other hand, counsellors venturing onto a client's territory – be it a private home or a factory canteen – where they are unsupported by the trappings of their own space, have much less power than in their own offices.

exercise **1.4**

To experience the differences mentioned above yourself, arrange to meet one of your clients in his/her usual or preferred setting. Note how different it feels to meeting in your office. Does it help or hinder the counselling relationship? Why?

Counsellors should be aware of these power factors when seeing clients. If possible, clients should have some choice about the meeting place; certainly they should be made as comfortable as possible in strange surroundings by allowing a little time for them to settle. It may be possible to minimise interruptions from the telephone; a sign could be put on the door, and those who often interrupt could be asked to respect the counsellor's wish for privacy at such times. Where other people, especially small children, are present, counsellors might decide to ask directly for the chance to talk in another room if someone else can supervise the children. Alternatively, counsellors could have some toys or games to occupy children. They might ask for the radio or television to be switched off or the volume turned down. If soundproofing is a problem, it might be useful to have quiet music playing in the waiting/reception area. However, outside their offices, counsellors will often have little option but to try to screen out or work around such distractions.

2 Counselling and culture

ince counselling involves cross-cultural aspects, all counsellors need to recognise, accept and strive to deal more effectively with cultural diversity in their work with clients. This involves knowing one's own values and culture, the social and political forces that shape clients' lives, culture-specific customs and beliefs, when not to counsel someone from another culture, and having an extensive repertoire of verbal and non-verbal skills.

Recognising diversity

For many years, traditional counselling theories and practices have been challenged as being monocultural, oppressive, elitist and racist (Sue, Ivey, & Pedersen, 1996). So numerous have become the critiques, commentaries and research reports on multicultural counselling that the awareness of and incorporation of multiculturism into psychology has been termed the 'fourth force in psychology' (after the first three: psychodynamic theory; cognitive-behavioural theory, and existential-humanistic theory) (Pedersen, 1991). In spite of the increasing focus on the topic, there is still an almost overwhelming diversity of viewpoints, opinions and approaches among current theorists and practitioners. This is illustrated by the many reactions, both positive and negative, that appear in Sue, Ivey and Pedersen's (1996) book outlining their theory of multicultural counselling. Ultimately, educators and counsellors may just have to accept the fact that 'it is impossible for any one person or group to capture the totality and multiplicity of [multicultural] helping approaches and to integrate them into a unified whole' (Sue, Ivey & Pedersen, 1996, p. 249).

The aims of this chapter are to elevate the importance of cultural considerations in counselling so that they become central considerations in every counselling relationship and to encourage counsellors to recognise, accept and deal more effectively with diversity in their work with specific clients. The placement of this chapter near the beginning of the book is intended to reinforce these aims. By introducing readers early on to cross-cultural considerations in counselling, it is hoped that their reading of the rest of the book will be done from a perspective that is more sensitive to the presence of cultural differences in relationships. The chapter does not present, however, a single view or model of multicultural counselling. Rather, its purpose is to challenge counsellors to acknowledge and value diversity among people and to seek more effective ways of dealing with cultural differences in their own counselling.

It has been argued that all counselling involves cross-cultural aspects since every client is different in meaningful ways from the counsellor (Pedersen, 1990; Speight et al., 1991). This view takes on even greater meaning if the term *culture* is expanded beyond its usual definition as 'the language, customs, religion, art and folklore practices of a particular ethnic group' (Ramondo, 1991, p. 70). Then factors such as age, culture, disability, race, sexual orientation, level of education, gender, socio-economic status and even physique become relevant considerations in counselling, since each may contribute to fundamental differences in lifestyle between the client and the counsellor (Weinrach & Thomas, 1996).

It is also the case that the differences in values and beliefs *within* a particular ethnic or cultural group may be as wide or wider than differences *between* groups (Sue, 1983; Weinrach & Thomas, 1996). To ignore this is to risk stereotyping members of a particular group by assuming that all members of that group have values, beliefs and ways of thinking that are alike. In counselling, therefore, it is less important to know what specific groups clients belong to than how they perceive themselves as members of those groups (Richardson & Molinaro, 1996).

This point has been addressed in New Zealand by Davies, Elkington and Winslade (1993) and by Su'a and Crichton-Hill (personal communication, November 1996)* in their respective models for understanding the different degrees to which New Zealand Maori and Samoan families living in New Zealand identify with their traditional cultures. For counsellors to assume that all Maori or all Samoans (or the members of any other cultural or ethnic group) identify with their traditional cultural background to the same degree is simplistic and counter-productive to an effective counselling process and outcome. Rather, counsellors need to have the skill, knowledge and sensitivity to accurately assess their client's level of cultural identity, and then to respond appropriately.

To aid this assessment process, Davies et al. (1993) described four degrees of cultural identity among Maori clients: (a) the influence of the dominant culture has been extensive and that of the traditional culture marginal; (b) the influence of the dominant culture has been considerable but the client also identifies to a moderate degree with his traditional cultural beliefs; (c) the influence of the dominant culture has been moderate while that of the traditional culture has been considerable; (d) the dominant culture has had little influence while that of the traditional culture has been extensive. Knowing which level best describes Maori clients is important in deciding how to proceed in counselling.

Similarly, Su'a and Crichton-Hill stress that an appropriate assessment of

---

* Samoans Tagaloa Su'a (cultural consultant) and Yvonne Crichton-Hill (social work trainer) of Christchurch, New Zealand, conduct cross-cultural training sessions for counsellors and social workers throughout New Zealand.

Samoan clients' identification with their traditional cultural values is a vital first task in counselling. It cannot be assumed that, because clients identify themselves as Samoan, their families live a traditional Samoan lifestyle. They have identified four broad (and they stress the word 'broad') categories of Samoan families living in New Zealand:

1 **Traditional families** adhere to Samoan culturally defined lifestyles. Members of these families will usually listen politely to the suggestions of outside professionals, or they may refuse any interventions because of a lack of understanding and the fear of being forced to accept another system of values, beliefs and customs.

2 **Bicultural families** appear to have adopted many aspects of the dominant or mainstream lifestyle and are the most receptive to outside ideas and interventions.

3 **Assimilated families** have adopted Palagi (European) styles of living and as a consequence are often isolated from the wider Samoan community.

4 **Generation-gap families** have traditional parents/elders and assimilated, New Zealand-born children. The parents and elders tend to assume that their own traditional cultural norms are the same as the norms of wider New Zealand society while their children often resist and resent their parents' forcing these traditional values on them as a means of controlling their behaviour. This situation often results in a generation gap, making it difficult for outsiders to work effectively with the whole family.

Obviously, treating all of these types of families in the same way would not be culturally sensitive or effective.

Gudykunst and Kim (1984) asserted that the processes involved in intracultural, intercultural, interracial and inter-ethnic communication were the same and could be described more accurately as *communicating with strangers*: 'anytime we communicate with people who are unknown and unfamiliar and those people are in an environment unfamiliar to them, we are communicating with strangers' (p. 15). In such interactions, the initial aim is to reduce the uncertainty that is present, and in counselling the aim is to reduce uncertainty in ways that do not stereotype, misrepresent or devalue clients.

There is current debate in the literature on multicultural counselling about the degree to which counselling is a universal, generic activity which transcends specific cultures (Fukuyama, 1990; Patterson, 1996; Vontress, 1979) versus a focused, culture-specific interaction (Locke, 1990; Ivey et al., 1993) in which each different cultural group 'requires a different set of skills, unique areas of emphasis, and specific insights for effective counseling to occur' (Pedersen, 1976, p. 26).

The first view, called the universalist perspective, focuses on the process of counselling and emphasises the primacy of the counselling relationship and the importance of rapport between client and counsellor (Patterson, 1996). Universal qualities in counselling are thought to be analogous to the core conditions identified by Rogers (1957): respect; genuineness; empathic understanding; communicating empathy, respect and genuineness: self-disclosure, and structuring the counselling process so that clients understand what will happen and why (Patterson, 1996). However, as noted by Pedersen (1996), even these core values have different meanings in different cultures, hence their universal nature is doubtful. Inherent in the universalist approach is the first of three possible errors that counsellors can make in deciding which approach to multicultural counselling is most appropriate. That is, the error of *overemphasising similarities* among groups (Pedersen, 1996). Examples of this type of thinking are illustrated by statements like, 'We are all one people' and 'Basically people have the same wants, desires, and needs the world over'. These ideas minimise differences, ignore diverse cultural perspectives and can support, intentionally or otherwise, continued majority dominance over minority interests.

The focused, culture-specific approach attempts to provide information and knowledge about the characteristics of specific groups and identify techniques that fit those characteristics (Patterson, 1996). When using this approach it is possible to commit a second error, that of *overemphasising differences* among groups (Pedersen, 1996). In practical terms 'attempting to develop different theories, methods, and techniques for each of these groups would be an insurmountable task' (Patterson, 1996, p. 228), and could result in counsellors becoming 'chameleons who constantly change their techniques to meet special needs of minority clients' (McFadden, 1996, p. 232). Moreover, the culture-specific approach has not been very helpful in the past (Sue & Zane, 1987).

A third error that counsellors can make in deciding which approach to multicultural counselling to use, is to assume that counsellors *must choose* to be either universalist or culture-specific in their counselling (Pedersen, 1996). An alternative and preferable position to take is to accept that 'multicultural competence in counseling might be universally valued but require different behaviors in each culturally different context' (Pedersen, 1996, p. 236). This is the middle position taken by writers such as McFadden (1993), Pedersen and Ivey (1993), and Sue (1981) (see figure 2.1). Essentially, this approach asserts that clients will be best served when counsellors 'emphasize an essential balance that acknowledges both similarities and differences' (Pedersen, 1993, p. 230). This is also the approach taken in this book – with the added proviso that effective cross-cultural counselling involves the consideration of factors usually thought to be outside the domain of therapeutic counselling: social, gender, economic and political (Waldegrave, 1990).

The context of cross-cultural counselling

One of the first steps in addressing your own limitations and needs as an effective cross-cultural counsellor is to be aware of and acknowledge the existence of current negative attitudes toward diversity in society at large and to examine your own beliefs about cultural differences in relation to those negative attitudes. There has always been opposition – more or less stridently expressed – to

Universalist:

Counselling as a generic
activity; transcends culture
(e.g. Fukuyama, 1990)

Focused:

Culture-specific;
stresses the uniqueness
of each group
(e.g. Locke, 1990)

X – – - – - – - – - – - – – - – - – - – - – - – - – - – – - - – - – - – - – - – – - · – - – - – - X

Multicultural approach:

Requires both universal
and culture-specific
considerations (e.g. Ivey
et al., 1993; Sue et al., 1996)

Figure 2.1 Continuum of approaches to multicultural counselling

recognising diversity in society. To some people it is anathema: unnecessary, unfair, undemocratic and even dangerous to treat some groups differently from others. This belief and variations on it can also be found among counsellors. In fact, many counsellors defend their lack of cross-cultural awareness and competence – or, alternatively, offer proof of their openness and tolerance – by saying such things as:

- We are all one people; we have the same thoughts, feelings and needs.

- It is dangerous and divisive to emphasise differences all the time. Doing that will only further divide society and create antagonisms between groups.

- I am a tolerant, open-minded person and I never oppress others.

- I have been trained to be empathic, respectful and genuine with all of my clients. I resent the suggestion that I am insensitive to other groups.

- Let's face it, minority groups must learn to fit in with the rest of society. I'm only helping them to do that more effectively. After all, it is to their advantage in the long run to do so.

- Counselling is all about treating every person as a unique individual; that's certainly what I strive to do.

- If you're a good counsellor, you automatically value and take account of your clients' cultural backgrounds. You don't need special training in cultural competence to do that.

- If we learn to be culturally sensitive to two or three groups, shouldn't we do the same for every group in society? I just don't have time for all of that!

Sometimes these statements indicate a lack of knowledge or information about the issue; at other times they can mask prejudice, or an insecurity about a counsellor's own competence, or a feeling of being overwhelmed by the complexity of the topic (Pedersen & Ivey, 1993). In each instance such views function effectively to deny others their rights, their personal and cultural integrity and to restrain their cultural development as people (McFadden, 1996).

---

exercise 2.1

1   Stop and examine your own beliefs and feelings in relation to these and similar statements. Do you see yourself in any of them? If you do, what are you going to do about it? What is a positive first step you can take to alter such beliefs?

2   If you hear these sorts of things being said by other counsellors, how do you react? What is your responsibility to them? The profession? What specific things can you do in response?

Following are seven suggestions for counteracting these sorts of statements (adapted from the Waitangi Workshops' *Programme on racism**).

1 *Decide how strong you feel* in yourself and about the situation before you challenge the statement. Remember, you don't have to respond to every situation.

2 When you challenge someone, *you don't have to win*. Merely expressing your point of view may initiate the process of change.

3 *You don't have to sit and listen* to such statements. You can leave. Ultimately, the changing of an individual's mind is not as important as challenging institutional oppression.

4 *Look for support* from others before challenging someone. If there is none, then decide if you are strong enough and willing enough to proceed.

5 *Always support others who challenge* such statements and make your support obvious.

6 Accept that there is *no simple answer to some prejudiced, oppressive comments*.

7 *Choose your time and setting*. Informal discussion in more relaxed surroundings are often more personal and therefore more difficult to handle than educating people in a formal setting.

Training for cross-cultural competence

Becoming cross-culturally competent involves counsellors in 'a process of liberating ourselves from a limited perspective on life – of becoming more fully human, with a greater awareness of and sensitivity to self, others, and the

---

* Waitangi Workshops, Box 35089, Otautahi/Christchurch, New Zealand.

relationships between them' (Gudykunst & Kim, 1984, p. 232). Many writers on this topic suggest that the following competencies and areas of knowledge are essential to 'liberating ourselves' and becoming a skilled cross-cultural counsellor (e.g., Leong and Kim, 1991; Ivey et al., 1993; Richardson & Molinaro, 1996). While this process may be difficult for some, and perhaps not always pleasant, there is no shortcut if the aim is to become more skilled.

The counsellor's orientation to others

Formal training programmes on cross-cultural counselling tend to emphasise the counsellor's personal values and orientation toward others as an essential competency (Leong & Kim, 1991). In order for counsellors to be effective in cross-cultural situations, therefore, it is suggested that there are certain personal values that all counsellors should hold. These include:

- a genuine, non-judgemental curiosity about others and their lifestyles;

- an openness and tolerance toward others that allows counsellors to approach them in a friendly, non-threatening way;

- a flexibility of thinking and an adaptability in behaving that enables counsellors to appreciate beliefs and behaviours that are different from their own and to interact with others appropriately;

- a confidence about themselves and their values that allows counsellors to respond to criticism or rejection (remember, not everyone will like or trust the counsellor) without feeling threatened or belittled;

- a respect for and acceptance of the complexity and diversity of other people's ways of doing, feeling, thinking, no matter how different they might be;

- a non-superior attitude that conveys an authentic appreciation for the values and beliefs of others.

When first reading them, counsellors may think that these personal values are idealistic and unattainable. However, taken together they describe people who have had a broad experience of cultural diversity, are mature, knowledgeable about themselves, accepting of differences and non-domineering toward others. In short, they describe desirable personal characteristics of effective counsellors.

exercise **2.2**

1   Answer these questions as honestly as you can. Because you may find it interesting to return to them a number of times during your training so that you can evaluate and modify your original answers, it would be useful to keep a written record of your responses.

a   What are your personal feelings and beliefs toward people from other cultures? How do you know this? Where do your feelings and attitudes originate?

b   Which of these beliefs have you had the longest? Which ones have been modified and why?

c   How much experience have you had with people from other cultures? What prevents you from having more? How have these experiences shaped and influenced your own values?

d   Which beliefs do you think you need to re-evaluate and change? Why?

2   Talk with as many older members of your extended family as you can to find out about your family's history, its traditions, rules and rituals. How are that history and those values expressed in your own beliefs? In your work?

3   Choose someone with whom you are at ease and comfortable when self-disclosing. Discuss your answers to the questions in #1 with that person. Make a commitment to explore your beliefs again at future date, sometime later in your training. Note whether your beliefs have changed and why.

The counsellor's knowledge of own culture

It is important for counsellors who are exploring who they are as people to learn about their own culture and their degree of identification with that culture. And, by extension, it is necessary for counsellors to gain a clear understanding about how their own culture-centred biases, values and beliefs impact on their counselling.

exercise **2.3**

1   Choose several pictures or objects that represent some important aspects of your own cultural heritage. Discuss these objects with others in the group. Describe the cultural values, ideas, or beliefs they embody and how those cultural values have influenced you as a person and as a counsellor. Note the similarities and differences among the group members.

2   Choose one of your favourite childhood stories or poems. Read it again looking for the cultural values and beliefs that it conveys. Discuss with others in your group how those values have influenced you as a person and as a counsellor.

3   Try to identify which values and beliefs help or hinder your work with clients from other cultures.

Counsellors' own cultural identity development is central to this process of understanding their own cultural identity. At this point it should be pointed out that when reading the professional literature on cross-cultural competence in counselling, it is easy to assume that counsellors are most often white, European and middle class and that their clients are of a different colour, ethnic background and/or nationality. This assumption is realistic given the predominant number of such counsellors over all others and the status and power differential that typically exists between such counsellors (who are usually members of the majority culture) and their clients (who are often members of a minority and, therefore, less powerful culture). However, it is important to stress that multicultural or cross-cultural counselling theory and practice is applicable to counsellors from all cultural backgrounds when they work with clients from another culture.

Ponterotto (1988) has developed a four-stage model that describes the white counsellor's multicultural development. Applying it to your own identity development may be enlightening and productive.

Stage 1. *Pre-exposure*: At this stage counsellors have virtually no awareness of cultural diversity or their own cultural identity and how that identity impacts on their work with their clients. Their counselling practices may be racist and oppressive to clients in ways they do not even recognise or understand.

Counsellors who continue to work at this stage of minimal awareness are in fact working unethically (Ivey et al., 1993) since many codes of ethics require counsellors to adopt a multicultural perspective so that they are sensitive to differences among clients due to such factors as age, gender, culture, and ethnicity.

Stage 2. *Exposure*: At this stage counsellors have become aware of multicultural issues, diversity, and the implications of these for their counselling practice. Probably for the first time they also begin to identify themselves as white counsellors and members of the dominant class in society. Personal reactions commonly include guilt, confusion, and a feeling of being overwhelmed by the complexity of cultural diversity.

However, merely being exposed to these issues does not necessarily enhance the counsellor's cross-cultural competence and, therefore, is not sufficient development.

Stage 3. *Zealotry and defensiveness*: At this stage counsellors usually become either multicultural activists or feel overwhelmed and retreat into a defensiveness about their monocultural work.

It is at this stage that educators need to be sensitive to each counsellor's personal reactions so that each can be supported and guided to the next stage of multicultural understanding and competence. Counsellors need to be helped to progress beyond their zealotry or guilt and begin to gain new understandings and new skills to enhance their cross-cultural competence.

Stage 4. *Integration*: At this stage counsellors begin to construct a coherent, sensitive multicultural overview of the counselling process and their part in it. Counsellors have a greater depth of understanding of the many issues involved, the limits of their own competence in the area, and practical, effective ways for working with clients from other cultures within those limits.

exercise **2.4**

1 Using Ponterotto's model (above), where do place yourself in your own multicultural development? How do you know this?

2 What do you need to do to progress to the next stage? List several specific tasks, learning experiences and/or activities that will help you move to a greater understanding and insight into yourself and your work with other cultural groups.

Knowledge of historical, social, political and economic forces

Knowledge of the forces that shape and have shaped people's lives, especially the lives of minority groups, is essential to an understanding of the institutional systems that act to oppress, restrain and inhibit the development of particular groups in society. To be effective, counsellors must know about the political, economic and social context within which their counselling takes place. Counselling, after all, is a political activity – it can liberate clients or oppress them. Therefore, it is necessary to understand the impact it has on clients. As Linda Smith (1989, p. 8), a Maori educator said, 'to be naive about the power which backs up your theory and practice (e.g., the validity of your theories, your credentials, your status, your wealth) and to be unaware of the power which has brought disempowered clients to your attention is to be grossly insensitive'.

An exemplary model which confronts, understands and takes into account these macro-social, -economic and -political factors in counselling has been developed by Waldegrave and his colleagues at the Family Centre in Lower Hutt, New Zealand. Their *Just Therapy* approach (1990) draws together both political and clinical concepts to enable clients and their problems to be seen in relation to structural problems like unemployment, poverty, injustice, racism and sexism. The approach helps clients to create new meanings for their experiences so that 'feelings of sadness, hopelessness, and self-blame, transform appropriately to feelings of anger, new possibilities of hope, and self-worth' (p. 25).

Another aspect of professional counselling that can be applied in an insensitive and/or oppressive manner is the counsellor's code of ethics. Most codes have a narrow cultural base and may, therefore, be interpreted in ways that ignore or violate the needs and realities of many cultural groups. For example, is it ethical or insensitive to apply a literal interpretation of confidentiality with clients who strongly identify with their culture's collective, family-based values? In these cases it is more likely that counsellors need to have the courage and good sense to alter or reframe particular guidelines so that their meanings and application are more culturally appropriate (Sue et al., 1996).

---

exercise 2.5

---

1   Start by identifying two or three specific political, economic and social
    conflicts and issues that exist among various cultural groups in your
    community. Read more about these differences so that you understand
    the various perspectives better. What suggestions would you have for
    resolving such conflicts?

2   Attend meetings, workshops or rallies at which members of various
    cultural groups are discussing their views of current issues, problems,
    conflicts. How do the views presented at these meetings differ from your
    own? How can you resolve these differences and incorporate them into
    your counselling?

Culture-specific knowledge

While acknowledging that there is a wide diversity of values, customs and beliefs
within cultural groups, it is nevertheless essential for counsellors to gain
knowledge specific to the cultural groups with which they work. This knowledge
may include – at the very least – rudimentary knowledge of customs, rituals,
language (including correct pronunciation of names and key words), beliefs
and values.

Another way for counsellors to increase their knowledge of specific groups
is by comparing and contrasting the different orientations of various cultures
to specific concepts, activities and values. This approach, called the analysis of
value orientations (Sue, 1981), helps to illustrate the diversity in orientations
that exist (see, for example, Ramondo, 1991; Richardson & Molinaro, 1996).

How could the orientations of the various cultural groups you work with be
described in relation to the following? What would be a specific group's
predominant or preferred focus, value or world-view? Examples of possible
orientations from Ramondo (1991) are given for several concepts (column one);
however, you may be able to think of others that are more useful and descriptive
for the particular groups with which you are familiar (column two). Compare
them with your own beliefs and preferred focus (column three).

1 Concept, value or worldview	2 Group and preferred focus	3 Your focus
Time (focus on the past, present or future?)		
Activity (focus on doing, being or becoming?)		
Relations with others (individual, family, hierarchical?)		
People and nature (harmony, mastery, fatalism?)		
Nature of people (good, evil, mixed?)		
Individualism/collectivity		
Use of authority (authoritative, authoritarian, autocratic?)		
Spirituality and religion		
Competitiveness/cooperation		
Work ethic		
Ways of thinking/reasoning		
Family composition		
Gender relationships		
Age and aging		
Knowledge and wisdom		
Justice/fairness		
Wealth		
Status		
Self-esteem		
Decision-making		
Expression of emotion		

exercise 2.6

1   Referring to the concepts listed, identify your preferred or dominant orientations. Are these the same as your parents'? Your close friends'? Your work colleagues'? How rigid are you in applying these styles? In which do you need to become more flexible?

2   Find someone from a culture different to your own with whom you can freely discuss beliefs, values and rituals. Find out as much as you can about their values while sharing your own. What did you discover about why another culture values things the way it does?

3   Make a list of five things you can do to learn more about the cultural groups with which you regularly work. Be specific. Next, set yourself a time-frame within which to do them. At various points, refer back to your original list to check your progress. As you accomplish each item on your list, add another.

4   Identify a local cultural or ethnic group with which you will be working. Following proper protocol, arrange to visit one of their local community functions, activities or church meetings. This means you will have to find out as much as you can about protocol and procedures beforehand. While attending, note the differences and similarities in values and practices from your own.

5   Learn common forms of greeting, salutation and simple discourse in the language of your clients. Learn them well enough to be confident about using them appropriately and correctly.

A broad set of skills and behaviours

Finally, it is necessary for counsellors to learn a broad set of skills and behaviours that allow them to respond appropriately to the diverse range of clients being seen. Having a repertoire of verbal and non-verbal skills should help counsellors to adjust their approach to the needs, values, and circumstances of their clients. For example, the skills identified and explained in this book can be adapted and applied in more culturally appropriate ways if you use the insight and understanding acquired in the preceding discussion of these four areas:

- knowledge of your own values and personal characteristics and how they are expressed in your work;

- knowledge of your own culture and the strength of your identification with that culture;

- knowledge of the social and political forces that impact on the lives of your clients;

- knowledge of the culture-specific beliefs, values and protocol by which your clients live.

Acquiring these skills can, and ought to, be done in multiple ways (see, for example, Sue et al., 1996):

- by attending as many training experiences and workshops on the topic as possible;

- by using supervisors, consultants and 'cultural guides' (see page 33) to comment on, critique and inform your work;

- by keeping up-to-date with the multicultural literature, including both commentaries and research reports;

- by being involved socially and politically with various cultural groups in your own community; there is no short cut to being involved with and accepted by local communities so that you are known to be supportive and trustworthy;

- by continuing to learn about the language and customs of the specific groups with which you work.

exercise 2.7

Think of a couple of times recently when you had successful and unsuccessful cross-cultural interactions, times when (a) you felt comfortable in and confident about the interactions; and times when (b) you did not feel so comfortable and confident. Now, try to identify or isolate the factors that contributed to the success or lack of success. What were these factors? Which ones would you use more of in the future? Less of?

Discuss your ideas with people from those cultural groups. Get their comments and feedback.

Pedersen and Ivey (1993) suggest that this developmental progression – from self-awareness to knowledge of wider systems and specific cultures, and then to the appropriate application of skills in cross-cultural interactions – provides a useful framework for accomplishing the following: training others; assessing the cross-cultural competence of individual counsellors; consulting organisations, and preparing cross-cultural counselling training materials. Nevertheless, it must be accepted that there is an enormous diversity of opinion, theory and practice in cross-cultural counselling. Because of this, it is necessary for both counsellors and trainers to accept that current notions of cross-cultural competence are dynamic and will continue to change.

It is natural to want to identify the theory and the set of skills that work. It is natural to want to find certainty in the form of one particular theory and a specific set of skills that will always work. Such certainty would be reassuring and welcome, but it is also unrealistic to expect it. Thus, when working cross-culturally, exceptions become the rule, and these can then become new rules.

The theory of *multicultural counselling and therapy* expounded by Sue et al. (1996) contains several such rules:

- Use the theory best suited to the cultural perspectives of the client.

- No matter how different they may be, counsellors and clients can usually find some common ground on which to base a relationship. However, counsellors need to accept that there will also be differences that may never be understood.

- The cultural identities of both counsellors and clients are constantly evolving. Therefore, counsellors cannot ever assume that they completely know their clients.

- Questions of culture (e.g., matching for maximum similarity) must take second place to client choice. Thus, the assertion that the only counsellors who should work with clients are those of similar race, ethnicity or gender can result in stereotyping.

- The notion of what constitutes counselling may need to be expanded to include a wide variety of related activities and interventions (see chapter 9).

- Cultural diversity may render many taken-for-granted ethical principles invalid.

- Cross-cultural counselling, by its very nature, contains a strong educational component, including the 'liberation of consciousness' (Sue et al., 1996, p. 22).

While the complexity and uncertainty of all cross-cultural competence may seem overwhelming to many counsellors, they should not use it as an excuse to avoid acquiring new knowledge and learning new skills and thereby to continue imposing their own cultural perspectives on their clients.

Practical suggestions

As a counsellor you can do a number of things beyond formal training to increase your knowledge of other cultures and to support an atmosphere of tolerance and acceptance within the profession. These are:

- challenging statements or actions that stereotype, demean or oppress others;

- examining work procedures, rules and policies for biases or hindrances to certain groups;

- continuing to learn as much as you can about other cultures, other groups, and current issues of culture, class and gender;

- continuing to build working relationships with people from other cultural and ethnic groups;

- finding ways to actively support the political actions of other cultural groups;

- respecting others' views, no matter how different they are from your own;

- avoiding decisions about what is good or best for others.

In addition, you will need to give thought to the following and decide how you will respond in your day-to-day counselling:

What terms/language will you use to describe yourself/your work? To some cultural and ethnic groups terms like therapy, treatment, counselling and clinical psychology may convey negative meanings (Sue et al., 1996). There may be more familiar or benign terms that could be used with some groups. Your job is to find out what those terms might be for the various groups with which you work (e.g., healers, shaman, medicine men (see Lee, 1996)). One way of doing this might be to consult local cultural advisers.

What is a cultural adviser and how should one be chosen? It is becoming more common for counsellors of one culture to consult with a cultural adviser who is from the same culture as the client (Smith, 1989). In some instances, this adviser functions essentially as a co-counsellor, guiding and advising both counsellor and client as the counselling relationship progresses. While potentially very beneficial, the use of an adviser is not without its problems. Since the role of adviser is a very powerful and influential one, advisers should be chosen with care (Su'a and Crichton-Hill, personal communication, November 1996) to ensure that such cultural advisers are thoroughly:

- knowledgeable about the client's culture, the presenting problem, and the counsellor's helping system/agency;

- knowledgeable about legislation relevant to the problem (e.g., child-care; sexual abuse; school expulsions; divorce and separation proceedings);

- knowledgeable about and experienced in the delivery of competent counselling/therapy/social services;

- knowledgeable about available resources for helping;

- familiar with the concept of confidentiality, both in its professional sense and its meaning within the client's culture;

- trustworthy;

- bilingual;

- acceptable to the client and the client's cultural group in terms of status or standing in the community.

Do you have the courage and self-confidence to tolerate possible criticism both for the cross-cultural work you do and the work you do not do? In trying to do the right thing for their clients, counsellors can easily get caught up in cultural controversies. To withstand these often stressful situations, they must be clear about their motives and methods, and strong enough to survive and learn from censure and public criticism.

Cautions

Even with the best will in the world, there are several serious challenges to counsellors who are striving to work in a culturally sensitive way.

1 Increasing your repertoire of verbal and non-verbal skills is certainly a laudable goal. But those skills must still be applied in ways that both fit with the cultural protocol and rituals of the client's culture and with the client's degree of identification with their culture of origin (Su'a and Crichton-Hill, personal communication, November 1996).

2 Becoming a more culturally sensitive counsellor still ignores the fact that most counselling theories and practices are culturally specific (that is, Western, white, middle-class) and that they do not acknowledge or adequately account for diversity across cultures (Smith, 1989; Sue et al., 1996). Learning to be cross-culturally competent should include increasing one's awareness of structural constraints in both society and the process of counselling (theory and practice) itself (Waldegrave, 1990).

3 An important consideration that seems to be ignored by most theorists and researchers is that *clients determine whether their counsellor is sensitive* to cultural and ethnic differences and possesses the skills to interact effectively within their culture. In the end it matters little how much formal training counsellors have received in multicultural counselling and how competent as cross-cultural counsellors they have been judged to be by their trainers if their clients do not also perceive them that way. For example, will clients want to work with a particular counsellor? What will they say to others in their community regarding the counsellor's work? About the counsellor as a person? Clients are, after all, the final arbiters in these matters, the ones that count, just as they are in judging the extent of their counsellor's empathy, respect or genuineness. In effect, 'the conditions [including cross-cultural skills] must be perceived, recognised and felt by the client if they are to be effective' (Patterson, 1996, p. 230).

   Perhaps the best that counsellors can do within present theory and knowledge is to strive for: (a) sensitivity to others' contexts, beliefs and values; (b) an increased awareness of their own context, beliefs and values; (c) greater knowledge about the various cultural and ethnic groups with which they work, and (d) the acquisition of generic and culture-specific skills that can be used as appropriate.

4 Counsellors must also keep in mind that no counsellor will be able to work successfully with every client. Some clients will like and respect a particular counsellor, while others will not be attracted to that person. Some will see the counsellor as sensitive and supportive while others will not. Having the sensitivity to know when not to counsel someone from

another culture and to whom to refer that person is an additional, though seldom discussed, cross-cultural competency.

5 There will be times when effective communication with a client from another culture breaks down for some reason. How the counsellor attempts to rectify the situation is more important than the breakdown itself. Perhaps the most useful counsellor characteristics in these moments are (Gudykunst & Kim, 1984):

- an intuitive sensitivity to verbal and body language that enables counsellors to recognise when communication has been misunderstood;
- an open-minded tolerance of differences in thinking, expressing oneself and behaving;
- an outlook on the world that is predicated on an assumed complexity of values, attitudes, behaviours;
- an ability to delay making definitive judgements about people until what they have said or done can be evaluated more fully;
- an ability and willingness to modify their own stereotypes of events, places and people.

Specific skills that may be useful to counsellors in recovering from such breakdowns or impasses include:

- an attitude of curiosity and a request for an explanation (e.g., 'I have never come across that before; what does it mean to you?');
- an admission of ignorance and a plea for help (e.g., 'I'm sorry, but I guess I don't understand that idea; can you show me how it works?');
- calling attention to a mistake and asking for forbearance (e.g., 'I think I just now said something wrong. I'm sorry if it hurt/embarrassed/insulted you. Could you help me to understand what I did more clearly?');
- self-disclosing embarrassment or discomfort (e.g., 'Right now I'm feeling embarrassed about my own inability to understand things from your perspective; is there something I could do that would help right now?').

If these sorts of self-effacing responses are used in a genuinely respectful way, clients will often help counsellors to re-establish effective communication.

6 In the end, it is probably the client who accommodates more of the counsellor's values, procedures and protocol than vice versa. The reality of most cross-cultural counselling is that clients decide whom they like and respect well enough to enter into a meaningful relationship with. Of course, the counsellor's training and cross-cultural skill may help the client to make this decision.

7 Finally, it seems that specific knowledge about particular cultures is almost always useful in cross-cultural counselling. Perhaps there is no short cut, and, whatever else they do, 'to learn how to work successfully with minority clients, students [counsellors] need to interact directly with them' (Nuttall et al., 1996, p. 131).

The counsellor and the counselling relationship

I n any interpersonal situation (whether group or one-to-one) in which people assume the role of counsellor, those people also assume a responsibility for their own behaviour, their knowledge of themselves, and their ability to relate effectively to others. Anyone who undertakes to be a counsellor must be prepared to interact as a real person with the client and to strive for an awareness of the factors involved in the process. As it is impossible for counsellors to be totally objective and rational, all who endeavour to be so deny themselves a most valuable source of counselling information: their own feelings, perceptions, hunches, and ideas.

A dynamic relationship

Counsellors should try to make good use of all sources of information in the counselling process. This means that counsellors must rely not only on their perceptions of and understanding of their clients' situations, but also on their own feelings about and reactions to what is happening at the time. This latter source is often purposely ignored because it is thought that subjective impressions are necessarily inaccurate and biased. They are, however, potentially the more accurate of the two types of information, provided counsellors can develop their self-awareness to a level that will enable them to identify and interpret correctly their own reactions and feelings. By contrast, their understanding of another person's situation is always compromised by several things: each participant has had different cultural experiences and therefore perceives events differently, the power and status of each is unequal, any communication from one person to another is inevitably prone to some degree of distortion and error. Counselling can be thought of as a dynamic relationship involving two people, and one in which the counsellor's knowledge of her/himself is as important as her/his knowledge of the client and of counselling principles.

This dynamic relationship is a process of defining and redefining the specific roles that counsellors and clients will play. Participants can decide how to respond to one another, but not *whether* they will respond. For example, in any encounter with another person, everything said or done communicates to the other person how one is willing to relate. If someone says, 'I don't understand what we are supposed to be doing', any response (verbal or nonverbal) by another person begins to define a relationship between them. How would each of these seven responses to the statement above begin to define a relationship?

1 'I don't either. Let's ask someone else.'

2 'Maybe you should listen more.'

3 'I don't either. What should we do?'

4 Shrug of the shoulders.

5 Say nothing, merely turn away from the speaker.

6 'Let me see if I can find out for you, OK?'

7 'We are supposed to be finding out more about each other.'

In the first example, the respondent refuses to assume a leadership or information-giver's role and instead tries to become an equal by admitting to ignorance and suggesting that both ask someone else. In **2**, a critical and/or instructive position is assumed that clearly indicates that the speaker should be more responsible. In **3**, after admitting not knowing, the respondent refuses to accept a leadership role and instead tries to get the speaker to take over or at least recognise that they both have some responsibility for solving the problem. The shrug will probably be interpreted as, 'Don't ask me; I don't want to get involved', indicating a desire for no further interaction. The action in **5**, no matter how it is done, clearly indicates the respondent's desire for non-involvement. Example **6** illustrates the respondent's willingness to accept a supportive leadership role. The final example gives the information requested by suggesting how the two should proceed. This same process of defining and redefining a relationship occurs in counselling. Every word, gesture, and silence alters how the counsellor and client will relate to each while together.

The counsellor's needs in counselling

Before seriously considering themselves counsellors, people should critically and honestly examine their own motivations for taking on the responsibilities of helping another person. Very simply, they should ask themselves: 'What do I expect from the relationship? What will be my satisfactions and rewards in helping others?'

Counsellors' reasons for helping are seldom entirely pure and altruistic, but all counsellors should be open to and aware of their motivations. After all, these motivations can profoundly influence their effectiveness. Just as the counsellor's choice of theory or model of counselling conveys autobiographical information, so too can choosing to be a counsellor be indicative of a person's own needs and values. For example, the effectiveness of counsellors who help others in order to avoid dealing with their own problems will be limited. Even if clients do not 'see through' them in a completely accurate way, their clients will never develop the confidence and trust in them that is essential for effective counselling. Similarly, counsellors who encourage their clients to confide in them because it gives them status and control will soon find that they will have only very dependent clients, as others will avoid them and their controlling behaviour.

Some counsellors may desire close contact with others but be unable to achieve these relationships in normal interpersonal situations. By becoming counsellors they are able to avoid facing up to their own deficiencies and to feel competent and fulfilled in working closely with others. There are others who counsel from a firm belief that they have answers to life's problems that should be shared with others. With the best of intentions they try to convert clients to their way of thinking but end up alienating many. Others counsel out of a sincere wish to help, with no other hidden motivation. Very often they are unaware of their own rewards and satisfactions. They may be viewed with some scepticism and distrust by the more suspicious or cynical client. Whatever the reasons for helping others, counsellors' credibility, and hence their effectiveness, will he enhanced by their awareness and acceptance of those reasons.

The first reasons that come to mind might not always be the most honest or accurate. Self-deception in this area hinders effectiveness and, as suggested earlier, real motives will be perceived by clients. Adolescents are particularly quick to identify the phoney adult or the counsellor who is only enforcing the prevailing rules in a 'softer' way. Discovering your needs and motivations involves you in an ongoing examination of your beliefs about yourself, your beliefs about others, and your commitment to learning more about yourself. Questions you need to answer are:

- What kind of a person am I?
- What are my strengths? Weaknesses?
- What do I need from others?
- What do I have to offer other people?
- What do I believe is right for others?
- How am I influenced by others' impressions of me?
- Why do I want to be a counsellor?
- Is counselling sufficiently satisfying for me?

Answering such questions is often difficult and may even be painful. However, effective counsellors should continually strive to know themselves better. Counsellors must be committed to continuous personal growth both in training and real life situations, and must have the courage and confidence to undertake the in-depth personal analysis they ask of clients. It must be stressed that personal development is an ongoing process, and that as a person changes, the questions above will require new answers. It will be necessary to periodically answer the questions: 'What are the rewards that keep me satisfied in my work? Should I continue to be a counsellor? Why?'.

Related to this ongoing process of self-analysis is the question regarding personal counselling for counsellors-in-training: should it be a requirement of training? There are several good reasons why counsellors would benefit from undergoing counselling during their training (Corey & Corey, 1989; Dryden, 1993; Kocet, 1994):

- it promotes self-exploration and enhances self-understanding;

- it enables counsellors to better understand and empathise with the client's experience of counselling;

- it enables counsellors to work through problems, blind spots and conflicts of their own that may compromise their effectiveness with clients;

- it allows counsellors to experience effective counselling at first hand and learn by modelling from their own competent counsellor.

However, making personal counselling *mandatory* is another matter. The position taken in this book is similar to that expressed by Dryden (1993): in the absence of clear evidence that such personal counselling enhances client outcome, personal counselling should be the trainee's choice and not a course requirement. Nevertheless, the material in this book, particularly in chapters 1, 2 and 3, emphasises ongoing personal development and career-long education if counsellors are to be fully professional. For many, this will include personal counselling; for others it will consist of related experiences such as participation in personal growth and development groups, educational activities and formal and informal self-study.

It is hoped that counsellors will experience what it is like to be a client at some time in their careers. This perspective can be invaluable in every counsellor's work and may be gained as a consequence of their recognising that their readiness or suitability to counsel has altered as their own circumstances have changed. In short, there will be times when they will have to sort out their own difficulties before they can resume counselling others. When this happens, the important thing for counsellors to recognise is that re-evaluating their beliefs, motives and levels of functioning through counselling will enable them to continue working more effectively and ethically with clients.

Perhaps the most important aspect of this process of continual self-development is for counsellors to adopt an ever-present attitude of self-assessment, of critical self-reflection toward their work, themselves and their relationships with others. Such an attitude is founded on cognitive flexibility, curiosity and the ability to tolerate ambiguity. The process of counselling must be viewed with positive fascination, optimism and a sense of challenge. When it ceases to be so, every counsellor must again answer the question: 'Should I [continue to] be a counsellor?'

exercise **3.1**

1   Discuss with four or five others your reasons for wanting to become a
    counsellor. Afterwards, evaluate your participation. How open, searching,
    and honest were you in your statements about yourself? Did you hold
    back some reasons and instead say what you felt was safe and acceptable?
    How did others feel about your degree of openness?

2   Counselling is often a difficult, uncertain process in which many issues
    and questions remain unfinished and unanswered. In pairs, answer the
    following:

    a   How much of this sort of discomfort can you tolerate?

    b   Are you secure and self-confident enough not to *need* client approval
        and admiration? How do you know this?

    c   To what degree do you like to be in control of situations and other
        people?

    d   Can you accept that many clients may never give you positive feedback
        or express their gratitude?

    e   Why do you want to be a counsellor?

3   When both people have completed the statements in activity 2, discuss
    the following questions in the larger group:

    a   How open, searching, and honest were you in your statements about
        yourself?

    b   Which statements were the easiest to complete? Which were the most
        difficult? Why?

    c   What did you learn about yourself?

4   Using the information and self-knowledge gained from the activities above,
    write a one-page statement of your present motivations to be a counsellor.
    Keep this statement and refer to it frequently as you progress through this
    book or your training course. Alter and amend your statement at any time
    you wish. Do not share your statement with others unless you want to do
    so.

The counsellor's personal cultural history

A major area of counsellors' self-knowledge is their personal history and its
influence on their present views of people and society. This topic was introduced
in chapter 2 in relation to developing cross-cultural competence. The focus here,
while similar and complementary, is on how counsellors' families-of-origin have
affected the way they think and feel about themselves – their values and beliefs
about religion, morality, politics and race and gender issues. It is helpful for

counsellors to focus on specific topics from their family-of-origin, such as who constituted the family and what kinds of relationships existed among its members, what rules operated and what sanctions and rewards supported them, how decisions were typically made and how the family dealt with tensions and crises. Discussing the content and composition of old family photographs can be a valuable aid to recall how the family actually operated and how it might still influence the counsellor's behaviour as an adult. It can also be helpful for counsellors to discuss their family history further back, by considering their grandparents and great-grandparents and the ways in which the grandparents' life experiences may still be relevant to their own.

exercise 3.2

1   Your own family-of-origin:
   a   Choose 3–4 early family photos (taken when you were about to 3 to 12 years old) to share with two or three other people. When describing your family as it appears in the photos, try to identify the roles various family members played, the rules for interacting that operated, and the groupings of children and/or adults that had a significant influence on your family's functioning. Try to gain a clearer understanding of how your family-of-origin has affected your present values and beliefs. This exercise can become so absorbing that you may need to set a time limit so everyone has an equal opportunity to share.

   b   Draw a family genogram going back as many generations as you can. Include as much detail as you can: names and ages of all family members; dates of birth, marriages, divorces, deaths and significant life events; occupations, illnesses, other life changes. Make notes of events, achievements and milestones. Look for interesting trends, repeated situations, significant events. If it is possible, talk to other family members and sort through old photos and family possessions. What conclusions can you draw about yourself, your values, beliefs, life decisions, abilities and interests as a result of completing a genogram?

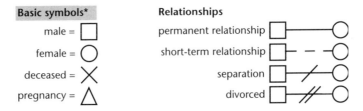

(*You may need to create your own shorthand or notations that help you summarise information in your genogram.)

   c   Draw a floor plan of the house in which you spent a significant amount of time as a child. Describe the floor plan to the others in your group. As you do this, look for significant factors that identify your family's functioning. For example, how were bedrooms allocated? Who was placed where? Which areas of the house were private? Public? Which activities could be done where? Why? Again, try to gain a clearer understanding of how your family-of-origin has affected your present values and beliefs.

   d   In groups of 3–4, construct a personal sociogram. Draw a pictorial representation of yourself in relation to others in your life (family members, co-workers, friends, distant acquaintances). What relationships and values regarding people are obvious? Where do those values come from in your life? How do your present relationships influence your beliefs about counselling?

Developing self-awareness

Becoming a counsellor involves the continual process of becoming more self-aware and increasing self-understanding. Two important behaviours in this process are for counsellors to take risks by revealing parts of themselves to others, and to be willing to ask for and receive feedback from others about how they affect others and how well their behaviour matches their intentions.

Risk-taking involves trying out new behaviours, sharing thoughts and feelings with others and attempting to do those things which might be difficult, that is, similar to what clients are asked to do. In these ways counsellors begin to discover more about their abilities and limitations, and how people perceive them and react to them.

exercise 3.3

1   In groups of two or three share information about yourself (i.e., self-disclose) by completing the following statements:

   a   Joining a new group makes me feel …

   b   I like people to think I am …

   c   When things are getting me down, I …

   d   At this moment I feel …

   e   I get embarrassed when …

   f   My biggest fear in social situations is …

   g   Doing this exercise made me …

2   When everyone has answered all of the questions, discuss the following:

   a   How did you feel while doing this exercise?

   b   Which questions were easiest to answer? Most difficult?

   c   Did you use objective and factual information about yourself to answer the questions, or subjective and 'feeling' information? Which is more revealing of yourself? Why?

   d   What did you learn about yourself?

This exercise can be made more or less intense or challenging by pairing participants with, for example, someone they know/don't know, like/dislike or trust/distrust, and by gradually introducing more personal and revealing questions.

exercise 3.4

The purpose of this exercise is to get you to take a small risk by doing something new or difficult. First, think of a situation or activity that you have wanted to change, challenge, confront, or attempt, but have never been able to do before. For example, you may want to meet a certain stranger, sort out a misunderstanding with a workmate, or volunteer to lead an activity. Second, think of ways in which you could accomplish your goal. Third, choose the way you think is the best and put it into action.

Later, discuss the results with others. Why did your attempt succeed? Fail? How do you feel having done it? Was it worth the risk?

Feedback from others provides counsellors with a valuable source of information. Counsellors must be prepared to learn from more than their own experiences so that they can change, modify, and be aware of which of their behaviours are appropriate and which are not.

In giving and receiving feedback, counsellors will be most effective if they observe the following guidelines:

- *Give* feedback when it is requested. *Ask* for it only when it is desired.

- Focus on specific behaviours and avoid sweeping, judgemental statements about a person's character or personality.

- Use simple, non-technical language when describing another's behaviour.

- Give feedback on behaviour the other person can control and change.

- Give feedback as soon after the event or behaviour as possible. Do not store it up for later use.

- Positive feedback is usually more effective than negative. People need to know their strengths as well as their weaknesses.

- Accept the feedback as given, without misconstruing or generalising the content.

- The receiver should have an opportunity to react to the feedback and check its accuracy with others.

exercise 3.5

Seeing yourself as others see you is a powerful method of learning about yourself. There are a number of structured situations that can be used to encourage constructive feedback and sharing of perceptions.

1 Pair up with someone you have had some contact with already. Complete the following sentences:
   a You seem like the kind of person who …
   b If you were angry, I would expect you to be …
   c If you were happy, I would expect you to be …
   d I appreciate you most when you …
   e If you were my counsellor, I would expect you to be …

2 Reverse roles with your partner. Speak as though you were that person. Try to describe yourself as you think your partner sees you as a person; as a counsellor. When finished, discuss what information/insights you have gained about yourself.

The counsellor's personal qualities

Although there is no specific set of personal qualities or characteristics that the effective counsellor must possess, the following are thought to be desirable: mental flexibility, warmth, acceptance of others, open-mindedness, empathy, self-awareness, genuineness, respect for others, non-dominance, objectivity, personal maturity, optimism and the ability to tolerate tension and ambiguity. To state that these are essential is quite another matter. Researching these qualities is complicated by a number of factors such as imprecision of language, problems of control and measurement, and usefulness of the results in other situations. Furthermore, such qualities are not absolutes and their presence or absence cannot be objectively determined. Rather, it is the client's judgement regarding the presence and degree of these counsellor qualities that is crucial, not the counsellor's own belief that he/she possesses them. In fact, different clients will prefer different counsellors, but usually for similar reasons. The implication of this is that educators cannot posit a best or ideal counsellor type, and selection procedures for training courses must take this into account.

In trying to describe the effective counsellor, the best that can be done seems to be to supplement research findings with expert opinion, personal experience, and common sense. Perhaps a more useful way of indicating the personal qualities desirable in the counsellor would be to describe three areas of counselling in which they are important: the counsellor as a model, the counselling relationship, and the counsellor's courage to counsel.

The counsellor as a model

Modelling takes place in most learning situations. Essentially it is a means of learning through imitating the actions of others. In counselling, clients imitate their counsellor's actions and take certain of their counsellor's beliefs and attitudes as their own. This process is inevitable and beyond the counsellor's control. However, counsellors should be aware of and accepting of themselves, their values and their behaviours, so that they present a consistent model for effective relating and problem solving. Such characteristics as being open, non-biased, non-judgemental, sensitive and caring can then be seen as directly related to effective helping.

The counselling relationship

It is widely accepted by practitioners and theorists that the relationship between counsellor and client is an important aspect of counselling. Effective counsellors are thought to be those who are able to establish caring, non-threatening relationships with their clients in which both feel safe and secure enough to interact as genuine, spontaneous people. The quality of this relationship can in itself be therapeutic and it depends very largely on the counsellor's being a real person. However, different clients may respond positively to different relationship factors. So, while it is safe to say that the relationship between counsellor and client is important, we cannot assume automatically that a particular kind of relationship is best for all clients. It is clients that are the final arbiters of which relationships are helpful and supportive.

The courage to counsel

In order to help others, counsellors need courage and self-confidence. There are many times when it would be easier for counsellors to opt out of helping: to ignore a plea for help; make excuses for not wanting to become involved with another person; or judge a situation to be hopeless, unrealistic, trivial, or outside their area of competence. To make a commitment to help another person carries with it responsibilities and uncertainties. All those who seriously intend becoming effective counsellors must be willing to accept those responsibilities and uncertainties and place themselves in situations of personal, emotional, interpersonal, and vocational risk. Counsellors must be prepared to function as whole and real people rather than as performers acting only within safely prescribed limits.

Role-playing as a counselling skill

Much of living and learning involves the playing of roles. This is particularly true in counselling, both in training to be a counsellor and working therapeutically with clients. Role-playing itself is not a unique or unusual form of behaviour. All relationships involve role-playing, since people relate to others as holders of a certain role, status, or position.

Role-playing is the process of acting the part of a real or imagined person. When used in counsellor training, it has a number of potential benefits for counsellors:

- By role-playing real situations early in training, counsellors can feel free to try new behaviours and make mistakes without worrying about adverse effects on actual clients.

- Role-playing enables counsellors to experience what it feels like to be a client and to develop ability and confidence in portraying and expressing feelings and ideas.

- Role-playing helps counsellors to learn by doing rather than by merely discussing techniques and strategies in an abstract and intellectual manner.

- Role-playing is useful in learning about the dynamics of forming and building a relationship.

There are difficulties in role-playing as a training device, however. Many people find it threatening. This threat should be faced and overcome by those intending to become counsellors. Also, some people are so guarded or unimaginative in expressing their feelings that they are ineffective in role-playing, or they portray clients who are difficult to work with, emotionally dull, and unresponsive. Those who have these difficulties should practise expressing their own feelings, even exaggerating them, until they are able to express easily and realistically a wide range of emotions. A related problem is that of trying to beat or frustrate the counsellor by playing an impossibly difficult client. The aim of role-playing is not to compete against a counsellor but to simulate a real counselling situation.

Role-playing may be criticised as being artificial. While there is some justification for this view, most role-players report that they very quickly forget about themselves and become totally engrossed in the part they are playing because the roles they are playing are really extensions of themselves. Thus, whatever the supposed difficulties of role-playing as a training device, it allows people an opportunity to experience new situations, practise new behaviours, reveal themselves in safety and gain confidence and skill in relating to others. If individuals persist in labelling the situation as artificial and refuse to take part, they may be avoiding something in themselves and should be asked to evaluate their stance. Role-playing, whether from detailed, scripted material or from wholly imagined material, is ultimately an expression of each player's self: beliefs, attitudes, and feelings.

In counselling, much of what counsellors ask or encourage their clients to do, or suggest that they should do, involves acting differently or changing aspects of their behaviour; in short, playing new or more effective roles. Counsellors should be willing and able to model the behaviours they want their clients to try.

---

exercise **3.6**

1   Group role-playing. Someone from the group plays the role of client while the rest of the group simultaneously plays counsellor. Clients can role-play any problem, concern or situation they wish. As the counsellors begin to respond, the client should deal with one response at a time, saying, 'Yes, that was useful or encouraging because …', or 'No, that was not useful or encouraging because …'. When a 'Yes' response is received from the client, the group should continue as though in a real counselling situation.

When finished, the 'client' describes what it felt like to be a client, and the exercise is repeated with another person playing the part of client. This method of role-playing minimises the threat to any one person by having several people play counsellor simultaneously. It also gives those playing counsellor some information about how effective their responses are, and at the same time encourages 'clients' to be aware of how they feel in that role and in response to what is said to them.

2   The large group divides into smaller groups of three or four. Two people role-play an interview situation as in the first exercise above. Those people not role-playing should act as observers and comment on how authentic the role-play seems and how helpful or otherwise the counsellor's statements seem. Repeat this situation until everyone has played both counsellor and client.

3   Finally, people should pair up and discuss real situations with their partners. Everyone has something they are concerned about and which they can safely share with another person. The topic does not have to be a major concern or worry, but it should be current. The counsellor's aim is to listen, understand, and respond as helpfully as possible. After 15 minutes, switch roles and repeat. This variation makes the situation more authentic and gives the person playing client the opportunity to experience what it is like to ask for and receive help.

Being an effective trainee

If you are a counsellor-in-training, you have some responsibilities yourself and some legitimate expectations of your trainers and supervisors. First, you owe it to yourself to be motivated, well-prepared, accepting of feedback, open to new ideas and honest with yourself. One of the most important things is to admit to and explore both your fears about training and the things about counselling you do not know, without shame or embarrassment. If approached in the right frame of mind, that is, 'I don't know, but I care and want to know', your uncertainties and ignorance can be used to enhance your learning by promoting an attitude of constructive curiosity, inventiveness and inquiry (Kerwin, 1994). When learning as part of a larger group, you should work co-operatively, constructively and supportively with others. You should also insist that your training include regular supervision of audio and/or video recordings of your counselling. One-to-one supervision of your work in this way is invaluable. There is no short cut, no matter how anxiety-provoking the process might seem to you.

Finally, you have a right expect quality training, adequate support, accurate feedback and patience from your trainers. Your trainers should be fair, neutral, well-prepared, knowledgeable and competent as teachers and supervisors. Insist on this. Remember, it is your training, so get the most out of it.

Chapter **4** Finding solutions to problems

wo models of counselling, problem-solving and solution-focused, are integrated to form the **finding-solutions-to-problems** approach. The seven stages in the model and the skills appropriate to each are outlined.

Brief counselling

The approach to counselling that this book presents is one example of a general category of counselling approaches called brief (or time-limited) problem-solving. Although the practice of planned brief counselling has as its primary focus the resolution of client problems in as simple and efficient a manner as possible, nowhere in this book will an optimum number of sessions or amount of time for counselling be recommended. Counselling should continue for as long as it is needed. But in this book, a key principle is that counselling should be planned and conducted within a limited time/minimal cost framework.

Planned brief counselling usually includes at least five components (Bloom, 1992, p. 157):

1 prompt intervention;

2 a relatively high level of counsellor activity;

3 establishment of specific but limited goals;

4 the identification and maintenance of a clear focus;

5 the setting of time limits.

In recent years the popularity of brief counselling has grown immensely, spurred by an increasing concern for efficiency and economy (Bloom, 1992; Gentner, 1991; Hoyt, 1991), the use of task-centred, homework-based approaches (Steenbarger, 1992) and the accumulating evidence of its effectiveness (Bloom, 1992; Steenbarger, 1992). There is even some evidence that most clients prefer brief counselling and that they benefit most from the first six to eight sessions (Eckert, 1993).

Counsellors working within brief models have as their goal helping clients to cope better rather than to 'cure' them, and they focus on immediate problems or symptoms rather than on underlying or unconscious concerns. In short, they accept and respect their clients' needs to continue functioning adequately in their day-to-day lives, to solve their problems quickly and to do so as cost-effectively as possible.

Solutions to problems: integrating the problem-solving and solution-focused models of counselling

The specific model of brief counselling presented in the following chapters, called **finding solutions to problems,** is an integration of two seemingly divergent, but actually similar, approaches: problem-solving (as in Dixon & Glover, 1984; Munro, Manthei, & Small, 1988) and solution-focused (as in de Shazer, 1985; 1988; 1991). It represents a process view of problems, that is, the problems that clients experience represent an ongoing series of unsuccessful attempts to resolve their difficulties rather than a deficit in personality or a dysfunctional family structure (Fraser, 1995). The counsellor's emphasis in this model is on identifying repeated patterns of behaviour rather than single causes, and on clients' perceptions of their difficulties and the meanings they attach to those difficulties rather than someone's objective diagnosis of it.

Approach #1: The problem-solving model

The problem-solving model of counselling does not differ in its essentials from approaches to the solving of problems that have been found useful in other contexts. Indeed, it is because of the wide applicability of problem-solving models to many aspects of human behaviour that the approach is so strongly commended here. The problem-solving approach recognises that problems in life are normal:

- that all people have them;
- that all people use some form(s) of problem-solving – however unsophisticated – and are therefore already familiar with the process;
- that some forms of problem-solving are more successful than others;
- that people sometimes fail to recognise that they already possess effective solutions to their problems;
- that people sometimes are too emotional, or lack motivation or clarity, to employ problem-solving successfully (Dixon & Glover, 1984).

In addition, the problem-solving model serves as a useful guide for counsellors beginning their careers, providing a positive, goal-oriented framework which offers guidance and direction, but still allows the counsellors freedom to choose from a range of styles and techniques. In other words, it is a robust, flexible approach that can easily accommodate ideas and techniques from other approaches.

Of the various models of problem-solving that have been proposed for counselling, the five-step approach by Dixon and Glover (1984) is simple, pragmatic and locates problems in the context of the client's social environment. Their systems-based approach has been extended in this book by adding two more stages: matters to think about prior to the first session, and the first things to consider in actually getting started. The first of these two stages includes counsellors' being aware of their own values about counselling and the possibility that pre-counselling changes have already occurred (Talmon, 1990; Weiner-Davis, de Shazer & Gingerich, 1987). The second involves the many things to be attended to before serious talking actually begins, things like building a trusting relationship, using available client background information, and effectively inducting the client into counselling. Thus, the seven stages used in the **finding-solutions-to-problems** model are:

1 pre-counselling considerations;

2 getting started;

3 problem exploration;

4 goal setting;

5 strategy selection;

6 strategy implementation;

7 evaluating success.

The exact stages necessary when working with each client, their precise content and the amount of time spent on each are less important than that counsellors recognise the value of being reasonably systematic and see in the model an effective decision-making process and guide for working with clients.

Approach #2: Solution-focused counselling

In solution-focused counselling, attention is centred on generating possible solutions to client problems rather than analysing the problems themselves. Solution-focused counselling can be thought of as a truncated version of the fuller process of problem solving. In effect, the focus of attention moves quickly to the goal setting and implementation stages. Far less time and attention is spent on forming a relationship and defining and exploring the client's problem. The approach, developed and described by de Shazer (1985; 1988; 1991) and Berg (1994; Berg & Miller, 1992), has been classified as strategic, systemic and social constructionist in its assumptions about knowledge (Berg, 1994; de Shazer, 1991; Guterman, 1994; Steenbarger, 1992). Social constructionism represents an approach to knowledge that disputes the existence of a world that can be known objectively and called 'the truth'. Instead, it assumes that there are multiple truths and, therefore, a variety of explanations that may fit each client's situation.

In practical terms this means that both clients' problems and their solutions are *co-constructed* by clients *and* their counsellors (Guterman, 1994). In solution-focused counselling, no assumptions are made about the 'true' nature of the client's problem. Rather, solutions are found for each individual client (Berg & Miller, 1992).

In brief, the central task of solution-focused counselling is to identity, amplify and reinforce those aspects of clients' lives that do not represent problems, but rather are constructive and desired, including any positive happenings that may already have occurred before counselling actually begins, that is, pre-counselling changes. One way of doing this is to look for instances when the problem is absent or not a problem and identify exactly what is happening at those times. Find out who is doing what. These exceptions to the problem – however small – can often then be repeated and their frequency increased. In effect, they become key behaviours for identifying and structuring therapeutic goals and solutions (Berg, 1994; Molnar & de Shazer, 1987). In this goal-oriented, solution-focused approach, the counsellor functions as a naive non-expert whose job is to find out, to be respectful of the client's inherent competence and creativity, and to convey optimism and an orientation to success to his/her clients. As a consequence, clients become co-participants in their own counselling (on a more equal basis) and both *identify* possible solutions to their predicaments and *choose* which one(s) they wish to implement.

Finding solutions to problems: an integrated model

These two seemingly different approaches are combined to form the **finding-solutions-to-problems** model of counselling. The addition to Dixon and Glover's problem-solving model of pre-session change questions and the addition of the process of identifying exceptions to problems provide the counsellor with greater flexibility in structuring the counselling process. In effect, the counsellor and client can choose whether and when to focus on:

- pre-counselling improvements (What is better and why?);
- problems (What's wrong? or, What's not working?);
- instances of client strengths, abilities and successes;
- exceptions to problems (What's going well? What's working?);
- goals/solutions (What's desired? What needs to be done?).

Since virtually all models of counselling can be seen as a form of problem-solving, either implicitly or explicitly, the problem-solving model as a meta-theory of counselling can be used as an overarching framework for integrating other approaches (Dixon & Glover, 1984, p. 5). Similarly, because it is process-based, the solution-focused model is general enough and flexible enough to incorporate the ideas and techniques of many other approaches. As Guterman (1994, p. 235) suggests, 'its formal content is posited in general terms that permit the incorporation of virtually any informal content during its change process.'

He described the model as a meta-theory that could explain most other theoretical ideas and concepts and still retain its theoretical integrity. The combination of the two approaches, called **finding solutions to problems**, results in a robust model of counselling that allows counsellors to incorporate content, constructs and principles of change from other theories of counselling should they choose to do so. How and when this is done will depend on what the client's needs are perceived to be. In spite of its ready compatibility with other approaches and techniques, however, the **finding-solutions-to-problems** model of counselling *on its own* is believed to be a coherent, effective and efficient method of dealing with most client problems.

Problems and solutions are closely related concepts. In a sense they are different sides of the same coin. Problems are instances when client attempts to solve or rectify matters have been unsuccessful, usually repeatedly so. When this happens, the tendency is to analyse the problem more closely so that what is wrong and why things continue to go wrong is understood more precisely. Once these details are known, a plan for fixing the problem can be devised and implemented.

On the other hand, in practice it is possible to solve problems without ever knowing what they are – as long as the solution is new and results in desired change. Nevertheless, solutions presuppose the existence of problems. Therefore, a solution-focused approach can be thought of as a form of problem-solving that avoids repeating unsuccessful solutions (that is, merely doing more of what has not worked) and, instead, identifies new solutions that do work (Amatea, 1991; Fraser, 1995). In effect, to know in detail what has not worked (i.e., problems, or failed solutions) can be a valuable, but not essential, step in discovering what will work (i.e., solutions that really are solutions).

Inevitably, counselling starts with problems because clients begin with 'problem talk' about the difficulties they are currently experiencing. At this point, counsellors can decide whether to engage clients in problem-solving or solution building. If the latter is chosen, clients will probably need help in shifting their perspective from problems (What's wrong?) to solutions (What's right?) since a solution focus will probably be dramatically new to them. A simple process for doing this has been described by Furman (SFT-Discussion List, email communication, 1/10/96) as follows: client disturbances (disorders, conditions – often with labels) should first be translated into problems (What is wrong? Why is it a problem?) and then into goals (What is desired? What needs to be done?). Once goals have been described, finding solutions or ways to accomplish those goals becomes more straightforward.

For most counsellors and clients the **finding-solutions-to-problems** approach represents an important – sometimes radical – shift in thinking. Counsellors trained in traditional theories of helping may find it difficult to pay less attention to difficulties, deficits and complications and focus more on client strengths, competencies and possibilities. For many, this shift from problems to possibilities requires the adoption of new beliefs and values about clients and the conduct of counselling (Friedman and Fanger, 1991): beliefs and values which give clients messages of hope, competence and choice.

A basic belief of the **finding-solutions-to-problems** model of counselling is the notion that 'clients need to feel in control of their lives as much as possible' (Berg, 1994, p. 61), a concept called 'empowerment'. Empowering clients means accepting that the client-counsellor relationship is collaborative and that clients are competent, capable and expert on matters affecting their own lives. 'It is an approach that respects the client's autonomy and personal, familial, and cultural boundaries' (Berg, 1994, p. 61). This belief in clients' competence is fundamental and central to the model of counselling presented in this book. Additional beliefs and values (Berg, 1994; Berg & Miller, 1992; Friedman & Fanger, 1991; Weiner-Davis, 1992) that are important include the following:

- The emphasis is on health rather than illness, strengths rather than weaknesses.

- Clients are empowered to feel in control of their lives.

- Effective counselling builds on those thoughts, feelings and behaviours that are already being used successfully by the client.

- Counselling is focused on the future rather than the past.

- Clients are regarded as capable of finding solutions to their own problems and are responsible for doing so.

- How problems came to exist or why they continue to exist are seen as relatively unimportant.

- Counselling starts with the simplest interventions before trying more complicated methods.

- Small changes can lead to bigger changes, a sort of ripple effect.

- No attempt is made to define the 'true' nature of the problem.

- Clients are not given psychiatric labels, nor forced to accept treatment.

- Counselling will usually be brief and intermittent rather than long-term and once-only.

The primary goal of the **finding-solutions-to-problems** model of helping is to help others resolve their problems as efficiently and quickly as possible, not just for them to understand their problems better. The aim is to help them cope more effectively with difficulties in their daily lives rather than to find a perfect, permanent cure.

Different clients will be able to move through the seven **finding-solutions-to-problems** stages at different rates and in different sequences. For example, for some clients, solving problems does not always 'mean that the client's problem needs to be explored in great detail or defined exactly or even talked about at great length' (de Shazer, 1988, p. 52). Other clients will want to pin down their concerns, understand them and describe them clearly in the form of some specific problem(s); still others may find it difficult to distinguish between big problems (costly in terms of time, money or emotional output) and little ones, or real problems as opposed to pseudo-problems (Manthei, 1990). For some it may seem impossible to think of alternative ways of doing things, while for others it may be impossible to see how they contribute to or have control over some aspect of the problem or a solution to it.

Counsellors will have to be aware of those steps of the process that clients find most difficult and move counselling to a more productive stage of the process. In some cases, this may mean going back to an earlier stage (e.g., problem definition or goal specification) when it becomes evident that the outcomes of that stage have not been accomplished. It is important for counsellors to keep in mind that, ultimately, the goal of counselling is to discover and increase desired, successful patterns of behaviour rather than merely understand faulty or dysfunctional ones.

Another important point about the **finding-solutions-to-problems** approach to counselling is that it can be used to teach clients a general model of coping which can be transferred to other situations other than the particular concern that brought them to the counsellor in the first place. Counsellors should, therefore, think of their role as including both guiding and educating clients. These roles can be fulfilled by making sure that the process of counselling is clear to clients; by working *with* rather than *on* the client; by encouraging the client to take as much responsibility for the process as possible; by crediting clients for the successes they achieve, and by spending time during the session discussing what has been learnt and considering how that learning might be applied in other situations.

Finally, although the focus of discussion and examples used in this book are on counselling individuals, the **finding-solutions-to-problems** model of counselling is equally applicable to counselling couples, families and small groups.

The finding-solutions-to-problems model of counselling

It is most important that counsellors be clear about where they and their clients are in the process of resolving clients' problems. Unfortunately, some counsellors miss out or rush through important steps in the process, for example by trying to move to a solution before the client's emotional state has been supportively and adequately recognised (e.g., Lipchik, 1994). Highly emotional clients are usually less able to think or act clearly, and may therefore have difficulty identifying exceptions or specifying concrete goals, both of which are largely cognitive tasks. Instead, they may need time to express and explore their feelings, to gain greater self-control and composure before continuing. Another common mistake is to seize on the first solution likely to solve the problem, without first considering what has already been tried (and has failed) and without considering several alternative possibilities.

Although each step in the **finding-solutions-to-problems** model is important and it is best to be as systematic as possible, counselling seldom proceeds in a strictly linear fashion. Thus, to have to return to an earlier stage does not necessarily mean that the counsellor or counselling has been ineffective.

Similarly, it may be necessary to spend only a brief time defining the problem before looking for exceptions to it and identifying desired goals. The important thing is to spend whatever time is required at each stage of helping.

It should be emphasised here that counselling that is planned, intentional and solution-oriented is often condensed into quite a short time. If there is a good working relationship and a high state of readiness on the part of the client, the necessary steps may be covered satisfactorily in a comparatively short amount of time, even in one session of less than fifty minutes. With complex issues or less motivated clients, however, it may take several lengthier sessions before the problem is clearly defined, goals are identified and satisfactory solutions are implemented. Recent research has shown that solution-oriented counselling can be, on average, as brief as three sessions per client (Berg & De Jong, 1996).

In the remainder of this chapter, the seven-stage **finding-solutions-to-problems** model is explained and the skills and considerations appropriate to each stage are listed. The fact that a skill is listed and described in relation to one stage but not another does not mean that it cannot be used earlier or later in the sequence of stages. Rather, the skills have been introduced at the point where it is likely that they will first be used or used to best effect. More detailed discussions of the skills and exercises for practising them appear in chapters 5, 6 and 7.

Stage 1: Pre-counselling considerations

Counsellors need to be aware that their own values and attitudes to counselling and to people are important factors in how they will approach counselling and how they will interact with clients. All counsellors need to know and scrutinise their own values, attitudes and cultural backgrounds and understand how these factors impact on their counselling. And since these beliefs and attitudes tend to change over time, examining them must be an ongoing activity (review chapter 2).

In addition, counsellors need to be aware that it is not unusual for clients to experience improvements in their problems before their counselling begins (e.g., Weiner-Davis et al., 1987). Often the decision to seek help signals an important turning point in clients' lives – from being overwhelmed, stuck or immobilised to beginning to deal directly and constructively with their problem(s). Therefore, one of the first tasks of the counsellor is to be aware of this possibility of pre-counselling change and to consider ways of triggering, supporting, encouraging and amplifying it. Several things need to be examined and thought about:

- the counsellor's values and attitudes (see chapter 3);
- stimulating pre-counselling improvement;
- 'Sowing the seeds of change' (Talmon, 1990);
- inducting clients into counselling;
- informing clients about counselling.

Stage 2: Getting started

At the point when the client appears for the first counselling session but actual talking has not yet begun, the counsellor is already thinking about and acting on a number of things. These include ways in which to establish a good working relationship with this particular client, what can be deduced about the client from available background information and what is salient about the client's appearance and manner. Things to consider include:

- How to build a trusting relationship.
- Is the client a voluntary or an involuntary client?
- Use of background information.
- Counselling as a reciprocal relationship.
- Positive first impressions.

Stage 3: Problem exploration

Once the client has been met and greeted, the client's reasons for seeking help are addressed. Exploring the problem, assessing client motivation for help, noting client strengths and abilities, and asking clients if they noticed any improvements in their problems prior to arriving for counselling (pre-session change) are important tasks at this stage. Also, it is important to find out about previous successful and unsuccessful attempts to solve the problem: what worked and what did not? Skills include:

- Encouraging exploration of problems and/or solutions
  Exploring pre-counselling improvements
  Compliments
  Open invitation to talk
  Sorting issues
  Coping questions
  Open and closed questions
  Topic following
  Using silence

- Demonstrating understanding
  Active listening
  Reflection
  Accurate understanding
  Thinking aloud

- Attending to feelings
  Identifying feelings
  Expressing feelings

- Assessing client problems and motivation
  Necessary expertise
  Choice/change problems

Identifying positive assets
Client motivation
Problem severity (scaling questions)

- Anticipating termination

- Engaging non-customers

- The language of counselling

Stage 4: Goal-setting

After the problem has been explored and previous attempts to solve it identified, this information can then be used in setting goals to solve it. These goals should be clearly defined, achievable, realistic and desired by the client. Useful skills at this stage include:

- Direct questioning

- Identifying possible goals

- Looking for exceptions
  Exception questions
  Miracle questions

- Sorting goals

- Gaining commitment

- Dealing with discrepancies

- Giving information

- Giving advice

- Influencing

- Interpretation

- Reframing

- Using personal examples

- Advising a delay

- Supporting and encouraging

Stage 5: Strategy selection

Once the client has identified a goal and is committed to pursuing it, it is necessary to talk about ways in which the goal can be achieved. Since there may be several possible strategies, it is necessary to select the one that is best and most likely to succeed. Skills at this stage include:

- Anticipating situations

- Providing models

- Role-playing
- Using rewards

Stage 6: Strategy implementation

The next step is to work out how the chosen strategy is to be implemented. In doing this it may be necessary to explore what additional information or skills are needed. Skills include:

- Making records
- Bodily awareness, relaxation, activities
- Thoughts and imagery
- Mixing strategies
- Summarising
- Designing a homework task
- Scheduling another session

Stage 7: Evaluating success

After the chosen strategy or solution has been tried, client and counsellor together need to evaluate its effectiveness. Was the strategy or homework task successful? Were there improvements? Can counselling be terminated? Is a referral elsewhere necessary? Skills and activities that are effective at this stage include:

- Assessing results
- Generalising results
- Referral
- Termination

An overview of the counselling process

What follows is a general outline of what is covered in the first and subsequent sessions of the **finding-solutions-to-problems** counselling. Of course, not all of the steps and the skills listed previously will be used with every client.

1 Pre-counselling considerations

a   The counsellor's orientation and values

In this model counsellors subscribe to certain values and have certain aims in mind. These are that counselling will:
- deliver brief, intermittent help in the simplest way possible;

- enable clients to cope more effectively with the concerns in their lives;
- treat clients as capable and possessing already the elements of effective solutions to their problems;
- help clients to focus on possibilities (What is wanted? What is working already?) rather than on problems (What is wrong? What is not working?).

b Fostering pre-session change

Can clients be contacted (e.g., by phone or mail) asking them to notice any changes that might occur before they have their first session? This method of anticipating pre-counselling improvements can help to plant the seeds of change and engender in clients an attitude of optimism and hope (Talmon, 1990).

> 'Between now and the first session, notice the things that happen that you would like to keep happening. This will help your counsellor to find out more about your goal and what you are up to.'

(Based on the pre-session change question in Talmon, 1990, p. 19.)

2 Getting started

a How best can the client be 'inducted' into counselling and the role of client?

What information can be given to clients regarding their rights and responsibilities; the conditions of counselling, such as costs; what to expect during the process, and how to make a complaint? What are the major aims of the counsellor's model of counselling?

b Pre-session change

The purpose of asking about pre-session change is to find out if things have already improved, even a small amount, and thereby orient the client toward possibilities and hope rather than problems and despondency. Therefore, the counsellor can begin counselling by asking if clients have noticed any improvements. This process may already have been initiated in Stage 1. If the answer is 'yes, changes have already occurred', the counsellor should then explore the reasons for those improvements and identify the factors over which the client has control. If the answer is 'about the same' or 'things are worse', the counsellor should explore the possibility that the client has managed to prevent the situation from being even more serious than it is.

> 'What have you been doing to keep things from becoming worse?'

Another useful question to ask is why clients have decided to seek counselling now. That is, what has happened that has made it desirable or possible to seek counselling at this particular time? Answers to this question often indicate significant shifts in thinking about problems and what can be done about them.

'Since the time you first contacted me and now, have things changed at all?'

'Have you noticed any improvements?' If the client says *'Yes'* ask *'What's different?'* and/or *'How did you manage that?'*

c   Assess the following

What specifically do clients want from the counsellor? Do they want a particular kind of help? A good and sympathetic listener? Advice? Knowledge from an expert? What previous experience of counselling have they had and how may that influence their present expectations? Once counsellors know what clients want from them, they must describe what role they are willing to play in response: listener? helper? information-giver? Is it best to refer the client to another source of help?

Counsellors should spend time assessing and considering the following: Is the client a voluntary or an involuntary client? What prior information about the client is available? What information is needed, but lacking? What are the client's emotional and physical states?

It is often useful to assess both the type of problem clients describe (is it a problem of choice or change?) and their readiness for counselling (are they customers or non-customers?).

3 Problem exploration

a   Encourage clients to talk freely and openly about their problems/concerns.

('What's bothering you?' 'How can I help you?') If necessary, deal directly with their hesitance or apparent reluctance to engage in counselling.

Problems can be simple or complex, single or multiple, of central or peripheral importance to daily functioning. Sort through the client's concerns and focus on the one the client chooses to address first. Next, explore the question of which solutions, both successful and unsuccessful, have already been tried.

b   Look for exceptions to the problem

As early in the process as possible, ask clients to identify and explore recent instances when the problem was absent and they felt that their situation was fine/OK.

'Was there a time recently when the problem was not a problem? Tell me about that.'

'What were you doing differently at that time?'

'What would others (family, spouse, friend) say about the times when the problem is not a problem?'

'What's happening in your life at the moment that you want to continue happening; what are the things that you want to experience more of?'

4 Goals (that is, the things clients will be doing more of when their problems are solved)

Explore exceptions (times when the problem is not a problem) for differences in the client's life that are important differences and within the client's control. Often it is useful to pretend that the problem has already been solved and to explore what the client's life would be like then. In this stage of counselling, the counsellor may need to point out discrepancies that arise or offer an interpretation of events or processes that help the client to adopt a new perspective or frame of reference.

Basically, establishing goals involves identifying aims that are realistic, clear, achievable, and desired by the client.

'What would you like to do that you cannot do now?'

'What would you rather have happening?'

'What changes would you like to see made?'

'If the problem disappeared, what is the first thing you would notice that was different?'

'What would others notice that was different?'

'What would tell you the problem was solved?'

5 Selecting strategies for accompanying goals

Explore the following: What needs doing to accomplish the goal(s)? What is already working well for the client? What are the client's strengths, abilities?

6 Implementing strategies

What particular task or homework can be assigned to ensure success so that the client will be given encouragement and hope for subsequent improvement? In essence, the preferred strategy is to identify what has already worked and to build on that. This can be done by first complimenting clients on the things they have already achieved and then deciding on a task that will enhance and amplify that success. If such homework is used, it should be clearly stated, be realistic and be achievable given the client's abilities. Homework will be seen as relevant and important to clients when its importance or necessity is explained in a convincing, credible way and clients believe they have a good chance of succeeding. The process of change should start with small steps and build on small successes. If it is used, homework should always be reviewed at the beginning of the next session/meeting.

The counsellor may need to use persuasion, give support or encouragement or perhaps even give advice in helping the client to carry out the homework.

'What do you need to do/learn/practise in order to be able to do that?'

'On a scale of 1 to 10, 1 being "very motivated" and 10 being "not at all motivated", how motivated are you to try this?'

'What would it take to move you from, say, a 4 to a 6?'

'What would it take to motivate you to try this?'

'How will you know when you are ready to do this? What is the first thing that needs to happen?'

7 Evaluating success

Begin subsequent sessions by finding out what has improved/not improved and why. Was the homework successful? If things are improving, enhance them, keep them going. Give clients credit for successes by complimenting them on their accomplishments. Identify the next steps that need to be taken.

Counselling can be terminated when clients are satisfied that they are coping adequately with their problems. In the case of a surprisingly large number of clients, one or two sessions are deemed sufficient, at least for the time being.

If things have not improved, review the problem definition, the goal, the client's motivation.

'What has improved?' (Anticipate success)

'On a scale of 1 to 10, where are you now? How did you manage that? How did you think of that?'

'What will it take to move one point higher?'

'Are the changes you have made so far adequate and satisfactory? When will you know that counselling is no longer necessary?'

Beginning the search for solutions to problems

I n this chapter the counselling skills in the first three stages of the finding- solutions-to-problems model – pre-counselling considerations, getting started, and problem exploration – are discussed and illustrated.

Stage 1: Pre-counselling considerations

Whenever it is possible to do so, counsellors need to review whatever information they have about clients and their reasons for seeking counselling before the first counselling session takes place. For example, if time has elapsed between the client's decision to seek counselling and the scheduled first session, it is quite likely that the client will have experienced some positive change in the problem. Although these changes may seem quite small and insignificant to the client, they are worth noting and exploring in greater detail.

In some settings, such as schools and medical centres, comprehensive records are usually available to be consulted by workers within that setting. If records are available, read them. What is the problem? How long has it been a problem? What has been tried previously? Who has referred the client for help? The credibility of the source of background information is another aspect to be considered. In other settings and circumstances, existing policies may prevent access to information about clients in order to preserve confidentiality. However, sometimes information will be offered directly by clients themselves, or they may give their permission for it to be released to specific individuals.

In addition, if counsellors work in settings where contact with clients can be made after clients' initial requests for help but before the first session, counsellors may want to consider whether information about themselves, the agency, the services offered, and the conditions of counselling might help to inform and reassure clients about what will happen in counselling. This information could be given to clients in the form of a personal information statement (also called a disclosure statement; Nelson & Nuefeldt, 1996) and would help to inform clients and the wider public about the services and treatment they can expect from counsellors. The following information could be included in such a statement:

- the counsellor's qualifications and certifications;
- membership of relevant professional associations and the code of ethics the counsellor follows;
- the types of work the counsellor is trained to do;
- a brief résumé of work experience as a counsellor;
- a clear, succinct description of the approach used and the way the counselling process is typically structured;
- a schedule of fees;
- hours of work and a contact address and phone number.

Sending clients a letter or phoning them before counselling starts is another way of helping them to engage in counselling, reducing their anxiety about counselling and fostering attitudes of hope and of competence rather than despair and incompetence. Such letters or phone calls could be used to inform clients of their position on a waiting-list (if applicable) and how the process of counselling actually works. Clients could also be asked to notice what solutions they have tried that have resulted in positive changes and any other ideas that they think might be helpful (Coles, 1995; Talmon, 1990). An example of such a question is:

> *'Between now and the first session, notice the things that happen to you that you would like to keep happening in the future. In this way, you will help [yourself and your counsellor] to find out more about your goal and what you are up to.'*
> (Based on Talmon, 1990, p. 19.)

Information of this sort helps to induct clients into the counselling process and the role of client by increasing their sense of hope, their expectation that counselling will be successful, their motivation to engage in counselling and knowledge of their rights and responsibilities as a client. It may also help them to focus on what is working and how they are already contributing to that success.

On the following page is one example of such a letter*.

---

* Based on an information statement provided by Te Ruru, a counsellor at *Soulutions Counselling Centre*, Christchurch, New Zealand.

The feel
BETTER Counselling Centre

Dear_____

   This letter is to welcome you to the **Feel Better Counselling Centre** and to give you information about what you can expect when you come to the Centre for counselling.

General procedures

Sessions usually last 50 to 60 minutes. If you are unable to attend a session, please give us at least 24 hours' notice; this will allow us to offer your time to someone else. If you miss a session without giving at least 24 hours' notice, you will be charged for the session at half your usual fee.

   At your first session, your counsellor will discuss with you how many sessions you can expect to have and how often your progress will be reviewed. Remember, you can choose to end your counselling at any stage.

   The Centre provides a professional, confidential service. Times when confidentiality cannot be assured will be discussed in your first session.

   Your counsellor may make written notes during your sessions. You can ask to see these at any time and be assured that they will be kept in a locked, secure place.

Things to ask about

You may wish to ask about your counsellor's experience, qualifications, preferred way of working, areas of expertise and professional affiliations. You may also wish to see the code of ethics that will be followed and the procedure for expressing dissatisfaction with the Centre or its services.

   All of the Centre's counsellors receive supervision. This process sometimes involves audio or video-taping, but this will only be done with your prior consent. You should always feel free to refuse.

Fees

Fees are negotiable. Please discuss this with your counsellor.
Individuals: _____ per session. Couples and families: _____ per session

Before your first session

At your first session, your counsellor will get to know you, and ask about your concerns and how you have tried to solve them. Your counsellor will want to know:

* if your problems have improved prior to your first session; and
* if they have, what have you done to make that happen?

So, between now and your first session, notice when your concerns are less severe. What is happening at those times that you want to continue happening?

Your counsellor will be _____ , and he/she is looking forward to meeting you at_____ (time) on _____ (date).

Yours sincerely,

exercise **5.1**

1   Write a personal statement that includes essential information about yourself as a professional counsellor. Try to include things you think clients would find useful and relevant to them. Discuss your statement with others who have done this exercise.

2   Design a letter that would suit you or your agency's circumstances. What information would you include about yourself, your workplace, the counselling process? Why? Discuss your letter with several others. What improvements would you now make?

Stage 2: Getting started

Building a trusting relationship

The first contact between a counsellor and a client usually has significant effects on what happens subsequently. A relationship of trust needs to be built up and sustained if change is eventually to take place. Clients will want to feel that their counsellor has the ability to see a situation as they do, to feel that the counsellor supports them and is able to assume their frame of reference. Clients will usually respond to a friendly, caring, and considerate manner and to being helped to be specific about their feelings and experiences. Sensitivity, respect, and empathy for individuals and their cultural backgrounds are among the most important factors in facilitating a counselling relationship.

Clients may wonder whether they are free to express their real concerns. In effect, they sum up the counsellor and the counselling situation while responding. They may ask themselves a series of questions such as: Am I welcome? Can I trust this counsellor? Is a supportive relationship possible? Will it be satisfying? Can this counsellor help me?

Answers to such questions will be provided not merely by words. Other means of communication, often more subtle and powerful, include the physical setting, the way clients are greeted, the counsellor's gestures and tone of voice, and the presence or absence of distractions. All of these convey messages to clients and contribute to their crucial first impressions of the counsellor and their expectations about counselling.

From the outset it is vital that counsellors be alert to the many factors that influence progress. These include being attentive observers of clients and of the whole physical and social setting; helping clients to express themselves in their own way, and being aware of their own role as a possible stimulus to clients and a model for them to follow. Counsellors should also explain their services and the conditions of counselling as early as possible. Information about counsellors and their way of working is often reassuring to clients, especially those who might be anxious or doubtful.

Because counselling occurs in a reciprocal relationship, counsellors' awareness of themselves also needs to be considered. This mutually-influencing, relationship-making phase is a dynamic one involving specific behaviours that can be identified and practised.

Is the client voluntary or involuntary?

It is important to consider whether clients have freely chosen to come, whether they have been persuaded, or whether their counsellor has asked to see them.

After the introductory greeting it is often helpful to deal with this issue straight away. Voluntary clients may be easier to work with initially because they have already made a decision to seek help. This implies at least some recognition of a problem and some desire to change. Sometimes, however, it may mask a desire to use the counsellor in a manipulative way.

In some settings, clients may perceive the counsellor as someone who can be used to ease pressures that are legitimately exerted by other people. As soon as counsellors sense that this may be occurring, they should test this hunch, if necessary by discussing it directly with the client. Coyness, guile, and game-playing on the part of the client should not be reciprocated. The counsellors' model of open and direct expression of feelings and perceptions is the best counter to clients' attempts to 'con' or use them.

With involuntary clients it can be productive to deal immediately with the client's reactions to being present. Counsellors may:

- State who referred the client.

- Give the reason for the referral, e.g., 'Your employer seems to be concerned because you have been very quiet lately and missing key appointments.'

- Tell clients what might be offered by the counsellor.

- Invite clients to express their feelings about being in this situation. Are they angry? Afraid? Puzzled? Uncertain?

- Emphasise that clients are free to remain or to leave. Often acceptance of the freedom to leave without being pursued is the first step in establishing the trust which will lead to a client's voluntary return.

- Be sensitive to possible differences in cultural or lifestyle values. Do clients feel belittled or demeaned? Try to see things through their eyes.

- Join clients by asking what needs to happen to convince others (those who sent them for counselling) that counselling is not necessary (Berg, 1994).

- Suggest that while clients may reject you as their helper, there are other sources of help for their problems. Provide relevant information about these sources if they are interested.

In some instances clients may continue to be reluctant or reticent about participating in counselling. Additional techniques for engaging these clients are discussed more fully in this chapter on pages 91–93.

What background information is needed?

The answers to this question will be determined by the counselling setting, the nature and extent of the problem, the purpose of the counselling, the relevance and availability of the background information and the preferences of the counsellor.

The setting

Detailed information may be more pertinent in the clinical setting of a psychiatric unit where long-term, residential treatment is to take place than in, for example, a Citizen's Advice Bureau where the contact may be limited to one visit.

The nature and extent of the problem

Comprehensive, detailed background information may be desirable if major personality change is sought but is unnecessary if the problem is one of learning certain skills such as how to be more assertive or how to conduct oneself during a job interview.

Purpose of counselling

If people wish to free themselves from patterns of emotional reaction and behaviour that have their roots in their upbringing, it can be important to know something of the family dynamics. However, if clients seek information on university course requirements, their legal rights as parents, or child development concerns, background information on them as individuals may not be essential or even relevant.

Relevance

Information about educational qualifications would be relevant in vocational counselling but probably not in marriage guidance. A social worker engaged in a welfare inquiry would be vitally interested in details of family income but this may be irrelevant to a school counsellor dealing with a conflict between peers.

The counsellor's preferences

In most instances, reviewing available background information is useful and therefore recommended in this book as sound practice. There are times, however, when counsellors might purposely choose to do otherwise:

- Sometimes counsellors may prefer to gain their impressions of clients and their analysis of problems from first-hand contacts rather than be influenced by background information. They may want to leave their minds free from preconceptions or from the interpretations of other people.

- Counsellors may prefer to obtain background information incidentally during the course of an interview.

- Counsellors may prefer to obtain information in a structured interview as a way of beginning a relationship.

The first sighting and meeting: a reciprocal relationship

Counselling occurs in a reciprocal relationship. From the start the client, as well as the counsellor, is observing and reacting (see column 3 of figure 5.1, page 72). They immediately begin sizing each other up. Each begins the normal process of observing, silently questioning, and attributing qualities and attitudes to the other. An internal dialogue such as that in column 2 of figure 5.1 may take place in the counsellor's mind.

Since this is happening anyway, in every first meeting with a client the counsellor should be aware of the following:

- The client's physical appearance
  Could it create problems for the client? Does it give clues about health? Self-image?

- Manner and bearing
  Does the client appear nervous? Withdrawn? Aggressive? Defensive? Passive?

- Movement and gestures
  Is the client still or moving? What is happening with the client's hands? Head? Feet? What are the possible meanings of these movements and gestures?

- Posture and stance
  Is the client standing upright? Hunched over? Standing freely? Supporting herself? What might this mean?

- Surroundings
  Is the counselling setting private? Relatively informal? Is the decor of the room warm and relaxing? Is there freedom from extraneous noise? Are the seats comfortable? Well-placed?

- Differences in social status
  Do the client's clothing, speech or mannerisms suggest a different set of cultural values, beliefs and practices? Poverty? Wealth? Social position? State of mind?

- Physical distance
  Is the client so close to you that either one may be threatened by the closeness? Are the counsellor and client comfortably apart?

- Eye contact
  Is the client able to look the counsellor in the eye or is eye contact avoided?

Positive first impressions

Success in counselling depends considerably upon clients' perceptions of the counsellor's manner and behaviour. Clients will be aware of and react to the counsellor's eye contact, posture, gestures, manner and appearance. They will react to the length of and delay in the counsellor's responses, amount of talk, and voice quality. And, in the end, it is the client who will decide if a working relationship with this counsellor is possible.

Initial interactions between counsellors and clients always involve some degree of cultural difference – broadly defined. Thus, 'the ease with which openings take place depends, at least in part, on the degree of [perceived] similarity... between the two participants' (Gudykunst & Kim, 1983, p. 179). When dissimilarity is present and obvious, the primary aim of both participants is 'one of uncertainty reduction or increasing predictability' (Gudykunst & Kim, 1983, p. 179). Counsellors usually bring this about through the use of techniques such as questioning, self-disclosure and altering the setting. Pedersen and Ivey (1993, p. 103) emphasise 'attending', or 'paying attention to what is happening and being said', as the foundation skill in culture-centred counselling. By paying attention to the client's eyes, body language and vocal qualities, and by using verbal tracking (Ivey, 1994), counsellors can gain clues about differences that exist and ways of beginning to bridge those differences in the counselling relationship.

The following description of a relaxed, comfortable counselling setting and opening is not intended to be a prescription for every counsellor to follow. All counsellors will have to find their own way, and one that acknowledges appropriate cultural protocol. However, since people tend to use eye contact more when listening than when speaking, good eye contact in counselling involves looking at clients when they are talking and using glances that express interest and acceptance. However, a piercing stare, look of blankness, or avoidance of a client's gaze may be disconcerting to the client.

The counsellor should sit in a position that is not directly in front of the client and far enough away so that both feel comfortable. Sitting slightly to the side of one another is usually reported to be most comfortable. Counsellors' hands should be kept relatively still and their facial expressions friendly. Slouching, playing with a pen, frowning and too much movement can be distracting.

Encouraging clients to talk freely is important in the initial stages. A warm, pleasant tone of voice, simple language and medium volume are usually the most effective. Counsellors who talk too much discourage clients who may well be made to feel that their ideas are not important. If counsellors can slightly delay responses and do so naturally, there is an increased chance that clients will talk and explain more fully. Short counsellor responses also encourage this, as does a minimum of interruption.

The following exercises are designed to allow the participants to experience a first meeting and the effects of various physical surroundings, gestures, eye contact, and other attributes, as discussed above. (Leaders may find it valuable to have course members do the exercises before reading those sections.)

Attribute	Counsellor's observations and questions	Client's observations and questions
Physical appearance	She is very thin and pale … Is she ill? Under strain? Her hair is untidy and her coat has a button missing … Is she under stress? It must have taken courage to come.	He's so tall … reminds me of my brother. Can I trust him?
Manner	She seems withdrawn, passive. Is she depressed? Reluctant to be here? Or, is this possibly a way of showing respect?	His voice is warm and gentle. His eyes are friendly and I like his smile.
Bearing	She is hunched over, holding herself. Is she afraid of me? Of the situation? Of revealing herself? Am I intimidating her? It must be hard for her.	He looks relaxed and calm but he is watching me very closely. He is upright but not stiff. His hands are at his side. He seems at ease. I've come this far; maybe I can I relax, too.
Movement Gestures	She has turned her head away from me, and is moving her left foot up and down. Is she very tense and anxious?	He is fairly still but not stiff and tense.
Posture	She is sitting hunched up, on the edge of the chair. Is she very tense? Defensive?	He is leaning back in his chair slightly. His hands are loosely clasped.
Surroundings	I've told the receptionist not to put any phone calls through for an hour. Hope she remembers. It's a bit cold… Should I ask her if she's warm enough?	It's quiet in here. I like the view and the colours. This chair is comfortable. Can I relax now? Maybe?
Eye contact	She avoids looking directly at me. But she does glance at me now and then. I'm not sure what this means just yet.	His eyes look warm. I want to look at him but I can't manage to keep looking at him yet. I think… I hope I can trust him.

Figure 5.1 A possible internal dialogue on first meeting

The exercises may be done as demonstrations in front of a large group or they may be done in small groups with one participant taking the part of the counsellor, another that of the client, and the others acting as observers/commentators.

1 Internal dialogue
   Have two people play the roles of counsellor and client. They should meet as though for the first time, be seated and then just sit in silence for a minute or so.
   Using headings similar to those in figure 5.1, have each participant write his/her internal dialogue. When each has finished, compare and discuss the dialogue. Notice different interpretations due to cultural differences.

2 Client reactions
   After each of the following activities, 'clients' should share their reactions to what happened. They may share with the whole group or with their small group only. Again, notice different interpretations due to cultural difference.
   a Physical conditions
      i Experiment with three chair positions.

      In which situation does the client feel most comfortable?
      ii Vary the counsellor's position in relation to a desk.

      In what way does the client feel differently towards the counsellor's being in each of these positions in relation to the desk? Are there any differences due to cultural factors? Discuss them.

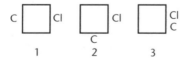

   b Eye contact
      i Counsellor looks at the ceiling, out of the window, at the bookshelf, anywhere but directly at the client.

---

* Throughout this book, exercises that are marked with an asterisk (*) have the answers provided in *Answers to exercises* at the back of the book.

    ii Counsellor makes eye contact with the client without staring her down. How is eye contact used differently in different cultures?

  c Movement, gestures, posture, stance

    i Counsellor sits upright at her desk, plays with a pencil, bends a paper-clip, taps a foot against the desk.

    ii Counsellor leans against the wall and waves his arms around while talking.

    iii Counsellor leans forward towards the client while already sitting close, with her/his knees almost touching those of the client.

    iv Counsellor sits on his chair in a relaxed way, hands held loosely, and leans forward slightly.

---

exercise 5.3*

[Adapted from D.W. Johnson, *Reaching out*, Englewood Cliffs, N.J. Prentice Hall, 1972.]

Counsellor's reactions

Ask what the counsellor's reactions are to what the client might be experiencing in the following scenarios. What values, beliefs or experiences might influence the counsellor's reactions? What cultural factors might be at play here?

a Client sits perched on the edge of the chair, twisting her hands and staring at the floor.

b Client sits upright holding herself tightly, hands clasped firmly and launches into a complaint in self-righteous tones.

c Client sits down and bursts into tears.

d Client refuses to speak.

---

exercise 5.4

Counsellor's awareness of own behaviour

1 Counsellor's voice quality

  a Form pairs. Make a tape of a segment of conversation. Comment on the quality of each person's voice, e.g., interest, clarity and friendliness. Is there any aspect of your voice you would wish to alter? Why?

   b Make a second recording in which both people try to vary aspects of their voice. Stop, replay, comment.

2 Counsellor's responses

   a The course leader and/or participants should make a tape of a segment of conversation demonstrating effective and ineffective use of timing and length of responses and interruptions. Group members should be invited to comment.

   b Alternatively, a segment of conversation could be role-played in front of the group.

Stage 3: Exploration

Initially the counsellor's goal is to enable and encourage clients to talk freely and openly about their concerns, feelings and fears. These skills are designed to help that process.

Encouraging exploration of problems or solutions

Exploring pre-counselling improvements

It is not unusual for clients to experience positive improvements in their problems – even very small ones – between the time they first decide to seek counselling and their scheduled first session (Lawson, 1994; Weiner-Davis, de Shazer & Gingerich, 1987). For many, this initial decision may in itself signal that counselling has already begun. Clients may experience a positive change in thinking or an increase in determination to overcome some problem. Consequently, it is not surprising that they might also begin to act or think differently and thereby experience changes in the intensity or nature of the problem itself, even before their first counselling session.

Therefore, one of the initial tasks in the first session is to find out if clients have noticed any improvements in their problem. If such changes have occurred, clients should be asked to describe whatever strategies or behaviours they may have been using to cause the changes. In effect, the process of solving the problem has begun and the client can be helped to explore ways to maintain, reinforce and perhaps accelerate those changes. Useful pre-session change questions include:

'Often people notice that things begin to improve before they even come in for counselling. Have you noticed any changes?'

'Are things any better?'

If things are not improved, it may be helpful to ask:

'Why aren't they worse than they are?'

Another useful topic to explore is why the client has chosen to seek counselling today rather than last week or last month. The answer to this question often indicates an important change in thinking, understanding or level of motivation, all of which may be productive in identifying and finding solutions that make a difference (Cummings, 1990).

> *'Why have you come for counselling now instead of coming last week or last month?'*

Compliments

As clients talk, counsellors should note all of the things that they are doing successfully or well. These behaviours and activities can be used to construct successful solutions to problems and concerns. Complimenting clients on what they are already doing well in an honest, sincere way helps to establish an atmosphere of possibility, hope and understanding. Compliments can also be used to optimise the counsellor's impact on the client, to empower clients and promote change (Wall et al., 1989). In most models of helping, the usefulness of complimenting clients has been underestimated (Berg, 1994) and underutilised (Wall et al., 1989).

Clients' thoughts, attitudes and behaviours that indicate a positive, constructive approach to problems are among the things that can be complimented. For example, clients can be complimented for turning up for counselling, for their patience in waiting so long, for their decision to seek counselling, their clear view of the problem, the manner in which they have coped, and their unwavering determination. In short, they can be complimented on any positive aspect of themselves that will enhance their self-esteem (Berg, 1994). However, remember too that there are individual and cultural differences in the preferred ways of giving and receiving compliments. For some clients, receiving direct compliments can be embarrassing and they may try to 'discount' them by diminishing their intended meaning (Manthei, 1981). For example, some clients may find the following compliment too direct: 'I admire the way you've been handling your teenage daughter's requests to stay out late'. As a result they may 'discount' it: 'I really didn't do anything; my friend suggested it'. An alternative, less direct way of complimenting clients is by phrasing compliments as questions, e.g., 'How did you think to handle your daughter's demands in that way?'.

Reframing (see chapter 6) problematic or difficult situations through the use of compliments can also be effective, e.g., 'It is good that you know your own limits so well and have decided that now is not the right time to take a stand on this issue'.

There are other methods for identifying clients' strengths and abilities. For example, Ivey (1994, p. 144) suggests using the 'positive asset search' to highlight clients' strengths and abilities. This is done by reflecting notable attributes or skills back to them, e.g., 'Even though things have not gone as well as you hoped they would, you haven't given up or lost your sense of humour'.

Open invitation to talk

If clients are invited to talk freely about any topic of their choosing, instead of being subjected to a series of questions, they are more likely to reveal their problems and/or desired outcomes. In part, the invitation to speak will be conveyed by the counsellor's posture, manner, gestures, and tone of voice. The words used will make the message explicit.

After clients have been received, greeted and seated, a statement can be made or a question asked that tells them they are welcome and recognised, and that their thoughts and ideas are valued. It should also say that the counsellor is ready to listen and help. For example:

'I'm glad you have come. How can I help you?' or *'What has brought you here?'*

'My secretary said that when you phoned you were concerned about ...' *'How has that situation changed?'*

Counsellors should use warm, accepting tones and words that are natural. They should avoid stereotyping beginning statements or using false humour. They should also be wary of using such terms as worry or problems unless the client has already used them. Occasionally counsellors are faced with clients who are initially reluctant to participate in counselling or resist doing so.

exercise **5.5***

In pairs, alternating the role of counsellor and client, give open invitations to speak to the following:

a A distraught mother whose teenage son is disrupting family life.

b A middle-aged man just made redundant.

c A teenage girl with a career inquiry.

Discuss the effectiveness of your invitations to speak.

Sorting issues

Some clients may respond to the counsellor's open invitation to talk with a torrent of problems or concerns. They may talk non-stop for several minutes and describe a number of related or unrelated problems. Since it is necessary for clients and counsellors both to fully understand and to clarify the client's concerns, counsellors can begin by responding in a way that will help clients sort the issues. This is done by simply listing the concerns clients have mentioned and inviting them to select the one that they think should be dealt with first.

For example:

Client: *'I've had it with my job! The work is too hard and the supervisor has it in for me; and my husband says I'm not earning enough – no ambition. And I've been losing my temper with the kids too much lately.'*

Counsellor: *'You have mentioned several things: the difficulty of the work; the supervisor's attitude toward you; your husband's concerns about your low pay and lack of ambition, and problems with your temper. Which of these do you think we should talk about first?'*

The skill of sorting issues indicates that the counsellor has been listening, is actively concerned, and is ready to focus on issues the client thinks are most pressing. Also, encouraging clients to think more clearly about their problems and to list them in the order they wish to deal with them, presents clients with the beginning of an effective model of **finding solutions to problems**. To aid this process, either the counsellor or the client can make a list of the problems as they are described. This will underscore the importance of being clear and will help to guide and structure the counselling relationship in successive sessions.

exercise 5.6

In pairs, alternating the role of counsellor and client, use the skill of sorting issues in response to the following:

1   'Nothing is going right. I hate myself, can't stand the sight of me! And when I'm home, the kids get on my nerves – always demands and problems. I never get any help from anyone – I always have to do everything myself.'

2   'Well, let's see. I guess it's really my own lack of self-confidence. I mean, I suppose I should know how to get a job, but I don't. How would I even start? And my husband doesn't really help things. He just criticises me for being lazy. What can I say to him? What should I do?'

Coping questions

There will be times when it is clear that clients have been dealing with multiple problems of a serious nature and they may have a need to vent their feelings and thoughts about them. While their circumstances and outlook can seem bleak and overwhelming at the time, it is also true that the fact that clients have managed and survived the situation is quite remarkable.

Once clients have given an account of their difficulties, the counsellor can compliment clients on their ability to cope and, in effect, move the focus away from their many problems. Coping questions (Berg, 1994) convey a message of hope and competence to people who often feel overwhelmed, when indeed their efforts to survive are almost heroic. For example, in response to depressed clients who see no bright spots in their situations and virtually drag themselves out of bed each day, counsellors may choose to focus on their resolve to keep going rather than the depression itself:

> *'So, when things are so bleak and you feel so discouraged, how do you manage to get up each day and look after yourself?' Or, 'What have you done to cope with these feelings before? What's the first thing you do to get yourself going?'.*

The client's answer usually indicates some small, positive things that can be complimented, built on and perhaps expanded, things that the client may not even be aware of doing. At the very least, having clients answer the question may show them that they have made some good decisions and that they do have strength and resolve.

Questions about coping strategies are also useful in crisis situations. To know how clients are managing personal or family crises can provide clues to possible solutions to those problems.

Open and closed questions

Open-ended questions or statements invite clients to continue talking by suggesting that they give more details about a topic they have introduced. For example:

> *'What is it about you that your mother respects the most?'*

Open questions are best used when explanations, opinions, and examples are needed. They are particularly important in the early stages of an interview when the aim is to find out as much as possible about the client's situation – the good and the bad. Beginning questions with 'Tell me... 'Describe...' 'What?' 'When?' 'How?' 'Why?', are useful ways of making clients open up.

By contrast, closed questions are best used when factual information or a 'yes' or 'no' response is all that is required. Closed questions tend to limit client responses and implicitly suggest that the clients' role is to talk less and answer only what is asked of them. A series of such questions or statements can sound like an interrogation. For example:

> *'It sounds as if your girlfriend trusts you more now.'*

> *'Yes.'*

> *'Do you trust her more, too?'*

> *'Yes.'*

> *'So, you're getting along better now?'*

> *'I suppose.'*

> *'Oh, I thought you'd be more enthusiastic than that.'*

> *'Mmm...'*

Before using an open or closed question, counsellors should decide what kinds of information are needed. Answers to open questions will tend to give counsellors fuller explanations, more complete information, and useful clues or free information to follow up and thus keep the interview going. Open questions also indicate to clients that they are free to lead the discussion where they want. Answers to closed questions, on the other hand, can be used to gather important factual information about clients (e.g., biographical, medical or employment situations) or confirm or disconfirm a point or an opinion. They can indicate that the counsellor is listening, is thinking about the client's problem and may be forming some hypothesis about the problem.

It is important to remember that open questions are not to be thought of as a 'good' counselling skill and closed questions as a 'bad' skill. Both have their uses and can be effective when used appropriately.

Note: Whatever types of questions are used, it is important to avoid asking several questions at once. This can be confusing to clients and experience indicates that they invariably answer only the last question anyway. Therefore, decide what to ask, ask it and wait for the client's response.

---

exercise 5.7*

1   Which of the following are open-ended questions?
   a   Do you like to argue with people?
   b   What convinced you that changing jobs this year would be a good thing?
   c   How do you usually handle those sorts of nuisances?
   d   Do you have to decide right now?

2   Rewrite the following as open-ended questions.
   a   Did you enjoy completing the job inventory?
   b   Did you leave school because you wanted to earn money?
   c   Have we got enough money to get home?
   d   Did you start the argument?

Topic following

Topic following is best thought of as an aim or focus, i.e., as attending to what it is that clients want to discuss, and not as a discrete skill. In fact, any skill a counsellor chooses to use can contribute to staying on the topic, or not. In essence, topic following means focusing on what the client has actually said rather than taking the topic in a new direction or adding to its meaning.

Topic following is usually preferable to frequent changes of topic, especially in the early stages of counselling before the counsellor has a clear and detailed picture of the client's concern. In later stages of the relationship, it may become more appropriate for counsellors to introduce new topics, return to previous ones or check the accuracy of their own hypotheses about the client's predicament. To use this skill appropriately, counsellors need to understand its purpose and to recognise when it is appropriate to follow the client's topic and when it is necessary to change topics.

Examples of minimal verbalisations that ensure that the topic is followed include:

'I see what you mean.'

'Tell me more about it.'

'Would you explain that a bit more?'

'Yes?'

'Mmm..'

'Your father?'

exercise 5.8*

Add a statement or question to each of the following client statements so that the topic is followed. As the conversation continues, use additional statements that topic follow.

a   'I can't seem to get a job. Whenever I go for an interview, they say they'll get in touch but they never do.'

b   'My parents insist that I get home by 12 pm whenever I go out. Sometimes that's just impossible.'

c   'I'm really worried. I can't get motivated to even get out of bed any more. I have no ambition, no energy.'

Using silence

Counsellors are often anxious about, or embarrassed by, silences during interviews. Silences, however, may be as revealing as the spoken word. Acceptance of clients' silences may emphasise to them that it is their right to determine the nature of the interview. It allows both counsellor and client time to think. It builds trust and may eventually encourage clients to be very frank in their revelations.

To use silence effectively, counsellors need to accept its worth, to feel confident about allowing it to continue beyond a few seconds, and to be sensitive to timing. Usually counsellors should let clients take the time they need to reflect on and formulate a response to a question. If, however, the silence seems to convey a strong sense of resentment on the part of the client, especially if the client is involuntary, it can be helpful to verbalise this.

---

exercise 5.9

1   When replaying a video or audio tape of one of your interviews, note all occasions when you used open versus closed questions, whether you followed the topic and whether you used silences appropriately. Note the effects of each skill.

2   Alternatively, during role-playing or actual interviews, an observer could be asked to note these things for you.

Demonstrating understanding

As clients talk, counsellors will want to demonstrate that they are listening carefully and understanding accurately.

Active listening

Listening is basic to counselling. Active, total listening is vital throughout every interview, but especially at the beginning when the counsellor usually takes a less verbally active part. Counsellors listen by focusing their whole being on their clients, concentrating on them, allowing their messages to be paramount. Such listening requires that counsellors use all their senses to get the total message. They listen with their ears to the words spoken and the tone of voice, with an open questioning mind to the underlying message, and with their eyes to the language of the body in its posture, bearing, and gestures.

Counsellors also listen to themselves. They note their reactions to the person, the messages they are receiving, the possible cultural variations present, and to the way they are coping with all of this information. This total listening is intended to communicate empathy, i.e., to show that the counsellor has heard, understood, and accepted what has been said. Being listened to this intently is a rare experience for most people, and some may be visibly nervous or self-conscious when they experience it. Counsellors must be aware when this happens and learn to listen actively but in a non-threatening way.

Active listening, like other skills, can be practised. When practising, be aware of the following:

- Your attitude. How do you feel about the client and how are those feelings influencing your perceptions of her/him?

- Your attention both to what is being said (content) and what is implied or hinted at (unstated or emotional message).

- Focusing on what the other person is trying to tell you, not on what you might say in response or how you can straighten out the mix-up.

exercise 5.10

Two group members are to have a conversation on an agreed topic where personal feelings will be expressed. This should take no more than three to four minutes.

a   One observer closes her eyes and listens to the client's words and summarises the message.

b   Another observer concentrates on the body language of the client.

c   The rest of the group can listen to the total message but also be especially aware of their own reactions to the client's statements. Compare and contrast the 'messages' heard by each observer.

Reflection

Reflection is a skill used to demonstrate and enhance understanding. Effective use of reflection conveys to clients that the counsellor is trying to understand, has understood correctly and accepts what they have said. Counsellors can reflect *content* by short, simple re-statements or paraphrases of the essence of what the client has actually said. Reflection of content condenses and crystallises in a fresh way the information clients have given.

Counsellors can also reflect *feeling*, that part of the client's statement that represents the emotional message. Often what is said (content) does not communicate the *real* meaning. Reflection of feeling focuses on this underlying or unstated message. In most instances, it is more effective to reflect both content and feeling in the same statement than either one alone.

Reflection should be used to demonstrate understanding, but more importantly, to facilitate the client's movement toward more complete self-awareness and self-understanding. It is appropriate and effective to use reflections of content and feeling at any stage of the counselling process. However, reflection is frequently overused, almost as though it were an automatic, unthinking 'verbal filler'. When used in this way, it can be repetitious and parrot-like and it may annoy clients. Listening to several recordings of your counselling sessions will help you to decide whether you are using this skill appropriately.

The following is an example of reflection:

Client: *'I don't think I could do it. I'd only fail. I ... well – I've never been able to face large groups like that before and I'm sure I couldn't now.'*

Counsellor: (content reflection) *'Your nervousness in the past convinces you it's not possible now and* (feeling reflection) *you're feeling a bit afraid to even try.'*

---

exercise 5.11

---

1   In the following exercise there are four client statements. After each one write (i) the counsellor response that best reflects the content of the statement, and (ii) the response that best reflects feeling, i.e., the response which indicates that you understand the client's attitude and the situation as it appears to her.

    Compare and discuss your answers with others doing the same exercise.

a   'No, I won't! I'm not going to tell you anything about my separation. I didn't ask to see you. The court ordered it! You're not getting anything out of me!'

b   'I really need your help. I just can't seem to get over his death. I just cry and cry – I feel awful. I wish it was me who had died – he had so much to live for.'

c   'Nearly two more years! Honestly, I just couldn't stand two more years of school. Oh, I can do it all right – I know I can pass the exams. But it's all so boring! I'm changing my mind about going to university.'

d   'Well, OK, it is at home. But what difference does it make talking to you about it? You wouldn't understand. You just don't know what it's like there day after day with all the tension and anger.'

2   Next time you are listening to an interview on a current events programme, notice how often the interviewer reflects the feeling of the person being interviewed as opposed to the content of what has been said. What seems to be the effect of each type of reflection on the person being interviewed?

Accurate understanding

In counselling it is necessary for counsellors to understand what their clients are saying and to be able to communicate that understanding to them. Understanding involves far more than merely hearing the words that are spoken. It first necessitates active listening. In addition, counsellors must rely on their perceptions of the client and their hunches about what is going on, but at the same time be careful not to interpret what they think clients have said nor take their meaning for granted.

Communicating understanding to the client involves reflecting or paraphrasing content and/or feeling and **'perception-checking'** which simply means that counsellors ask their clients how accurate their reflections have been. Effective use of perception-checking demonstrates the counsellor's interest, understanding, and openness of mind.

Finally, accurate understanding involves not only immediate understanding, but also clarifying what is obscure. Therefore, counsellors should not hesitate to say that they do not fully understand. Rather than assume things about the client, counsellors should ask, even if the answer seems very obvious.

exercise **5.12**

Following is a list of counsellor responses or 'perception checks' that can be used to see if you understood correctly. They are included to give you some ideas of how this skill can be implemented.

- Is what you're saying…?

- You seem to be saying…

- As you see it…

- Let me see if I understood correctly. You…, is that right?

- Am I correct in assuming that you…?

Using short client statements (see exercise 5.11), counsellors can use leads like those listed above to check their understanding of what has been said. In addition, the following client statements may be used for counsellors to practise accurate understanding, that is, reflecting content and/or feeling and then checking their perceptions.

a 'I think I can do it, but sometimes I don't know. Anyway, I guess it's worth a try.'

b 'I'm not sure how I feel. Sometimes I'm angry about my marriage; other times I just don't care. But it does bother me.'

c Client sits quietly, looking sad.

d 'I've got to get help. If you don't do something, I'll never get started.'

e 'Things are fine now. Thanks. I guess you won't want to see me next week.'

1 Counsellors should write down their responses and then discuss them with others to make sure that each response shows that the counsellor is trying to understand the client. For example, the counsellor might write the following in response to client statement a: 'Deep down, you don't sound as though you really want to try. Is that right?'

2 When counsellors are able to write effective responses, they should try responding orally. Again, the responses should be discussed so that each counsellor is sure that accurate understanding was demonstrated.

3 Individuals can make up client statements of their own to suit their particular work or personal situations.

4 When listening to a dialogue or interview on television or radio, count the number of times the interviewer uses perception checking to clarify his understanding of what has been said.

Thinking aloud

When counsellors think aloud, it has the effect of demystifying the process of counselling and empowering clients by informing them about the counsellor's approach to counselling. Revealing the counsellor's musings, questions and strategies to clients allows them to then participate as more informed equals. This skill can be described as a form of psycho-education, that is, teaching clients about the process of **finding solutions to problems**.

The skill of thinking aloud has three specific uses: (a) to explain to clients what is happening in the counselling process, (b) to reveal to clients the counsellor's thinking and thereby include clients as more informed participants in the counselling process, and (c) to explain the reason for a sudden change in topic.

In the first instance, the counsellor's aim is to allay clients' doubts, hesitations, or suspicions about what is happening. Usually, short, clear explanations will reassure clients, help them to make sense of what is going on, and demystify the process. For example:

> *'I need to know some specific information about your son's medical condition before we discuss further the ways in which his behaviour is disruptive at home.'*

In the second instance, the counsellor's aim is to be open and forthright about his/her thinking in a way that conveys confidence in the client as being both competent and equally responsible for the outcome of counselling.

Example 1

> *'I'm a bit stumped. Maybe we need to discuss ways that you could manage your fear so you could be alone at night before looking at other solutions. What do you think?'*

Example 2

> *'There's at least two ways of confronting your supervisor about this situation but I'm not sure that's what you want to do. Maybe we need to look at any other possibilities you have thought of first.'*

Occasionally a client says something that leads the counsellor to believe that a shift in topic could be productive. Rather than making an abrupt change which may leave the client feeling puzzled or irritated, the counsellor can think aloud. For example, during a vocational interview, the counsellor may have a reason for broadening the discussion to a new or related field of work. Lest this switch seem inexplicable or too abrupt, the counsellor could think aloud:

> *'I know you are interested in medical laboratory work, but there are very few vacancies in that area right now. As an alternative I wonder whether you have ever considered a career in pharmacy management. It is possible to take this up without having studied commercial subjects at school. Your science and maths are strong and could be used in both pharmacology and business studies. What do you think?'*

Attending to feelings

Identifying feelings

The ability to perceive and respond appropriately to other people's feelings is important if counsellors are to help clients talk about what is on their minds or what underlies their difficulties. Counsellors must be sensitive to more than just the content of a client's message. Very often the way in which clients speak is more important than the words they use to express themselves.

Responding to feeling is a powerful technique because of its intimacy and the fact that it communicates acceptance of and empathy with the client. In normal social interactions, feelings are regularly disguised and controlled. Thus, when someone perceives our feelings accurately, it tends to have a profound effect on us. We usually react positively to the person who has understood us, and we feel reassured that our feelings, whatever they might be, are justified.

The first requirement for dealing with feelings in a counselling situation is to be able to recognise when feelings are being communicated and precisely what they are. Client statements often contain or imply feeling but do not specifically describe the feeling involved. Therefore, counsellors should encourage clients to specify and identify what they feel; counsellors should not rely solely on their own interpretations of what clients might be feeling, no matter how obvious the feelings might appear to be. If feelings remain unspoken, they may dominate the relationship and inhibit finding solutions to the problem. Often merely recognising and expressing a feeling is enough to lessen it, control it, accept it, or shift one's attention away from it.

Counsellors can simply and effectively clarify this by asking some variation of the following:

'So, what are your feelings about yourself now?'

'What is your reaction to your successes this past week?'

'You certainly look pleased. Is that how you're feeling?'

Expressing feelings

The measure of any counsellor's success in working with feelings in a counselling situation is largely determined by his/her ability to recognise his/her own feelings as they occur and to use them (or not) in a manner that is most helpful to clients. Using feelings effectively can mean a number of things. When counsellors openly share their feelings with clients, they may be modelling desirable behaviour or enhancing a climate of trust and honesty. Similarly, open expression of feelings can sometimes relieve interpersonal tensions and demonstrate to clients that feelings themselves need not be overwhelming or disabling. Even when not directly communicated to clients, counsellors' feelings can be used constructively. For example, once counsellors recognise a feeling within themselves, they should next determine whether it is the direct result of their interactions with clients or whether it arises out of their own personal experience. In both instances, counsellors can make constructive use of their feelings beyond merely expressing them to clients.

---

1   Think of a situation in which you were very angry. Of the following, which would you prefer to have had said to you? Why?

    a   'You know, this whole thing might not be as bad as you think.'

    b   'This whole business has really made you mad!'

2   Take part in a role-play using short client statements that are designed to provoke some feeling in the counsellor. The following client statements are given as examples:

    a   'You never say anything! You just sit there nodding and saying yes all the time. I thought you were going to help me!'

    b   'You're so easy to talk to. You seem to understand everything I say and do. I just know you will do something for me.'

    c   'You lied. You said that what we talked about here was just between us, but this morning the teacher asked me if I had talked to you yet. You had no right to tell him I was coming.'

    d   'What's the matter with you? I've said I don't know but you don't seem to believe me. If I knew what to do, I wouldn't be here.'

    e   'Leave me alone. (Long silence)…'

Counsellor role-players should respond to each client statement by identifying their own feeling reactions to the client. For example, the counsellor may feel hurt or guilty or even angry in response to client statement **a** above.

Assessing client problems and motivation

In this book, assessment does not mean assigning a diagnostic label to clients or placing them in some category of dysfunction. Rather, assessment as used here refers to five things: (a) counsellors deciding whether they have the knowledge and expertise necessary to work with a particular client; (b) the general type of problem presented by the client; (c) a listing of what has not worked and what strengths, successes and abilities the client possesses; (d) an estimate of the client's motivation to solve her/his problems, and (e) the client's estimate of the present severity of the problem. In essence, counsellors need to begin thinking about who will benefit from counselling and how that benefit might be achieved. Assessment is more like a map or plan of action (Berg, 1994) than a label to describe what is wrong.

Necessary expertise

Every counsellor must assess whether it is appropriate to begin and continue working with a particular client. It is, after all, unethical for counsellors to work outside their areas of expertise. In addition, counsellors will need to assess the client's ability to engage in counselling, identify goals and implement them. Questions you need to consider when making this assessment include:

- Can I work with this client? Do I have the requisite training and experience?

- Should I refer this person? Is other, more appropriate, help available?

- Is the client's thinking process lucid, or is it significantly impaired? Can I engage the client in sensible, purposeful conversation?

- Is there a common understanding regarding problem definition, something for which there is an attainable and useful goal?

- Does the client appear to have abilities and skills that can be used to implement desired goals and/or behaviours?

If you decide you cannot or should not work with a particular client, then you should make an appropriate referral (see chapter 7). When this happens, it is not necessarily a sign of failure. Rather, it may be evidence of sound professional practice.

Type of client problem

Leona Tyler (1969) devised a useful method for categorising problems. Use of this simple dichotomy can immediately clarify and focus the process and goals of counselling.

Choice problems involve making a decision. Before doing that, however, the client may need to either survey the possibilities more carefully or make a firm commitment to a course of action. Either way, a suitable method of decision-making is needed.

Change problems involve doing something new or different by removing existing obstacles or creating new possibilities. Usually action is called for, which sometimes means learning new skills.

In cases in which it is not yet clear if the problem involves a choice or some kind of change, further discussion and exploration is needed before deciding whether to work toward changing or making a choice.

Identifying positive assets

Early in the counselling relationship counsellors should begin to note things that clients have tried that have not worked (to avoid doing more of the same), those things that clients are competent at (a positive asset search; Ivey, 1994), or have already succeeded in doing (exceptions to the problem; see chapter 6). These skills, abilities and successes can then be used to identify goals and implement them. In other words, the client should do more of what has already been successful.

The client's motivation

It is useful to know how motivated clients are to solve their problems in order to structure their counselling appropriately. Solution-focused therapy (Berg, 1994; de Shazer, 1988) describes three levels of client motivation and how to respond to each: visitors, complainants and customers. In this book two of these types, visitors and complainants, have been combined and called non-customers. Since the goal with all clients is to discover the things for which they are customers, a simple dichotomy has been found to be practical, useful and adequate especially for counsellors unfamiliar with the model.

Non-customers are clients who are not yet ready or willing to engage in counselling. Sometimes they may have been sent for counselling against their will, in which case they are usually unwilling to admit to a problem and they see counselling as unnecessary. Other non-customers may be happy to talk about their problems but have no commitment to doing anything about them. They may see themselves as victims who have no part to play in finding solutions to the problems. In both situations, counsellors should compliment these clients for their willingness to attend, comment on any notable client insights or abilities they have observed, suggest that clients think about something they could do in their situation that would be new and different and invite them to return for another session.

Since non-customers are not ready to participate fully in counselling, assigning them substantial, behavioural tasks should be avoided. The aim should be to congratulate them on what they have done and ask them to return, thus allowing them more time to change from being non-customers to customers for some aspect of change.

Customers are clients who are willing to talk about their problems, ready to do something about them and motivated to put ideas into action. When working with customers, counsellors should proceed to explore the problem, identify exceptions to it, set specific goals and implement steps to accomplish those goals.

Estimating problem severity

Once the problem has been identified and explored, it is useful to establish its present level of severity. This provides a benchmark, a reference point for gauging subsequent progress and success. A useful technique for doing this is by use of a scaling question (Berg, 1994; Kiser et al., 1993). For example, clients are asked to rate the present seriousness or severity of their problem on a 1 to 10 scale, 1 being 'extremely severe' and 10 being 'the problem is no longer a problem'. Although a client may respond by saying '2', the number itself has no objective meaning. It merely represents the client's subjective estimate of its severity at that time. An immediate follow-up question could be 'What has to happen for a 2 to become a 3?' or 'How does that compare with last week? Last month?'

Note: The direction of the scale which indicates improvement (whether ascending or descending) is not important – as long as the concept being scaled and the descriptions of the end points are clear to clients.

Scaling questions can be used to prioritise problems and assess their seriousness, to gauge the client's level of self-confidence, motivation to change, self-esteem, quality of relationship (e.g., marriage). As long as they are clearly stated, scaling questions can help make concepts and ideas that the client may be having difficulty explaining, more specific.

In summary, clients' motivations can change during counselling: non-customers can become customers and vice versa; clients can be customers in the case of one problem but not another. When an accurate estimate of the type and severity of the problem is combined with the client's motivation to solve it and a list of the client's strengths and abilities, a plan or map of counselling has been constructed that will focus and guide the process of **finding solutions to problems**.

Anticipating termination

Determining progress in counselling should be a part of every session. Berg (1994, p. 13) even suggests that 'termination should begin with the first meeting'. If problems are defined and goals clearly specified, the point at which to terminate becomes more obvious. If counsellors introduce talk about terminating early in counselling, clients are led to expect brief, focused, successful work. Key questions that can be asked, even in the first session, include:

> *'How and how soon do you anticipate the problem will be solved?'* (Talmon, 1990, p. 28)

As a follow-up to a problem-severity scaling question where the client rated the problem as a 6 (10 is 'no longer a problem'):

> *'How high would you have to be to feel you no longer needed to come for counselling? How long do you estimate that to take?'*

Engaging non-customers

Non-customers, sometimes called reluctant or resistant clients, are part of every counsellor's experience. Faced with non-customers, counsellors can choose to accept their reluctance at face value, i.e., as an unequivocal refusal of help. Alternatively, they can sensitively attempt to engage the client so that the real meaning of the reluctance may become clear. Many non-customers may need only to find reassurance, honesty and the right invitation from a counsellor to begin a relationship. When working with such clients, it is essential to allow them time to feel comfortable and develop trust, to refrain from pre-judging their moods, motives, and needs, and to try out more than the normal variety of invitations to talk or participate. Essentially, the counsellor's task is to find a way of enabling non-customers to willingly become customers for change. The following five sections describe a number of ways in which non-customers or hesitant clients can be helped to engage in counselling.

Interpreting the client's silence

Silence can express many things: anger, fear, boredom, respect, embarrassment, sadness, contempt. Counsellors should make every attempt to understand the possible meanings of silence. In doing this, particular attention should be paid to the client's movements, gestures, and physical appearance.

Interpreting clients' feelings can be accomplished by written means. For example, clients may respond more readily to a written observation or a simple drawing than to the spoken word.

Mirroring as a form of interpretation can be used to highlight dominant aspects of a client's behaviour. In this technique, counsellors imitate movements, gestures, or postures that seem meaningful. Mirroring can be a provocative form of interpretation and may elicit a strong response, positive or negative.

Immediacy is recognising what is going on between the counsellor and the client at a particular moment and communicating this constructively. It should be done tentatively, however, and expressed only as an opinion.

Example 1

'I'm feeling that you are becoming irritated with me right now.'

Example 2

'It seems to me that you're reluctant to be here.'

Encouraging non-verbal responding

These techniques are intended to encourage the client to initiate exploration and self-disclosure without having to verbalise thoughts and feelings.

It is often effective to invite clients to draw or write down thoughts or feelings they find hard to verbalise. Alternatively, clients can be encouraged to express thoughts physically, e.g., by acting, miming or posturing.

Having once engaged clients to act out thoughts or feelings, counsellors can ask them to exaggerate specific behaviours. Repeating a gesture with emphasised movement may help a client to clarify its meaning and the personal feelings that lie behind it.

Working at the client's pace

In some cases, dealing with the non-customer's reluctance indirectly will foster trust and the development of an appropriate relationship. Counsellors should try taking non-customers for a walk; giving them some small non-counselling task to do; allowing them to remain while the counsellor continues with other work. The client may simply need time to get to know and trust the counsellor enough to begin talking.

Clients can be asked to bring photographs of themselves, their families or friends that they are willing to share and discuss. Some of the techniques described earlier can then be used to comment on and interpret the photograph.

The counsellor can try changing seating positions and/or other activities. In some cases, a mere change of position or activity will result in a client's being more willing to interact.

Responding to the talkative non-customer

Some non-customers will readily verbalise feelings such as hostility and anger, or interact in over-compliant or evasive ways. The effect is the same: avoidance of meaningful contact with the counsellor.

As in the case of the silent client, counsellors should pay particular attention to the talkative client's movements, gestures, and physical appearance.

Counsellors should also be sensitive to voice quality and use such information in responding. In many instances it will be productive to have clients repeat particular statements, phrases, or words. This repetition can serve to highlight underlying feelings and to clarify meanings.

If video equipment is available, clients can be recorded and then asked to view themselves and comment on what they see.

Explaining the counselling process

In some cases, clients' refusals to engage in counselling can be largely overcome by explaining the counselling process, how it works, and what the client can expect from the counsellor. The mere fact that counsellors are prepared to reveal their motives, intentions, thoughts, and feelings can act as an incentive and model for clients to do likewise.

Counsellors should be aware of the possibility that even cooperative clients may show reluctance when certain topics are introduced. Counsellors should also remember that they do not have the right to persist in efforts to engage unwilling clients. Reluctance may show something more than a temporary reticence. It may indicate a message that should be heeded: 'Leave me alone!' In the face of continued resistance, the counsellor should try referring the client elsewhere or simply end the contact.

The language of counselling

Because language is so central to social interactions and can have such a powerful effect in defining reality for various groups, it is important to use it in ways that will allow clients to change their perceptions of people and events. Language, after all, is 'the medium through which personal meanings are expressed and constructed' (Berg & De Jong, 1996, p. 388). Clients can change, therefore, by seeing their present difficulties as having new, more useful and less limiting meanings.

Counsellors also need to be aware of their own use of language and how it fosters or inhibits the client's view of their problems and their relationship with the counsellor. The following two sections describe ways in which both clients and counsellors can alter their use of language within the context of the counselling relationship.

The client's use of language

All counselling is a process of mutual influence and interaction, and language is a major tool in this process. Counsellors need to be more aware of how clients' use language to describe their situations and to figure out ways to use these descriptions to enhance the client's ability to change in desired ways (Berg, 1994).

Clients' use of language can also indicate aspects of their functioning and their concerns that may not otherwise be readily apparent. For example, unusual emphases ('I'd never admit anything to *her*!'), striking omissions ('I'm scared.' – About what?), and elaborate rationalisations should prompt a counsellor to seek further explanations and/or consider possible meanings behind what the client has said. It may also be helpful to get clients to talk less when it appears that their verbosity helps them to avoid their anxieties and uncertainties. Sometimes, too, the counsellor can help a client to deal with issues more directly and positively by suggesting that the client use different words or phrases.

Additional ways in which counsellors may help clients to alter their use of language includes directing them to do the things listed below. Counsellors can also model these preferred uses of language themselves and thereby indirectly reframe clients' perceptions of their situations (Johnson & Miller, 1994). This implicit form of modelling can effectively change clients' attitudes, beliefs and behaviours, and help them to discover new possibilities for solving their problems.

- Use the active rather than the passive voice ('I did it', rather than 'It just happened to me.');

- consider future action rather than dwell on past difficulties ('So, what do you need to do first?', rather than 'I've never been given a chance!');

- rephrase current concerns so as to neither overstate nor minimise them ('It's hard to face her right now', rather than 'I'll never be able to face her again.');

- speak in concrete, specific terms rather than abstract, general terms ('I yelled at my younger sister today and she told my parents about it', rather than 'I'm useless!');

- use 'want' instead of 'need' when that is what is really meant ('I want her to love me', rather than 'I need her to love me.');

- drop frequently used qualifiers like 'maybe', 'may', 'possibly' when those are used to cushion critical statements or avoid taking a stance ('I can stand up to him!', rather than 'Well, maybe I can stand up to him.');

- repeat a particular statement, phrase, or word to highlight and clarify its real meaning ('You didn't do it; I let you.' Ask the client to repeat 'I let you!').

The counsellor's use of language

Counsellors should also be aware of their own typical language patterns. The importance of this is often overlooked. There is enormous potential for counsellors to influence their clients' decision-making and actions through the latter's adopting the counsellor's style. Following are descriptions of five aspects of a counsellor's language with illustrations of how these aspects can be used to contribute to a more effective and open counselling relationship.

1 Establishing rapport, developing a relationship:

Virtually every counselling theory emphasises the importance of establishing a trusting, working relationship with the client. To accomplish this, counsellors can try several things. It is a sign of sensitivity to and respect for other people and their cultures if counsellors can understand and speak some of their language, both formal and colloquial. This may include only greetings, salutations and common expressions, but even this basic knowledge can be evidence of a sincere effort to understand the client's culture. It is also imperative that counsellors use non-sexist language and avoid using terms that may be derogatory or demeaning to particular groups (e.g., the aged and those with disabilities). Counsellors should also be able to engage in appropriate forms of small talk, to observe, even if briefly, the rituals of courtesy and socially appropriate greetings.

The language used in this rapport-building stage is usually simple and part of everyday usage. Initially, counsellors should listen for key words and expressions in the client's speech. These expressions can give counsellors insight into how clients define their situations. Counsellors can then use this information to help them join in with or blend with a client's behaviour or conversational style. In practice, this could mean talking less or more, light-heartedly or seriously, rapidly or slowly, each depending on the client's style; or actually mimicking in a sympathetic way particular gestures, movements or expressions.

2 Understanding the counsellor's preferred language:

Counsellors have their own idiosyncratic use of language. Typically clients may either consciously or unconsciously imitate their counsellor's dominant language features. Counsellors may notice that they repeatedly use feeling words, or behavioural labels, or references to cognitive processes, or figures of speech, or polysyllabic words. While these language habits may not all be counter-productive in themselves, they could well impede the progress of counselling.

3 The intended message versus the actual message:

Counsellors should aim to interact with their clients in purposeful, intentional ways. However, it is often the case that the counsellor's intended message is not what is actually said. For example, the counsellor may use warm, supportive words but convey an underlying impatience or coldness; or, the counsellor may change the topic of discussion merely to clarify an earlier client statement but in so doing convey an impression of being bored with the client. Furthermore, if counsellors need to know about something, they should ask. For example, if it is important to know how a client is getting along with his spouse, the counsellor should ask directly rather than hope that a vague, general inquiry like 'How are things at home?' will elicit the desired information.

When discrepancies occur between what was meant and what was actually said, the client may be left feeling unsure and confused. To overcome this, counsellors can endeavour to say exactly what they mean by being more specific and more open (see *Thinking Aloud*, p. 86).

4 Statements or questions as autobiographical material:

Counsellors' use of language can reveal much about themselves as well as what they are trying to accomplish with their clients. For example, questions that might mask autobiographical or self-statements: 'Shouldn't you first sort out your feelings toward your father?' should be examined. It may well be that it is the counsellor, and not the client, who has a need to examine familial relationships. If the autobiographical content of such statements arises out of the counsellor's own situation rather than the client's, this needs to be recognised and dealt with in ways that are appropriate to the needs of the client.

5 Using language to engender success::

Finding solutions to problems depends in part on having a positive, optimistic view of change. Counsellors can engender such an orientation by emphasising success rather than failure, possibilities rather than problems, competence rather than incompetence, the future rather than the past (see *The client's use of language*, p. 94). Specific questions can contribute to this sort of 'solution talk' (Furman and Ahola, 1992):

'How did you manage to do that?' (Berg, 1994)

'When (not if) *things are better.* ... (Berg, 1994)

'So, what will you be doing when the problem is no longer a problem?'

Related to this is the notion of the client as expert, the person who knows most about the problem situation and how to solve it. Adopting an attitude of curiosity or not knowing ('How did you do that?' 'Tell me about that.'), can encourage clients to explore, explain and accept greater responsibility for finding solutions to their problems.

In addition, counsellors should avoid using technical language and terms that are negative and convey hopelessness and an inability to change. Using language that promotes a new, positive view of things can encourage an active attitude of change.

1   Ask close friends and other counsellors to describe what they regard as your typical verbal and behavioural mannerisms. Find out what their reactions to those habits are. Which ones would you want to alter and why?

2   Audio or videotape a series of counselling role plays or real interviews. Replay them and note your verbal and behavioural mannerisms. Ask others to comment on the effect they seem to have on your clients. Which ones would you want to alter and why?

Chapter

Developing the search for solutions

nce the problem has been explored and previous attempts to solve it have been identified, the process of **finding solutions to problems** moves to goal setting. The skills involved in this fourth stage are discussed and illustrated in this chapter.

Stage 4: Goal-setting

After an agreed upon problem has been defined and previous unsuccessful attempts to solve it identified, this information can then become the basis for setting goals and constructing new ways of solving the problem. Since the problem is what brought the client to counselling, its solution is usually what is happening in the client's life when that problem is absent (Molnar & de Shazer, 1987). That is, what changes do clients want in their lives? The aim of counselling then becomes finding ways to implement or increase those problem-absent activities.

The way in which the client's goal is stated can make a great deal of difference to the effectiveness of counselling. For example, if the client is unable to formulate a goal, or can do so only in vague, general terms, it will be impossible to know how to reach it or when it has been reached. Counsellors should therefore help clients say what they want to achieve in language that is as precise and unambiguous as possible. It is important, however, for the goal to be meaningful to the client, and that it does not merely represent someone else's wishes for the client. This stage of counselling may necessitate the counsellor's taking a more active and leading role than in the earlier stages of counselling.

Direct questioning

As the name implies, direct questioning is the skill of focusing the discussion on a specific point. It is used to help clarify an issue the counsellor feels would be worth exploring further. This skill is usually used sparingly until clients have been given ample opportunity to examine their situations at their own pace and in their own manner. When used, the direct question or probing question is usually more effective if it is open rather than closed. This allows clients maximum freedom to respond and avoids a situation where questioning resembles an interrogation.

Example 1

Client:	'My managing supervisor didn't keep his promise to me.'
Counsellor:	(closed) *'Did you try reminding him of it?'*
	(open) 'How does that affect your relationship with him?'

Example 2

Client:	'Mum's OK. We get along fine. She seems to understand me. Dad's all right too, I guess.'
Counsellor:	(closed) *'Are you sure you give your father a chance?'*
	(open) 'You don't seem too sure about Dad. How do you get along with him?'

Looking for exceptions

Once the problem has been identified, even if only vaguely, clients should be encouraged to look for exceptions, that is, times when the problem is absent, less serious or able to be tolerated. It is at least as important to know what it is that precipitates solutions to problems as it is to know what triggers the problems. Therefore, find out what is happening when the problem is not a problem – what the client is thinking, doing, or feeling; who is doing what; what seems to cause the desired change. Answers to these questions will most likely contain clues to both achievable goals and possible solutions. In general, the more concrete, behaviourally specific, realistic and achievable the goal, the more likely it is that it will be achieved and the easier it will be to evaluate success (Dixon & Glover, 1984). It is important to start with simple goals and progress in small steps. This helps ensure success and build client self-confidence.

Exceptions questions

Traditional problem solving (analyse the problem, identify its causes and then remove them) is a tried and true method for dealing with difficulties. If we '"remove the bad things" [we] will be left with the good things' (de Bono, 1994, p. 45). However, the same author acknowledges that there are times when a specific cause cannot be identified or when there are so many causes that it is impossible to deal with them all. In these situations it will obviously be more productive to use a different approach.

Since problems can be thought of as solutions that are not working successfully, it is often more useful to explore what is happening when things are going well (Berg, 1994; de Shazer, 1988). Seldom do problems exist all of the time. Therefore, at the times when the problem is not causing distress, clients may be thinking in ways or doing things that are effective solutions already, even without realising it (de Shazer, 1988). Exploring these good times may uncover or reveal deliberate or accidental thoughts or behaviours that are, in effect, successful solutions. As clients describe these exceptions they may be surprised and even flattered to know that they are already doing things that are working well which in turn might mobilise them to work harder, recall other successes and view their situation with more hope and confidence. Questions that are useful for identifying and exploring exceptions are:

> *'Are there times when things are not so bad?'*

> *'What is going on then? What is different? Who is doing what?'*

> *'What did you do to control your anger in that situation?'*

> *'How did you figure all of that out?'*

> *'How did you manage to get to work on time three times this last week? What was your strategy?'*

> *'Is this something you think is useful? Can you do it again?'*

> *'How can you keep this going? What has to happen?'*

Miracle questions

There are times when clients may be unable to think of exceptions to the problem or cannot identify a goal or something they would like to work towards. They may be so stuck that they cannot think beyond or visualise a life outside of their despondency and difficulties. The miracle question (de Shazer, 1985) is a useful device to enable people to pretend, to transcend the present and imagine a better state of affairs. Pretending is part of everyone's experience and may help explain the success of miracle questions in assisting people to decide where they would like to get to and how it might be done. The typical miracle question goes like this:

> *'Suppose when you go to sleep tonight, a miracle happens and the problems that brought you in here today are solved. But since you are asleep, you don't know the miracle has happened until you wake up tomorrow; what will be different tomorrow that will tell you that a miracle has happened?'* (de Shazer, 1988, p. 94)

Counsellors can alter it to suit a particular context, client or problem. It is often sufficient to say, 'Let's pretend for a moment that all your problems are solved. If that happened, what would be different?' The playful, make-believe nature of this question often engages clients, lifts their spirits and allows them to think laterally about their situation. Counsellor trainees are often sceptical about miracle questions and worry that clients might answer with impossible scenarios, such as winning a huge sum of money or being cured of a terminal illness. In fact, in most instances clients' miracles are surprisingly down-to-earth and readily achievable. A variation of the miracle question that helps to focus on 'achievable miracles' is: 'Given your physical, financial or other limiting circumstances, what would make a significant difference in your future?' (Lipchik, 1994, p. 37).

In pairs, alternating the role of counsellor and client, interview each other about a problem the other is facing. Early in the interview ask (a) a series of exception questions (remember to follow up with 'Tell me more.' or 'What else?' – see *Topic following*, chapter 5); and (b) the miracle question.

Discuss the answers to those questions and the client's reaction to the questions themselves (e.g., How useful were they? What effect did they have on your thinking?).

Identifying possible goals

Most clients will be able to readily identify goals, or solutions to their problems. If encouraged to do so, they can describe alternatives that are more satisfying and achievable. This is a basic tenet of **finding solutions to problems**, and probably the most important aspect of this approach: 'respect people's resources and creativity, and never underestimate their capacity for creating more hopeful and satisfying lives' (Friedman, 1994, p. 220).

However, sometimes clients can get stuck and become constrained in their thinking by negative feelings, anxieties and rigid logic. At such times they may find it impossible to envision new outcomes, or alternative ways of behaving. One possible cause of this 'stuckness' can be an over-reliance on what de Bono (1971, p. 13) called *vertical thinking*, or thinking that only interprets situations in the most probable way. It is a process of thinking that is constrained by a logical, step-by-step path of progression and a rigid set of rules to guide that progression. An alternative way for both counsellors and clients to deal with problems and their solutions is to think laterally. This type of thinking can be stimulated in a number of ways (de Bono, 1971):

- by viewing the problem from a new and arbitrary perspective (e.g., to view counselling not from the perspective of problems that need remediation, but from a perspective of desired outcomes that may or not be related to the original problems);

- by adopting a new attitude or habit of mind in relation to problems (e.g., switching from an emphasis on what has not worked and why it has not worked to focusing on what is possible). According to de Bono (1994, p. 39) 'possibility may be the most important work in thinking. Possibility allows speculation. Possibility permits vision.';

- by deliberately distorting a dominant idea or problem (e.g., carry it to its extreme; exaggerate it);

- by purposely being illogical (e.g., use the elements of fun, humour, chance and surprise to create new, undiscovered possibilities).

Counsellors should understand the implications of these more creative ways of thinking and use them in their work with clients. In this way, counselling will emphasise possibilities rather than an absolute answer, reconciling contradictions rather than rejecting what is wrong, perceptions rather than facts, action rather than description, what can be rather than what is (de Bono, 1994).

---

exercise 6.2

The playful, creative nature of adopting a new perspective can be used to illustrate the difference between focusing on problems and focusing on solutions and how each can contribute to finding solutions to problems.

a   Have someone first play the role of the 'problem'. Have another person interview the problem. What helps it to stick around? Remain potent? What are its weaknesses?

b   Next, have that person play the role of the solution. What helps it to grow? What keeps it healthy? What undermines or stifles it?

This exercise can also be used with clients in actual counselling to help clients gain insight into their situations and to discover possible ways to bring about changes.

Some clients express their goals in general terms. In the behaviour-change phase of counselling, the first job of the counsellor is to help clients to be clear and specific about their goals. Counsellors may do this by helping clients break broad, general goals into smaller, more manageable ones, to plan practical steps towards a goal, or to choose one specific goal from a number of possible goals.

A useful technique to assist goal setting is to encourage clients to think of alternative ways of behaving. This encourages them to be practical. For example, getting answers to the following kinds of questions should help clients to express their goals so that practical steps to achieve them can be worked out:

'You're getting upset at the way your children react to you. What would you like them to do instead?'

'What would you like to do that you cannot do now?'

'What is the first thing that you would like to do better?'

'Are there times when the problem is not present?'

'What is happening at those times?'

Answers may be stated in the form of goals such as these: *'Have more fun with the children.' 'Be able to study better.' 'Stop nagging.'* Helpful though these goals are, each should be made more precise. 'More fun with the children' might come to be defined in several different ways – playing a game with them for at least 20 minutes every day, or swapping a joke every morning, or reading a story at some time every day. The goal of 'more effective study' might be specified as reading and taking notes without a break for 40 minutes at least twice a day. Negative goals such as 'stop nagging' need to be put in positive terms so that there is something definite to aim for. 'Stop nagging' might then be changed into 'making a specific request, at the right time, and once only'.

---

exercise 6.3*

1   Label each of the following as either 'G' (a general goal) or 'S' (a specific behaviour): (a) playing poker; (b) being a good conversationalist; (c) feeling on top of the world; (d) asking open-ended questions; (e) improving work habits; (f) relaxing in the evening; (g) inviting two friends to lunch; (h) driving the car; (i) feeling competent; (j) tolerating no nonsense; (k) doing yoga for 5 minutes daily; (l) setting the table. Check the answers at the end of the book and discuss them with others.

2   Write a specific goal for each of these general goals: (a) losing weight; (b) improving my appearance; (c) standing up to my father; (d) getting fit; (e) not boring other people; (f) getting on top of the job; (g) taking a break. For each goal, list the goal behaviours suggested by the group.

Sorting goals

If clients are able to identify multiple goals and a number of desirable directions in which to proceed, it may be necessary to sort goals (see *Sorting issues*, chapter 5). Since it is easier to focus on one or two small, achievable goals rather than attempt too much all at once, counsellors can list the goals clients have mentioned and invite them to select the one or two that can be accomplished first or those that are seen as most critical to a successful start.

Example 1:

Client: 'I need to get going earlier each morning, plan my work day more clearly, budget better and make sure I exercise at least three times a week.'

Counsellor: *'You have mentioned several things that you think will help you feel more in control of things and be more effective in your studies. Which one should you do first so that you will feel more ready and able to tackle the others?'*

Sort goals in response to the following:

1 'When I am relaxed, my anger is under control. One way I have discovered I can do this is by having 15 minutes to myself when I get home from work. Also, when I leave my work at the office, I'm happier and seem to have more time with the family. Drinking less leaves me fresher and less tired in the morning, too. So, there are lots of things I can do.'

2 'There are so many things to do; I've just got to get started! I'm going to lose five kilograms, take up squash, learn to meditate, read for pleasure more often, start looking for a new job on Monday and make sure that I spend more time with my friends.'

Gaining commitment

Clients' motivation to change their behaviour is a major factor in counselling. It is best if they choose and specify their own goals, for they are then more likely to work hard to achieve them. But counsellors who have developed good working relationships with clients can also offer suggestions as a way of prompting their thinking. Counsellors should ensure, however, that clients commit themselves fully to their goals and that they accept responsibility for them. If counsellors neglect to do this, clients may blame them for any failures. Counsellors should take care that clients pursue goals that they see as being realistic and desirable, and ones into which they are prepared to put time and effort. In other words, counsellors should make sure that clients show themselves to be customers for accomplishing those goals.

In getting such a commitment from the client, skills described in the following pages may be useful. The skill of influencing might be needed to convince those who give up easily and who express fatalistic attitudes, saying, 'It's just hereditary – my mother was exactly the same.' Without pushing too hard, the counsellor could give one or two carefully chosen examples, using ordinary language and citing details that seem close to the situation in question: 'Many parents have been able to stop children's temper tantrums in just a week or so, and without getting upset themselves.'

Scaling questions (see chapter 5) can be used to assess clients' motivation to change or their commitment to act. For example, 'On a scale from 1 to 10 where 10 is "extremely committed to changing", where are you now?' The client's answer can be followed by other questions such as 'What would it take to increase your commitment by one point? What's the first thing that you would have to do?'

The counsellor might find it helpful to formalise an agreement with clients in which specific activities are listed. If clients find it difficult to take action in a certain situation, asking them to write down their plan in simple direct language could be useful. And if it would be useful, clients could even be asked to sign and date a written statement or contract. For example:

> *'I agree to practise the behaviours we have discussed: how to enter the room with confidence, introduce myself, and call the meeting to order in an authoritative manner. I will do this three times this week just before each meeting. After each meeting I will write down all the things I did well and also those things I still need to work on. I will bring this record to the next session so it can be used in planning what needs to be practised next.'*

Notice that this contract sets out:

- Exactly what the client is to do.

- How often it will be done.

- How this information will be used at the next session.

Such contracts should be decided jointly by counsellors and clients. Provided that tasks are relevant to their problems and are realistic and simple, it is highly likely that carrying them out will be satisfying to clients. It is important for clients to be motivated and to participate actively in planning for change. Requiring them to develop and execute tasks in this way helps to ensure their involvement.

exercise 6.5

1 Role-play in counsellor/client pairs. The client's role is to express doubts about being able to do certain things. Assume that the client has little formal education. Give examples of the exact words you would use to convince him/her that it is possible to learn to:

   a Stop children's temper tantrums.

   b Ask for help from a welfare agency.

   c Refuse overtime work.

   d Make a complaint about service received from a welfare agency.

2 In pairs, plan a contract which follows the three basic rules. Choose any topic, e.g., a physical fitness programme or a new way of reducing anxiety about speaking to large groups.

Dealing with discrepancies

Dealing with discrepancies involves the skill of honestly and directly pointing out to clients that their descriptions of themselves or their situations do not seem to match the way in which the counsellor or others might see the same situation. To avoid this skill being overly confrontational and challenging, counsellors can adopt an attitude and tone of voice which conveys the message 'help me understand what's going on here'. In effect, counsellors can make it clear that of course there will be logical, positive explanations for discrepancies – if only the client will help them understand what they are. Discrepant behaviours can involve such things as strengths or weaknesses that a client refuses to acknowledge, misinformation or lack of information, reluctance to put a stated intention into action, or a refusal to see another's point of view.

When pointing out a discrepancy to clients, counsellors should focus on present feelings and behaviours and not on what clients have said or done in the past. To use this skill effectively, counsellors must be able to:

- use their own feelings and perceptions to identify client discrepancies as soon as they occur;

- be able to state those perceptions in a clear, simple, non-judgemental and genuinely curious way;

- decide when it is appropriate to tell clients what their view of the behaviour or statement is and the specific reasons for that reaction;

- Allow clients the opportunity to respond.

Highlighting discrepancies will sometimes be perceived by clients as criticism of them and may, therefore, jeopardise the counselling relationship. But, if successful, this skill can greatly speed up the counselling process or overcome a block or barrier. If a helping relationship has already been developed, pointing out a discrepancy is less risky and may in fact be seen as a positive challenge and helpful by the client. A useful way to highlight a discrepancy is to use the sentence form: 'On the one hand, you… and yet on the other hand, you… Can you help me understand that contradiction?'

Example 1

'You say constantly that you are going to get up on time and get to school, but you seldom do. I'm curious about how that seems to you.'

Example 2

'You keep saying you love your wife, but you don't seem to want to make her happier by staying home more often. What am I missing here?'

Example 3

'Right now I hear you saying things are getting better, but you have been mistaken about that twice before. What's different about this time?'

exercise **6.6**

1   Form groups of three. In each group, decide who will first be counsellor, who will be client and who will be observer. The counsellor and client are to role-play the first situation below. The counsellor is to identify any discrepancy that appears in what the client has been doing or saying. The observer should make sure that the counsellor points out a discrepancy and does so in a way that allows the client some freedom to respond.

2   When finished, people in each group should swap roles and repeat the above procedure until each has had a chance to function as counsellor.

Role-play 1: You suspect the client is experiencing sexual problems in his marriage because, although the client insists there are no problems in this area, he refuses to discuss any aspect of sex, looks embarrassed and always manages to change the subject when you bring it up.

Role-play 2: The client insists she wants to change her critical and sarcastic way with people but she consistently refuses to discuss specific ways of altering this behaviour.

Role-play 3: The client keeps making negative statements about his artistic talents in spite of a number of compliments from others and praise from his art instructor.

exercise **6.7**

Think of some situation in your own life in which you could have benefited from having a discrepancy pointed out to you. Write a statement in which you identify that discrepancy. Choose another person with whom to share your statement. As you do this, try to be aware of how you are feeling as you do it and why.

Giving information

There are many times when simply giving information is the most useful thing to do. If clients ask for factual information that is directly relevant to their problems, it should be clearly, promptly, and simply given.

Counsellors at the start of their careers, often having been told to be wary of giving clients information, are sometimes reluctant to answer direct questions. They feel they should not answer until they are absolutely certain that the 'real' problem has been identified. Thus, they may be evasive and tend to probe beyond what the client has already revealed. This behaviour can be irritating and confusing to clients.

Another situation that causes counsellors difficulty is when a client asks them direct, personal questions. Again, in most cases a direct, simple answer is best, even if it is a refusal to divulge the information. Clients will be more confused by and suspicious of a hesitant, evasive, or equivocal reply than they will by a direct refusal.

Below are examples of giving information and handling direct questions from clients:

Example 1

Client: 'Has my doctor talked to you about me yet?'

Counsellor: *'No. If you'd like her to talk to me, though, you may tell her that I would be happy to do so.'*

Example 2

Client: 'What do you think I should do?'

Counsellor: *'Well, I don't really know. And, besides, it's more important for you to be able to answer that question. So, I wonder what you would like to hear me say?'*

Example 3

Client: 'Have you ever smoked pot?'

Counsellor: *'Yes, I have tried it. What were you hoping to hear?'*

In the first example, the counsellor gives a simple, negative answer to the client's question and then offers to speak to the doctor if that is what the client wants. An alternative response could have been, 'No. What would she want to talk to me about?' This alternative is more direct and possibly more threatening to the client but potentially effective in addressing the client's concern. It is often useful to follow your direct response to the client's question with an invitation to talk or with an open question about the client's feelings or beliefs. For instance, in the second example the counsellor avoids making a decision for the client and then invites the client to express his/her own preferences. In the third example, the counsellor answers the client without any explanation and invites the client to explore the matter further.

Giving advice

If counsellors are following the model of counselling outlined in this book, advice will be given very infrequently, only when requested, and only after careful listening has ensured that the counsellor understands the client's situation. It is a skill that is easily misused. Advice-giving is open to game-playing in that it places the counsellor in the role of expert (and all such experts are sooner or later shown to be fallible). Also, it may be a manoeuvre by clients to avoid taking responsibility for themselves or to avoid looking at an issue fully. When advice is given, it should be based on reasons the client has previously offered in support of one particular option over others. When this is not possible, counsellors should state the reasons why they feel a particular option might be better for the client than the other options. Seeing things from this new perspective may then at least give clients feedback about themselves.

Client: 'Even after all our talking I can't decide which job to take, the sales position or the warehouse foreman's job.'

Counsellor: *'Well, you could try sales. As you said yourself, you've already had some experience in that area, you want a job that pays a base rate <u>and</u> commission, you have expressed concern about a job involving much lifting and you like the company's management structure. What do you think?'*

Sometimes the counsellor can use advice-giving to help a client make a decision. For instance, there are times when a counsellor suspects that a client who professes to be undecided actually prefers one option over the others. When this situation arises, the client's preference becomes obvious (through verbal and non-verbal signs) as soon as the counsellor purposely advises another course of action. This type of advice-giving should be used sparingly and only after the counsellor adequately understands the client's situation.

Influencing

Influencing and persuading clients to change their attitudes, beliefs and behaviours are central tasks in every counselling relationship. In fact, it is impossible to avoid influencing (and being influenced by) clients. Counsellors should not deny that such influencing takes place, but rather understand the process more fully so that it can be used more effectively.

There are times when it seems that all the client needs is a push to get started or make a decision. However, when used too frequently or without a complete understanding of the client's situation, attempts to persuade will usually be unsuccessful. Counsellors also risk disappointment if they too confidently believe that they know what is best for clients, and then clients choose another course of action. Like advice-giving, influencing is open to game-playing in that any failure can be blamed on the counsellor for offering the wrong solution.

Client: 'It's no use. I just don't feel comfortable in that situation.'

Counsellor: a *'I'm sure you can do it, especially if you follow the way we practised it here.'*

b *'If you don't, I'm afraid I can't help you any more.'*

Note the difference between the two counsellor responses. When would each be most effective and why?

Interpretation

Interpretations are alternative or additional explanations of, or insights into, a situation. When used in counselling, they can help clients to understand the meaning of events by presenting different views of their problems. Interpretations will be more helpful and less like expert pronouncements if they arise out of information clients present rather than wholly from the counsellor's experience and theoretical knowledge.

Counsellors should remember that an interpretation is merely one possible explanation or perception of an event. Clients may have entirely different and equally valid explanations based on historical, cultural and/or personality factors that are different from the counsellors'. Counsellors should offer their interpretations tentatively, allowing clients sufficient opportunity to modify them. In effect, interpretations then become hypotheses (about thoughts, feelings, behaviours, problems) that clients can consider and analyse. When used in this way, interpretations can be thought of as a form of thinking aloud in the sense that counsellors are including clients in their analysis of problems and the construction of possible solutions.

Read the following counsellor interpretations. Both are based on what the client has previously said and both offer the client the chance to reject or modify the counsellor's statement.

Example 1

'From what you have said about your father, it seems that you are really very frightened of him. Is that how you see it?'

Example 2

'You sound as if you're extremely embarrassed about being overweight. Perhaps your aggressiveness toward others is an attempt to cover your shame. Could that be right?'

The skill of interpretation can have negative aspects. It can be an impersonal technique that emphasises the superior status and expertise of the counsellor. Also, too often clients will accept interpretations as authoritative, fatalistic explanations and may cease working to change things. Offering clients interpretations can be valuable in counselling, but presenting them as expert pronouncements serves only to satisfy a counsellor need, not a client need. Finally, it is a mistake to think that a counsellor's effectiveness can be measured by the ingeniousness or frequency of the interpretations used.

━━━━ exercise 6.8 ━━━━━━━━━━━━━━━━━━━━━━━━━━━━━━━━━━━━━━

1   Think of how you felt at some point today. Try to think of as many interpretations of these feelings as you can. For example, you might begin by remembering that you felt annoyed at being misunderstood. Then try to

think of all the possible explanations for that feeling (e.g., 'She asked for my opinion but then didn't really seem interested – I felt foolish trying to explain.')

2   Which explanation seems to be the best? Why?

---

exercise 6.9

Write down as many possible explanations or interpretations as you can for the first client statement below. Then discuss your interpretations with others to find out which ones satisfy the requirements of an effective interpretation (e.g., based on what the client has said or directly implied, add new meaning to the situation, are presented in a way that allows the client to reject or modify it).

a   'I've really messed things up with that teacher. I hate the class, the work, her. I'm really worried about my attitude.'

b   'I'm finished. That factory job is too dull... I'm sick of putting the same piece in each crate hour after hour. I'm tired, bored, unhappy...'

Reframing

Helping clients to think about themselves and their difficulties in a different, more creative way is called reframing. It is a type of influencing, interpretation, or lateral thinking (see *The language of counselling*, pages 93–97), that substitutes a new and more positive meaning for a set of events or circumstances. Provided the counsellor understands the client's situation and the reframe is believable, it can free the client to think or act in new, more creative ways (Berg, 1994; Ivey, 1994). In order to reframe successfully, the counsellor must be able to generate several interpretations in response to the client's problem and to articulate one that will be plausible, positive and readily accepted by the client. Reframing is a skill that can be used very early in the counselling relationship, especially when complimenting clients on skills or strengths that they themselves are unaware of. For example, a counsellor may reframe a client's indecision as a necessary period of contemplation, or an intuitive wisdom about going slow when faced with a complex issue.

---

exercise 6.10

Write as many reframes as you can for the following characteristics: stubborness; unsociable; a controlling spouse; a critical teacher; shyness; a family that engages in constant fighting. Share your responses with others in the group.

Using personal examples

Many times clients have reported that they were unaware that others had experienced similar concerns or worries to theirs and had discovered ways of overcoming them. Therefore, it may seem to counsellors that it would reassure and support clients to hear that the counsellor had experienced a similar situation and what was done to cope with it. Hearing this form of self-disclosure can be an important factor in clients' decisions to begin searching for solutions to their own problems.

The example below illustrates three necessary aspects of an effective self-disclosure: it should be succinct, it should be relevant to the client's concern, and the focus of the interview should quickly move back to the client.

> Client: 'I just can't face a group. I get nervous and forget what I am supposed to say.'

> Counsellor: *'Yes, I know that feeling well. I was so frightened of groups it almost kept me from becoming a teacher. But I'm sure that if we work on it, you can overcome your fear.'*

However, caution is urged in using this skill. It is the author's experience that he has almost always regretted using personal examples. They tend to divert the focus away from clients and detract from their feelings of being most important and central in the relationship. To understand this, think of a situation in which you were talking about something of importance to yourself, and another person began telling of a similar experience of their own. How did you feel when the focus shifted from your story to theirs?

Advising a delay

Sometimes it is prudent and effective to advise the client to delay making a decision or take some action, in effect, to do nothing for a period of time. This is especially so when (a) important information about the concern will become available in a short time (e.g., the result of a spouse's job application will be known early next week); (b) the client is unrealistically panicky about things and feeling pushed to make a hasty decision (e.g., the client, a father and a solo parent, feels it is time he was more decisive and that he should decide right now whether to propose to a woman he has known for only three months); and (c) the problem has been exaggerated beyond what is realistic (e.g., a man whose write-up of a project at work was criticised has decided that he has no future with the company and should quit his job immediately).

In most of these examples delaying the decision allows the client to gather more information about the situation, to become more clear about an attendant concern, or to clarify what the concern actually involves. Convincing clients to put off deciding or acting can be problematic: in many instances delaying will have to be presented to them (i.e., reframed) as a positive, decisive act. For example, it may be possible to prioritise specific steps in the decision-making so that finding out whether his wife's job application was successful becomes

the first, necessary step in deciding how to restructure the family budget (see
(a) above).

Supporting and encouraging

Used skilfully, support and encouragement of the client as a person who is
capable of coping, can be extremely reassuring and energising. Much of the
feeling of support and encouragement may be conveyed non-verbally through
eye contact, facial expression, smiling, posture, and tone of voice. However,
when using verbal means to convey support and encouragement, counsellors
should cite specific strengths and abilities as well as affirming the whole person.
Compliments (see chapter 5) are an obvious way of doing this.

Note the differences among these three counsellor responses. Which is least
judgemental and why? Which is the most obviously supportive or encouraging?

Client: I have really worked at changing and I think I'm finally getting
somewhere.

Counsellor: a   *'That sounds great! That's what I was hoping to hear.'*

b   *'You sound more positive now. I'm glad to hear it.'*

c   *'I knew you could do it; never doubted it for a minute.'*

7 # Completing the search for solutions

nce one or more goals have been chosen, the final three steps in the counselling process are to work out a strategy for achieving them, implement that strategy and then evaluate what was achieved in relation to what was desired. These are the stages of strategy selection, strategy implementation and evaluating progress.

Stages 5 and 6: Strategy selection and implementation

Once clients have selected one or more goals to aim for and these have been expressed in terms that are as specific as possible, the next step in the process is to work out how to achieve these goals. Useful questions at this stage are 'What might be a good first step at this point?'; or 'What would be one small thing you could do to begin moving toward your goal?' For some clients the task at this point is really one of choice: they may already have the resources needed to achieve the goal, but are finding it difficult to establish priorities or to choose between alternatives that seem equally attractive but may be incompatible. Often the gathering of information and the use of some systematic method of decision-making are sufficient to decide what needs to be done and how to do it. Occasionally, clients may need help in following up on the implications of their decision. Unproductive client behaviours at this point include continuing with things as they are, letting others make the decision, and making a hasty, ill-considered decision (Manthei, 1990). Counsellors need to be alert to these behaviours and address them directly; for example, by using the skill of dealing with discrepancies (see chapter 6).

For those clients who already know what it is they want to achieve, the task is one of change, that is, how to alter their present environment, their own behaviour or that of other people, or the way they think about the problem. The counsellor's task at this point is to help clients expand those areas of their lives that are desired and already functioning satisfactorily (Molnar & de Shazer, 1987). These solutions are most always generated by clients and it can usually be left to them to work out in detail how to put the solutions into practice. If asked, most clients will already have useful ideas about this process. However, at times counsellors may need to provide planning, teaching, and support to help them get started.

Selecting strategies

Anticipating situations

Clients should be made aware of the many factors that contribute to success. Among these is the importance of first practising only in those situations in which the chances of success are very good. Careful planning is essential. Clients should be helped to choose the best time and place to start, to decide on possible things to say and do, to imagine how they want to look and feel, to consider likely reactions of others and themselves, and to anticipate their responses to these different reactions. Counsellors should encourage clients to anticipate success, even if thinking about the situation beforehand makes them anxious.

The prospect of failure can also be discussed, because it would be foolish of counsellors to guarantee success. While the emphasis should be on the positive aspects and on planning for success, clients should be encouraged to think of failure as 'nothing lost', and as an opportunity to make better plans for the next occasion (see *Reframing*, chapter 6).

exercise 7.1

Write out a detailed plan to handle each of the following tasks. In each case, try to anticipate what could possibly happen and work out a plan to deal with each (e.g., 'If she says this, I'll say that'):

1   Expressing first your doubts about, then your firm opposition to, something you had previously agreed to.

2   Talking with a domineering supervisor about two aspects of your job that you want to see altered.

Discuss each plan with a partner.

Providing models

Modelling means providing a good example or pattern of behaviour for clients who do not know how to act appropriately in some situation. At one level, modelling could mean simply showing an actual example, e.g., a client's note-taking might be improved by seeing a sample page done by a fellow student.

Usually, however, modelling refers to more complicated interactions and for this reason modelling is commonly demonstrated in two ways – both completely, without a break, to show the total effect, and also in segments so that the separate skills can be isolated for observation and practice. Counsellors can act as a model during a counselling session. A peer or colleague of the client's can act as a model in the client's ordinary social setting. A model can also take the form of a special presentation of the target behaviour, e.g., on film or video tape.

There are some obvious advantages and disadvantages to these alternatives. The most serious disadvantage is that the performance of the peer or colleague cannot be controlled or repeated. It is best if counsellors can emphasise the vital parts of the performance and repeat those that they wish to highlight still further. Slight exaggeration can sometimes help in emphasising salient points.

After the modelled behaviour has been presented, clients can be asked to imitate the model. They should then be encouraged to rehearse the behaviour, with the counsellor giving immediate feedback in the form of positive comments and suggestions about improvements that are needed. Clients should be reminded of the importance of such behaviour rehearsal in their own time. The procedure for effective modelling may be summarised as follows:

- Ask clients to demonstrate how they typically act in the situation that is problematic.

- Break the situation into more manageable parts by isolating effective and ineffective aspects of their behaviour for observation, discussion, and practice. Compliment clients on aspects of the behaviour that they are already doing successfully or effectively.

- Choose one or two of the ineffective behaviours and demonstrate a more effective way, several times if necessary, exaggerating the parts that cause difficulty.

- Ask clients to rehearse the behaviour they have just observed. Give helpful feedback and compliment them on things that they have done well.

- Continue rehearsing until a smooth, natural performance is achieved.

- Repeat this process with other, more complex aspects of clients' behaviour.

When using modelling, it is important to begin with simple aspects of a client's behaviour. This helps to ensure that the client will experience success and will thus be willing and confident to attempt more complex behaviours. It is usually easier for clients to master simple non-verbal skills before attempting more complex verbal skills.

exercise 7.2

Plan modelling sessions with your partner, breaking up each of the following situations into two or three segments, each containing specific behaviours. Consider every detail – appearance, timing, gestures, posture, sequences, words, tone, facial expression. Then carry out each modelling segment, with your partner giving feedback on your performance.

a   Entering an office to ask for a job.

b   Making a complaint about how a medical examination was conducted.

Role-playing

Role-playing means acting out how another person with a particular title or function usually behaves. It is obviously akin to modelling and behaviour rehearsal, and all three are often used in conjunction with one another. But role-playing usually implies a less prescribed way of behaving. The emphasis is more on feeling what it is like to act in a certain manner, sometimes with the further implication that the role, being different, is unfamiliar. The roles should not be played for long: three or four minutes is all that is necessary.

For example, a parent plays a different role from a son or daughter, as does a nurse from a patient, and a counsellor from a client. If people pair off and play one of these roles and then switch to the other, i.e., *reverse roles*, they might begin to experience what another person feels or thinks. As a result, those taking part would probably be better able to appreciate what actually goes on in such pairings. If they are professionals, such learning may help them to be more effective in their work. In addition, the many opportunities for direct learning in role-playing and role reversal make them practical skills for counsellors to use in helping clients to change.

Both in role-playing and in role reversal, clients should be encouraged, even coached, to enter fully into the parts they play, with all the feelings, gestures, words, tones, and volume that are typically used. The more convincingly the roles are enacted, the greater the number of learning opportunities and change possibilities that are offered to clients.

---

exercise 7.3

Try short role-plays and role reversals for each of these situations:

a   mother/daughter conflict

b   welfare agency receptionist – applicant for assistance

c   friend – recently deserted wife

Using rewards

There is a substantial literature describing how to change people's behaviour in various settings (families, work-places, schools, institutions) by systematically altering the associations between events or 'bits' of behaviour. The general name for this method of changing behaviour is *reinforcement*, which refers to the way in which one can increase or decrease the likelihood that certain events will occur. As a general rule, behaviour which is regularly and immediately followed by pleasant experiences tends to be repeated. Such behaviour is said to be rewarded or positively reinforced. On the other hand, behaviour which is ignored or has unpleasant consequences is less likely to be repeated.

In everyday life things often seem to be more complicated than that and to follow either different rules or no rules at all. This is partly because what is rewarding to one person in a particular setting may not be so to others in that setting or to the same person in a different setting. Generally, however, the apparent complexities and contradictions arise from the fact that people have not observed accurately enough what is in fact occurring. For example, the very threats and naggings that are intended to stop a child's misbehaviour at home frequently have the opposite effect. In an apparently perverse way they serve to reinforce the unwanted behaviour. Often this is because misbehaviour is all that the adult has responded to, and the child gets little or no recognition or reward for good behaviour. Frequently in such a situation, all desirable behaviour passes unnoticed and without commendation of any kind, and the only adult reaction (notice, even in the form of nagging) is to misbehaviour. One of the most effective ways of dealing with a child who is misbehaving, for example, is by ignoring this behaviour if possible, and instead making positive comments (see *Compliments*, chapter 5) about appropriate behaviour. This must be done immediately after it occurs, so that the desired behaviour is reinforced. Parents and teachers using such tactics for the first time are often startled at their effectiveness.

Counsellors can help clients to plan changes based on careful observation of exactly 'what is reinforcing what'. The combination of rewarding desired behaviour and ignoring inappropriate behaviour is especially powerful, although it may not be sufficient or appropriate in every case. It is nevertheless widely applicable; problems arising in groups, in family relationships, and in supervision or training situations can often be resolved by altering the reinforcements.

Most of the counselling techniques used in the beginning and developing stages have 'rewarding' effects. Good eye-contact, open questions and compliments are rewarding in that they help clients to feel accepted and encourage them to keep talking. Topic following and reflections have similar effects. Almost all techniques in the early stages reward sharing, openness, problem-exploration, and the search for solutions.

Effective counsellors use techniques selectively to influence the course of a counselling session. By talking about or showing interest in client remarks which refer to insights and possible solutions, for instance, counsellors are rewarding positive attitudes and solution talk. If at the same time counsellors ignore or cut off long complaints and harrowing tales (i.e., does not reward them), they are in effect saying, 'Let's stop this talk and see instead what we can actually do about solving this problem'. While it is possible for counsellors to ignore something that clients particularly want and need to talk about, clients will almost always raise the topic a second time if it is important to them.

These simple, selective rewarding techniques are appropriate skills to teach to some clients. For example, clients lacking in conversational ability might be coached by counsellors in basic attending skills. Used in social situations, these skills act as rewards to speakers who are thus encouraged to respond to clients by conversing with them. Clients should be urged to practise such skills in their own time and to report on their effects. Responding skills would likewise be valuable as general social skills.

Counsellors should remember that reward techniques can operate in either direction, and that clients may use them on the counsellor, as well as vice versa.

Another useful reward technique involves getting clients to make a list of satisfying activities for themselves, or for another person for whom they feel responsible. Their lists might include the following: tending plants, chatting on the phone, walking the dog, listening to music. Their adolescent sons or daughters might have a list like this: having a driving lesson, playing pool, going out with friends. In both instances, clients should be encouraged to list as many items as possible, at least a dozen. The list can be regarded as a kind of menu from which satisfying activities can be selected.

All of these activities can then be used either as rewards to be enjoyed *after* a certain disliked task has been performed, or as substitutes – *instead* of some self-defeating behaviour. In the first instance the satisfaction of a coffee break or listening to favourite music might be made to depend upon having done all chores or studied for two 40-minute periods. In the latter case a client may be urged to consult the list and choose an activity whenever he/she is becoming tense, or bored, or depressed. Thus, instead of sinking further into unpleasant thoughts and feelings, the client might invite a friend to lunch or go out to the shops, and thus counter the depression or boredom.

exercise 7.4

1   Selective reinforcement

Notice that each of the following client statements includes references to both a feeling and an action that might be taken. Identify both parts of each statement, and then make up a simple reflection comment that reinforces the action part. For example:

> Client: I get so annoyed! They just won't do what I tell them!

> Counsellor: *You would like them to co-operate with you more?*

a   'Actually I am pretty low just now. I wish I could get more work done.'
b   'My husband and I just don't do things together any more. Perhaps we're bored with each other.'

2   Reinforcement menus

Make a list of activities that might be satisfying to you if you were in each of these situations:

a   A young mother with two children under three years, living in a new suburb.
b   A woman recently widowed, no family, 45 years old.

For each situation make a composite list from everyone's contributions.

Implementing strategies

Making records

Recording is a simple but very important skill because it provides one of the most powerful means of prompting and documenting behaviour change. Clients who feel that they accomplish little should be urged to keep a detailed diary of how they spend their day, including the times that things do and do not get done. Parents who complain about their child's misbehaviour or teachers concerned about an unruly class should be helped to organise a recording system showing (a) what happens just before and just after each misbehaviour and also how often the misbehaviours occur, and (b) how often the desirable behaviour occurs and what is going on at those times.

Recording should be focused on one or two observable behaviours that are at the centre of the issue and that can be counted. Instances of both the desired and undesired behaviours should be recorded. Observations based on generalised behaviours and vague problems lead to useless records. It is impossible to get accurate information about things like inattentiveness/ attentiveness, or disobedience/obedience without being precise about what these descriptions mean and how they are exemplified. Counsellors should help clients to clarify the problem by asking them specific questions ('How many questions did you ask in that time?' 'How many times was she out of her seat during the lesson?') and following those up with 'What did you do to make those desired things happen?'

Strictly speaking, recording is not a counselling skill, but it is such a valuable aid to making good decisions about change that its importance must be stressed. Counsellors should urge clients to gather relevant information about their behaviour and the behaviour of others when considering behaviour change. In some instances, keeping an impersonal, accurate record can induce change without the use of any other skills or methods.

---

exercise 7.5

1 Choose a familiar TV advertisement and practise recording one behaviour, e.g., How often is the name of the product or service presented? List all the adjectives used. How many different camera shots are used?

2 Watch two people talking to each other. In different one-minute segments, record separate behaviours, one to each segment, e.g., number of head movements, leg movements, arm movements. Compare your record with that of a partner.

3 Imagine that you are finding it difficult to fit everything into your day. Make a log of your activities yesterday from getting up to going to bed. Describe the activities in detail. Keep the log in at least half-hour segments. Explain to a partner in what respects this was a typical day, and in what respects it was unusual.

Bodily awareness, relaxation, activities

As part of the processes by which behaviour is changed, it can be very helpful for people to become more aware of and in control of their bodily sensations. Heightened awareness can help clients to identify their feelings more precisely. Counsellors can help clients to make use of such material by getting them to identify their bodily feelings and understand the reasons for them, and take steps to deal constructively with them.

Bodily awareness techniques can also be used to help clients to gain more control of themselves. Systematic relaxation is an especially useful technique for this. Transcendental meditation, yoga, moderate exercise and engaging in a preferred or pleasant activity (e.g., reading or listening to music) are other examples of techniques with similar purposes. The advantages of relaxation are that it is easily taught and easily learned. In addition, relaxation can conveniently be used in a wide variety of real-life situations. It can also be useful as an adjunct to other counselling skills.

Relaxation is achieved by gradually loosening muscles in all parts of the body so that there is no tightness or tension anywhere. Full attention is required, so that different parts of the body are relaxed in sequence. It is possible to attain either complete relaxation, so that the whole body is limp, or partial relaxation, which can be used as a way of coping with particular tensions, for example in the neck or stomach. Different degrees or levels of relaxation can be reached, from simply removing muscle tension to attaining a state of rest approximating sleep, sometimes in fact going to sleep.

Counsellors who sense that their clients are very anxious may help them to relax by getting them to do a few simple exercises. This may help them to face their problems more calmly in counselling and in their everyday lives.

'How about just leaning right back in the chair and taking three or four deep breaths... Slowly now, fill up your lungs... Slower yet, just relax your arms...'

Relaxation can be used in preparing for some especially tense situation, such as an interview, examination, or important meeting. Counsellors should encourage clients to use relaxation skills while actually in tense situations. Relaxing also can be a calming respite after a worrying or upsetting experience or physical exertion.

The reduction of tension by taking up some physical activity is another useful way of helping clients to change their behaviour. A game that demands some exertion of energy and permits some social interaction often reduces tension and can serve as an excellent reward. For some, solitary physical activities may be preferred. Physical activities can reduce the many stresses that come from modern living – mentally and emotionally demanding experiences and repetitious, solitary, and/or sedentary occupations. Similar functions can be served by many other pursuits such as dancing, hobbies, games, arts and crafts, and playing and listening to music. It would be wise to encourage clients to include in every 'reinforcement menu' some physical or creative activity.

Thoughts and imagery

The ability to deal directly and constructively with clients' mental activity is another important counselling skill. The client's thoughts, ideas, and perceptions are obviously important throughout counselling, so much so that their uses in changing behaviour are often overlooked. A good example of how imagery can be used is shown by the ways in which relaxation is taught. Besides the usual method of directing clients to relax various muscle groups, counsellors may encourage them to recall or imagine events and situations which help the physical processes. This imagery encourages the loosening of a client's muscle tension. Physical tightness in the body may be reduced if clients can call up images associated with calm, comfort, and rest. Counsellors prompt clients to do this by using colourful language and a soothing tone of voice:

> *'Imagine you are on soft cushions in a dimly lit room with quiet slow music playing.'*

> *'Notice how slow, and deep, and easy your breathing is now.'*

> *'Feel all the tightness seeping away as though you were in a warm bath.'*

At various points in a counselling relationship, thinking and imagination can be profitably used to help the change process. For example, counsellors should encourage clients to use similar sorts of descriptions and language to fill out what they mean by such general terms as 'a real scene', 'not so good', 'feeling better'. They should try to get clients to think, imagine, and describe things in concrete and colourful detail in response to such questions and requests as these:

> *'Tell me how you're feeling right now, when you're saying that you feel trapped. What does your body seem to be saying to you?'*

> *'What does he do then? What's going through your mind when he says and does those things?'*

Some clients seem to have too active an imagination, and most of their difficulties seem to arise from the way they concentrate on negative aspects of their thoughts. These people become more and more anxious and resistant to change because they constantly anticipate failure, and as a result they avoid facing up to things. In whatever ways they can, counsellors should help clients to stop dwelling on these aspects. Counsellors can reinforce talk about alternatives, they can ignore references to negative aspects, and they can point out in a rational manner the self-defeating nature of such thoughts. They can also elicit from clients 'reinforcement menus' of images which have pleasant associations, and clients can then be urged to use them whenever negative images intrude. Such a programme of 'guided fantasy' would of course need to be supported and supplanted as soon as possible by more active steps to bring the images into reality.

exercise 7.6

As counsellor, plan how you would encourage a client (your partner) to think positively, and in concrete detail about:

a Going to bed in a relaxed way.

b Getting ready for work on a Monday.

Mixing strategies

Systematic relaxation is a notable example of a technique which involves several different counselling skills in combination. Once the various skills of counselling and change processes have been mastered, counsellors are urged to combine them as they see fit. Many combinations are possible, and books on counselling often describe these as mixed or multiple strategies. Skills developed by cognitive-behavioural counsellors exemplify such approaches well by combining, for example, imagery, bodily awareness, and role-playing. Assertion training programmes likewise demonstrate how counsellors can help people by using a mixture of strategies. Typically such training involves the use of rational planning, imagery, modelling, and role-playing, followed by careful rehearsal of actions, words, and feelings. The result is that people who usually are not able to say what they want to because they are either too timid or too domineering, learn to express themselves more effectively.

Summarising

Near the end of the session it is useful for counsellors to review what has taken place. This can be done mentally, or by actually informing clients that the counsellor is now going to take a break (Berg, 1994) to think about what has happened for a few minutes. Whether this is done in the presence of the client or not is up to the counsellor to decide. What is important is that the counsellor is able to review and make sense of all the information that has been gathered in the interview. The purpose of this review is to identify those things the client has been doing well and the things that have not worked, to decide on the client's level of motivation and to identify a task that the client will be confident about and willing to carry out.

The skill of summarising is a way of doing this in a clear and orderly fashion. Summarising is the process of tying together the essence of what has been communicated during part or all of the counselling session. It brings together the main highlights of what has occurred, thereby clarifying what has been accomplished and what remains to be done. When summarising, counsellors should pull together the salient points, state them as simply and clearly as possible and ask clients for their reaction to the summary particularly whether they feel it is accurate.

When summarising, counsellors should also compliment (see page 76) clients on their abilities and accomplishments. Compliments communicate confidence in and respect for clients' ability to solve their problems themselves, give them the credit for successes already achieved, and increase clients' self-esteem and motivation to continue working. For example:

Counsellor: 'Let's see if we can put all of this together. On the one hand you feel lonely and isolated, especially with groups of people. On the other hand, you say that there are times when you are able to overcome your shyness and approach strangers on a one-to-one basis. So, you are clear about wanting to get to know others and you have begun to discover ways in which you can do that. It's obvious that you have thought about this a great deal and have begun the difficult process of sorting through what changes you need to make. That sort of motivation is often a difficult first step for people, but one you have already tackled. Not everyone is able to do it; how did you learn to do these things?'

It is sometimes just as useful to have clients summarise what has happened or been discussed. This enables counsellors to get a better understanding of the client's view of things and helps clients see what progress they have made.

---

exercise **7.7**

Summarising

1   Discuss a topic with a partner. The topic should be something of concern or interest to both people. Note that this need not be a role-play situation in which one person is designated counsellor and the other client.

Every few minutes ask someone (the leader, trainer, or a person designated as timekeeper) to interrupt and ask that each person should attempt to summarise what has happened up to that point and compliment the person's effectiveness and positive actions in the situation they are describing. Before allowing discussion to continue, make sure that each person agrees that his partner's summary and compliments were accurate.

2   Notice how often the interviewer in a radio or television news or current affairs panel discussion uses the skills of summarising and complimenting.

Designing a homework task

If clients are customers and have been able to express their goals in specific terms, the counsellor can suggest something to be done as homework, or, preferably, ask clients to state what task(s) they will undertake next. This is a way of ensuring that the process of solving problems continues outside the counselling session and it gives clients the opportunity to continue doing those things that are already working well, to implement additional solutions, to practise new behaviours and perhaps to learn new skills. Effective homework tasks are ones which clarify the things that clients have already been doing well and specify what action(s) they can take to extend such successes. Normally, to be effective homework should be:

- clearly stated (what to do, when to do it, where to do it and in what amount it should be done);
- presented convincingly enough for the client to understand it and accept it as a relevant, important task;
- manageable and relevant to the client's level of motivation (that is, is the client a customer? See page 90);
- measurable and designed to ensure success (accomplishing small tasks can build up the client's self-confidence and lead to greater successes);
- reviewed at the next session. This can be done by asking early in the next session 'What's better?', or 'What things have improved since our last meeting?'

Homework will be more successful if it involves:

- behaviours over which clients have control;
- things clients have already shown they can do;
- the simplest, least complicated, first step forward;
- things that have already been identified as successful or desired;
- doing something different if present behaviours are not working.

Deciding on a homework task for clients should not rest entirely with the counsellor. In fact, it may be more useful simply to ask clients what they plan to do next, especially if they are customers for change (see chapter 5). In most cases, clients will be able to describe exceptions to the problem, and embedded in those exceptions will be solutions they have already been using with some degree of success. Counsellors need to focus on these successes to find out which ones can be repeated and extended (Berg, 1994).

If the client is not a customer, that is, someone who is not yet ready to work toward solving the problem, the counsellor can summarise the points discussed, compliment the client for attending and showing interest in obtaining help, and then invite the person to return. Berg (1994) suggests that a thinking or observing task may also be appropriate for such clients. That is, they can be invited to 'think about what it would take for you to approach a stranger and begin a conversation without feeling so self-conscious', or 'notice what happens the next time you talk with someone you don't know. How does the conversation start? What do you do? What's different about that situation?'

When a homework task has been agreed to, the session is terminated and, if necessary, another interview is scheduled.

---

exercise 7.8

Homework

First, state a specific goal for each of the general goals listed below. Then write a homework assignment that might lead to achieving each of these goals:

(a) losing weight; (b) improving my appearance; (c) standing up to my mother; (d) getting fit; (e) controlling the class better; (f) getting on top of the job; (g) taking breaks at work.

For each goal list the behaviours suggested by the group.

Scheduling another session

There is nothing sacred about the once-a-week, 50-minute counselling session. There may be good reasons for having sessions of longer or shorter duration, of greater or lesser frequency. Counsellors should ask themselves and their clients: Is one session sufficient? Is another session necessary? If so, what would be the best amount of time between this session and the next? Clients are often quite clear about when the best time for their next session will be. In some cases it may be useful to offer a more open-ended invitation to come again, that is, to come back when clients themselves decide it is necessary.

Stage 7: Evaluating progress

If goals have been precisely stated and suitable solutions selected and implemented, the important task of evaluation can be relatively straightforward. It will be a matter of checking what has been achieved against what was hoped for. A useful question in evaluating progress made in **finding solutions to problems** is: 'How satisfied is the client with what has been done?' Counsellor and client should decide in advance how the evaluation will be made – by regular checks on progress towards the goals, or by a delayed check on the outcome as a whole. One means of doing this is by using scaling questions, e.g., 'Where do you have to be on your problem scale so that you no longer need counselling?' If the client's problem is a 7 or 8 on a scale of 10, 9 may be sufficient. Rarely do clients express the need to achieve a 10, or perfection. Most clients recognise that life is not without problems and that they would be happy enough just to be able to cope adequately.

If the outcome is not satisfactory, it may be necessary to go back through part of the process again. The client's motivation would need to be reassessed; perhaps the problem would need redefining; goals and/or solutions may not have been appropriate or achievable. The counsellor may even wish to seek outside consultation or refer the client elsewhere.

Once counselling has been successful, termination can occur and the counsellor can be confident that the client has been empowered to solve similar sorts of problems in the future. Termination can, however, be open-ended, allowing clients to return for counselling as needed.

Assessing results

As soon as possible after clients have carried out the homework task, counsellors should discuss the outcomes with them. A useful first question is 'What is better?', and as a follow up, 'How did you do that?' (Berg, 1994). The factors that contributed to the client's success should be identified, highlighted and explored further by asking how the client managed them, what was done to make them happen, whether these sorts of changes are the right ones, and whether they can be made to happen again. The client should be complimented on his/her good work and made to feel that further progress is possible.

Scaling questions are useful here to get some idea of the progress that has been made, e.g., 'Last time we met you said the severity of your problem was at a 2; where is it now?' If it has improved, to a 4, for example, counsellors can compliment clients, ask how they managed to bring about such an improvement, and discuss what it would take to move from a 4 to a 5. This process can be repeated in subsequent sessions as often as necessary.

If there is no improvement, or even a deterioration, counsellors need to slow down and go back to an earlier stage of the counselling process. When this happens, it is useful to explore what is worse, what has kept things from becoming even worse than they are, and how the client has managed to cope with the situation (Berg, 1994).

Essentially, the counsellor's task still remains the same: to find those things – however small – that are going well or improving, even if the improvement is slight. In these cases, consulting with a supervisor or outside expert can be invaluable. Counsellors need to accept that they will not be successful with every client and that not succeeding does not always have to be someone's fault. The most important thing is to decide on what to do next so that there are renewed *possibilities* for solutions rather than continuing failure.

exercise **7.9**

In pairs, one person tells of an actual or imagined experience in which the outcome was successful, but about which there had been some uncertainty and anxiety beforehand. Begin with an example from Exercise 7.7. The other person compliments the client and asks questions that bring out reasons for the success. Then reverse roles.

Generalising results

Generalising results is the skill of pointing out to clients that they can follow the process used in counselling and apply the same solution-finding process and communication skills to other aspects of their lives. For example, the **finding-solutions-to-problems** approach followed during counselling could be made explicit to the client with suggestions about how it could be used in the future.

> *'You may have noticed the process we've been going through during our counselling sessions. First of all we clarified your problem, then identified things that you were doing that were already effective, and then we set some goals. Later we worked out how to reach these goals, had you try them out and then discussed whether they had been achieved. You might like to go through a similar process when you have other family or work concerns to solve.'*

One way of helping clients generalise the skills and process of **finding solutions to problems** to other situations is to provide them with written material that they can take away with them as a reminder. It is also useful to suggest that as part of their counselling, clients who are so inclined might like to read appropriate books or articles that address their specific problems: 'Reading about the thoughts and life situations of others has long been one of the human forms of healing, education, and prevention' (Ballou, 1995, p. 55). When used to supplement counselling, this form of bibliotherapy can be a successful adjunct intervention for clients who are interested, willing and not too severely disturbed (Ballou, 1995). Most bookstores have a section of self-help books designed to help readers better understand their concerns and worries. In addition, such books often provide practical information that may be helpful in reducing anxiety or enhancing specific skills.

Referral

When counsellors decide that their clients have needs that they cannot meet, they should consider referring them to another agency or individual. Assuming that they have first appraised their client's needs carefully, they should adopt the following principles and procedures.

- Counsellors should first find out whether another agency provides the necessary services. This requires a thorough knowledge both of community resources for helping (e.g., employment, residential care, medical, recreational, rehabilitative, educational), and of their policies, programmes, costs, and limitations. It is also important for counsellors to know each agency's specific services and its relevant statutory limitations.

- Having selected an appropriate agency, counsellors should then discuss the case with the person in the agency who would probably receive the referral, taking care, however, not to disclose confidential information about their client.

- If a referral seems appropriate, it should then be discussed with the client. Counsellors should prepare clients for referral, explaining honestly and clearly their decision to refer to a particular agency. They should encourage the client to voice reactions to the proposal and express his/her thoughts about the actual decision. Counsellors should also take into account the possibility that clients may think that their problems are insoluble if the counsellor cannot help them further. Counsellors should be prepared to discuss this reaction with clients.

- When a referral has been agreed upon, definite arrangements should be made so that clients know exactly when and where to go and for whom to ask. In some cases, the counsellor might decide to accompany the client on the first occasion.

- Counsellors should take care to provide the referral agency with relevant information about clients, including:

  a a clear statement of their problems or needs;

  b a summary of the help that has been given;

  c a request for a specific service;

  d an indication of their feelings about referral.

- Once the referral has been completed, counsellors should be prepared to co-operate in some way if asked to do so by the referral agency. Whether they continue to be actively involved in the case or not, counsellors should seek a progress report from the agency so that they can assess the usefulness of the referral.

In all decisions regarding referral, counsellors should be guided by their professional estimate of their clients' best interests. In dealing with them, counsellors should continue to be open, honest, and supportive, and should act only with the client's consent.

Termination

Termination of counselling may occur at any time – most obviously when the client's goals have been reached. It may also result from an agreement at the outset that only one topic or problem would be dealt with, or that there would be a specified number of sessions.

The termination phase should begin with the counsellor and client jointly reviewing and summarising what has happened in counselling. The decision to terminate will be made when clients can show that their goals have been achieved to a level of satisfaction that is acceptable to them. Client progress can be charted using graphs of the frequency of desirable behaviour; regular, repeated estimates of problem severity, and regular reviews of specified goals. If 'termination talk' was introduced into counselling early – even in the first session – the decision about terminating will usually be less problematic. An appropriate note to end on could be the counsellor's preparedness to continue counselling on a 'call-me-if-you-need-me' basis, coupled with an expression of confidence in the client's ability to cope.

Besides keeping clients' estimates of their readiness to cope alone in mind, counsellors should be aware of their own reactions to terminating. It is understandable that counsellors would regret losing contact with clients who, for instance, had been pleasant to work with, had made much progress, and had openly expressed their gratitude. Or, it may be difficult to lose fee-paying clients if finances are tight. However, the counsellor's primary considerations must be the client's best interests, well-being and independence from the counsellor.

review exercise 7.10*

1   Using a verbatim transcript of a counselling interview, identify the skills used in every counsellor lead. Compare your answers with those of others. This exercise will help you to review many of the skills discussed in this and the previous two chapters and will indicate those about which there is still some uncertainty.

2   With the client's permission, record a counselling interview using an audio recorder. Analyse the interview as follows:

   a   Transcribe verbatim two sets of 15 consecutive interactions from any two sections of the interview.

   b   Critically analyse the transcribed portions of the interview by identifying the skill used, its intended effect and its actual effect. In addition, look for patterns of skill usage, indications of a typical style, and any inappropriate leads or assumptions that influence the course of the interview.

This exercise can be repeated over time. It can serve as a check on one's progress, proficiency, and effectiveness. See the brief example in the Answers to exercises.

3   Make a brief video or audio programme illustrating the effective use of a skill or skills. This is an excellent way of demonstrating a working understanding of particular counselling skills.

exercise 7.11

This exercise provides an opportunity to practise, in one interview, steps two to seven in the **finding-solutions-to-problems** model of counselling (refer to the outline of stages and counsellor's tasks in chapter 3).

1   Divide into pairs and decide who will play the role of counsellor and who will play the client. Using one of the role-play situations described below (or situations that are of current concern to the participants) the counsellor leads the client through the **finding-solutions-to-problems** sequence described in this and the two previous chapters. The counsellor should move from one stage to the next only when the first has been satisfactorily covered.

2   When finished, the participants should swap roles and repeat the exercise, using a different role-play situation (below).

3   When both persons have had the opportunity to be counsellor, discuss the usefulness of the **finding-solutions-to-problems** model in the larger group setting. For example, people may want to comment on how easy the sequence was to follow, how useful it was as a guide or indicator of progress, or its relevance to real counselling situations.

Role-play 1: The client begins by saying he would like to be more at ease in groups.

Role-play 2: The client says that his children are able to manipulate him too easily.

  # Working as a professional counsellor

B eing a professional counsellor involves performing a number of tasks in a competent, effective and ethical manner. It also means being aware of current social, legal and therapeutic developments and applying them in the professional practice of counselling.

In addition to learning the skills that are appropriate to a particular model of counselling, counsellors need to develop a professional orientation to their work. Professionalism is defined as 'internalized attitudes, perceptions, and personal commitment to the standards, ideals and identity of a profession' (Spruill & Benshoff, 1996, p. 468), and for counsellors this means performing certain professional activities that contribute to effective counselling.

Initial training

Those who want to become counsellors need first to acquire training that is recognised as being the best that is available and that offers qualifications or credentials that are widely recognised within the profession. Training programmes should be carefully evaluated and compared before one is selected. Without specifying a preferred course content, it may be mentioned that there are several factors that are desirable in a training course of quality. According to Binder (1993), the course should:

- be coherent and well-structured;
- contain both didactic and experiential components;
- teach specific skills and procedures;
- integrate didactic and skills components in an effective way;
- be progressive, that is, begin with simple skills and move to more complex ones;
- use multiple sources of feedback to students;
- include up-to-date information on developments in the profession.

Other aspects of training courses/programmes to check on include the methods of assessment used (Are they relevant? Is practical work as well as written work assessed?); the amount and kind of supervised work with clients (Are recordings – audio and/or video – required? Is live supervision used?); and whether there are opportunities to observe practising counsellors at work. Finally, people seeking training should check with a professional counselling association about the status of a course (Is it accredited? Is its qualification widely recognised within the profession?).

Once a decision has been made to enrol in a particular course, it becomes the individual's responsibility to participate fully and seriously (see, *Being an effective trainee*, pages 47–48)

Continuing education

In order to better meet the needs of their clients, counsellors should continue learning and developing their competence for as long as they practise counselling. In fact, professional counsellors have an ethical responsibility to do so, even after completion of a formal course of training (Pawlovich, 1994; see appendices A and B). The purpose of this education is to better meet the needs of their clients by ensuring that counsellors both maintain and extend their expertise and competence. To encourage further learning and ensure continuing competence, a number of professional counselling associations have made ongoing education a requirement of re-certification or renewed membership. For this reason it is useful for counsellors to keep a record of all the educational activities they undertake each year.

There are numerous educational and training opportunities through which counsellors can broaden their knowledge, extend their expertise, sharpen their professional judgement and keep informed of developments in their own and related fields of helping. Examples of such activities include:

- reading research articles and other professional literature: commentaries, case studies, professional and ethical debates, legislative developments related to counselling;

- attending training seminars and workshops;

- teaching others – preparing and presenting training sessions for colleagues, students, volunteers or conference attenders;

- becoming involved in local organisations that are working for change in mental health services;

- contacting and visiting specialist helping agencies;

- seeking personal counselling when needed;

- being open to feedback from both colleagues and clients;

- making a special study of a particular area of work, e.g., aggression, sexual abuse, adolescent suicide, eating disorders;

- supervising others;

- updating a personal theory of counselling at least every two years by reflecting on and reassessing how beliefs, practices and theory have been modified or confirmed by actual work experience (see chapter 1, exercise 1.2);

- attending personal growth or development experiences led by professional facilitators;

- being involved in some significant cross-cultural experience or programme at least annually.

Association membership

Becoming an active member of appropriate local and national counselling organisations is another form of continuing education. This means more than just paying the annual subscription and occasionally reading the newsletters. Non-participation can be short-sighted and self-defeating since a strong association benefits private and non-private practitioners alike. Therefore, professional counsellors are those who are active participants in the organisation's politics, in the development of policies and the regulation of counselling practices. Ways of doing this include attending conferences and annual general meetings, participating as both a presenter and a listener, holding office and/or being a member of a committee or working group.

Commitment to a code of ethics

Essential to competent counselling practice is following a recognised and respected professional code of ethics (see appendices A and B). In practice this means knowing what such a code contains and behaving accordingly. For clients, the knowledge that their counsellor is bound by a professional code of practice will increase their confidence and trust in the counselling relationship.

A code of ethics is a general set of guidelines the purpose of which is the protection and enhancement of the client's well-being. However, no single code will provide a complete set of simple, clear-cut directives for every possible situation a counsellor might face. For example, most codes of ethics reflect a largely male, Western view of mental health practices and in many instances they do not adequately address the fact that clients have diverse cultural backgrounds. In practice, therefore, they have to be modified or reframed in order to counsel in an effective cross-cultural way. For these reasons, it is imperative that the professional counsellor be able to demonstrate competence in ethical decision-making.

Counsellors need a working knowledge of several areas if they are to exercise sound ethical judgement: the contents of the code of ethics they have chosen to follow; what is accepted as good practice by the professional association to which they belong; the content and accepted interpretations of relevant legal statutes (e.g., the law relating to confidentiality, client privacy, reporting of child abuse). In most codes of ethics there are both specific standards which describe ethical practices and broad ideals or principles that can be aspired to and used as a more general framework within which to assess the counsellor's work. For example, the five general principles found in the New Zealand Association of Counsellors' code are (see appendix B):

- *Autonomy*: respect for people's right to make decisions that affect their own lives. This requires counsellors to fully inform clients of the limitations of counselling and the theory, model or approach used.

- *Not doing harm*: the avoidance of any practices or processes that are likely to cause harm to clients. This requires counsellors to work within the limits of their competence and to follow accepted codes of ethics.

- *Beneficence*: acting in ways that promote the welfare of clients. This means acting in the client's best interest, with good faith at all times, and understanding and being competent to deal with clients' diverse cultural backgrounds. It also includes consulting with other professionals when appropriate and staying up-to-date with laws that pertain to counselling.

- *Justice*: a commitment to fair and equitable practice and the promotion of social justice.

- *Fidelity*: being honest and trustworthy in all professional relationships.

When faced with an ethical dilemma, many inexperienced counsellors are disappointed to learn that there is no handbook of ethical practices to which they can refer to find out exactly what to do. Since there are seldom simple right or wrong answers to complex ethical dilemmas, it is imperative that counsellors should be clear about and able to justify the decisions they make. One way of achieving this is to employ an effective model of decision-making to determine a course of action. Corey, Corey and Callanan (1988) have outlined a useful model (see below). Whatever model is used, counsellors will also need to draw on their own values, experience and knowledge of cultural variations in making ethically sound decisions.

- Identify the ethical dilemma. Does it involve ethical, legal, and/or moral considerations?

- Identify the issues involved. Focus on the important aspects and discard the irrelevant ones.

- Review the code of ethics. Does it offer a possible solution?

- Seek advice or supervision. Review the process by which decisions were made.

- Consider possible courses of action and their consequences.

- Choose and justify the best course of action.

Personal values and beliefs are important in counselling and can influence ethical decision-making. Therefore, it is important that counsellors should be aware of these values and how they affect their work. What are your beliefs and values about each of the following? How might those values influence your practices in these areas of counselling?

a   Self-disclosure to clients.

b   Being totally open and honest with clients.

c   Having strong positive or negative feelings about clients.

d   Clients of a different religious or sexual orientation from your own.

e   Clients whose values are markedly different from your own.

Research and writing

Professional counsellors are those who are active as researchers, writers and commentators on counselling practices and current developments in the profession. However, their research and writing do not have to be of the formal, academic sort. Professional writing can be anything from formal research reports to commentaries on local issues. All counsellors at least should keep clear, systematic data on their own practice and clientele that will enable them to describe who uses their services, to evaluate their effectiveness and to generate questions about best practice that other researchers may pursue. The point is that counsellors need to be involved in the development of their own profession. Finally, counsellors should check the code of ethics they follow to see what guidelines are provided for researching and writing (see, for example, appendix A).

Receiving regular supervision

Ongoing supervision of both counsellors-in-training and experienced, practising counsellors is widely recognised as both desirable and essential to the development of effective skills and attitudes and the maintenance of effective counselling services. So important is it thought to be that some professional counselling associations have made it an ethical requirement for practising members to be in supervision (see the codes of ethics in appendices A and B). In the following pages, the process of supervision is described and ways in which both participants can ensure that the process is made more effective are outlined. Although the discussion focuses on one-to-one supervision, it is also common to conduct and/or receive supervision in groups.

The general model of supervision presented here allows for a variety of theoretical orientations to be used. It is not a prescription for the right or only way to conduct and receive effective supervision. However, if counsellors and supervisors follow these suggestions when initiating and conducting supervision, they should notice not only their own respective improvements in self-assurance and effectiveness, but can also be more confident that clients will be receiving more effective help.

Although counsellors-in-training can learn a great deal by supervising one another's work, supervision is a skilled, professional activity and those who are interested in supervising others should seek training in the necessary knowledge and skills. There may be formal courses, seminars, workshops and conferences on the topic offered locally. Professional counselling associations usually can provide such information.

What is supervision?

There seems to be general agreement regarding just what supervision is (i.e., a formal monitoring relationship that ensures that counselling services are being delivered effectively and competently, and that enables counsellors to more accurately identify their strengths and overcome their limitations in their practice of counselling). Counselling supervision comprises at least four elements: monitoring safe, effective practice; the use of actual recordings of counselling sessions; a developmental progression; time limits to maximise benefits.

The first and probably most important element of the supervision relationship is concerned with client safety. Monitoring counsellors' work involves determining whether they are practising in a safe, ethical and effective manner. Because of the private, confidential nature of counselling, it is very difficult to assess its quality and effectiveness. Supervision is one step towards ensuring that counsellors are accountable for their work and that their clients are protected. Monitoring is an essential aspect of supervision and should be recognised as central by both participants. It should not be put aside or denigrated as being unsupportive or authoritarian.

Monitoring means that the supervisor assumes some degree of responsibility for the work of the counsellor. This does not imply, of course, that the counsellor is absolved of all responsibility. In order to fulfil this monitoring function and to protect themselves, supervisors should:

- meet regularly with the counsellor;

- keep brief, factual notes of supervision sessions (e.g., What cases and concerns were discussed? What was decided? What progress is being made? Is the counsellor practising in a professional and ethical manner? (see the section in this chapter on *Note-taking*, page 147);

- review counsellors' business practices, including how they advertise themselves and their services; their procedures for record keeping, fee setting and fee collecting; their commitment to ongoing training;

- include at regular intervals the use of audio or video recordings of counsellors' work and/or conduct live supervision sessions (when the supervisor sits in on a counselling session to observe the counsellor directly).

The third element has to do with the developmental nature of supervision, and assumes that counsellors progress from a state of being less effective, confident, self-critical and/or collegial to a state of greater effectiveness, confidence, insight into their own work and/or collegiality. By its very nature, supervision for counsellors-in-training is a process of growth, from a state of less knowledge and experience to one of increased knowledge and experience. The extent of this growth may be less dramatic or obvious when experienced counsellors are supervised, but even then there is a focus on increasing counsellors' ability to assess their own effectiveness and reflect critically on their practices. In these situations the supervisor's role may be more akin to that of consultant than of trainer/teacher.

This developmental aspect of supervision implies that over time counsellors progress from a lesser state to a more accomplished state. In other words, supervision that is initially productive and effective may become less so over time as the counsellor-supervisor relationship becomes more predictable, comfortable and collegial. Therefore, to keep it challenging and fresh, supervisors should be changed periodically, say every 12 to 24 months.

There are a number of models for conducting supervision, each having a different focus. Firstly, supervision can be thought of as a form of *tutoring/teaching* (specialised knowledge and skills acquisition are the primary goals). Secondly, supervision can be similar to *counselling* (personal growth, support and self-insight as they relate to the counsellor's practice of counselling are the goals). Thirdly, supervision can be used to *review client progress* (details of particular clients and their therapeutic needs are the focus). Fourthly, supervision can examine the counsellor's method of *case administration* (the goals are more effective work organisation, reporting and case management). The fifth model focuses on *surviving and thriving as a counsellor*, whether in private practice or an agency, and can include aspects of each of the first four. However, its central aim is to enhance the counsellor's understanding and effective management of influence, power, agency politics and business practices.

All counsellors, whether experienced or inexperienced, can benefit from focusing on each of the five types of supervision at different times. However, deciding which focus is most appropriate for a particular counsellor at a given time will depend on a number of factors: the counsellor's level of experience (the beginner will have different supervision needs to the expert), theory of counselling, and work setting; the supervisor's model of counselling and approach to supervision; the contract negotiated by supervisor and counsellor.

Who benefits from supervision?

In most instances counsellors perform their services unobserved, in the absence of any accountability checks. Since the quality of these services is vitally important to the recipients, to the agencies providing them and to the professional counselling associations promoting them, supervision is one means by which that quality can be ensured. Supervision also helps to protect the rights and welfare of clients and emphasises the responsibilities of counsellors and agencies to their clients.

More specifically, for *counsellors* supervision serves to foster professional and personal development by extending their knowledge, experience and skills. It can be an intensive learning experience provided in an atmosphere of support and encouragement. Also, since counselling is a stressful occupation in which burnout and infrequent rewards seem to be accepted as inevitable, supervision can provide counsellors with much needed emotional replenishment. Finally, supervision provides counsellors with a means of assessing their job performance. Critical feedback from supervisors helps counsellors to explore and modify aspects of their performance.

For *clients*, supervision can function as a form of quality-control on the services they receive. Very seldom do clients have an effective, clearly delineated means of participating in the structuring, delivery, or evaluation of counselling services. As the recipients of counselling they are in an inherently less powerful or one down position vis-à-vis the counsellor and the helping agency. Supervision, if it is searching and rigorous, will go some way to ensuring that counselling services are more effectively and sensitively provided.

For *employing agencies*, supervision can result in the provision of better overall counselling services. Administrators will have less need to worry about the performance of counsellors who are receiving competent supervision. For example, since supervision can be effective in reducing job stress, it is reasonable for agencies to assume that counsellors receiving effective supervision will be less stressed and will be actively engaged in their own professional growth. Hence, they will be better able to cope with the rigours of the job and to provide more effective services generally.

For professional *counselling associations*, effective supervision will help ensure that their standards for professional practice and development are met and that the public can seek services from their members with greater confidence and safety.

Supervision can also benefit *supervisors*. Providing supervision to other counsellors develops supervisors' awareness of their own personal styles, counselling skills, beliefs and values. Providing effective supervision to counsellors can also prompt supervisors to identify and overcome their own professional weaknesses, for example, to be more direct, more specific, more problem or task focused during supervision itself.

Who should supervise?

Supervision will be of greatest benefit when counsellors select experienced, trained supervisors they trust and respect and who will challenge them as professionals. Is it necessary that the supervisor should work in the same model as the counsellor? No, not if both participants are able to be open, flexible and willing to learn. In fact, differences in assumptions, theories and practices can be a useful catalyst for new learning and identifying existing biases.

Counsellors should avoid asking someone who would have the dual role of supervisor and immediate superior or evaluator. Neither person should be able to use their position or status to unduly influence or manipulate the other.

How does one find a supervisor who will meet one's needs?
It is up to individual counsellors to arrange supervision for themselves by approaching a preferred supervisor and negotiating the practical details of the relationship. One way to locate potential supervisors is to contact the local branch of a national counselling association. The association's secretary may be able to provide a list of local, approved supervisors. Another way is by asking other professional counsellors for the names of supervisors they judge to be competent. It is necessary as well to ask other counsellors for their opinions about various supervisors' strengths and weaknesses in the supervisory role and their areas of counselling expertise. Other things to consider include the supervisor's sex, age, race, cultural background, and theoretical orientation.

Since supervision can be crucial to counsellors' professional development, they should be confident that the person they ask to be their supervisor will be competent to meet their needs. To achieve this, counsellors will need to talk to potential supervisors about their own expectations and the supervisor's beliefs about supervision. Therefore, the first step in seeking a supervisor should be to determine what one wants and needs from supervision and be able to express those things clearly. Counsellors will also need to decide whether their interpersonal style and personality are compatible with those of the supervisor. Will the relationship be honest, open, and challenging? Counsellors should seek a supervisor who will stay in the role of supervisor for the entire session. Supervision, after all, is for the benefit of the counsellor, and that is where the focus should stay. A counsellor's supervision time is precious and should be jealously protected from misuse and interruptions.

Supervisors, too, need to be clear about their beliefs, methods and orientations regarding supervision. The decision to provide supervision should be made only after a thorough discussion with the counsellor. Finally, it must be remembered that both participants are free to choose with whom they will work, under what conditions, and for how long.

Useful questions to consider when looking for a supervisor include:

- Whom did you approach to be your supervisor, and why?

- What desirable qualities or qualifications did you see in your supervisor?

- How will those qualities/qualifications enhance your growth as a counsellor?

Where should supervision take place?
If possible, supervision should occur in a neutral, professional setting that provides comfort, privacy and a sense of purpose. This minimises interruptions

and serves to emphasise the importance of the supervision process. If supervision must take place in the counsellor's office, efforts should be made to avoid being interrupted, e.g., close the door and post a notice asking not to be disturbed. Notify the receptionist that no incoming calls will be taken.

How often and how long?

Ideally, supervision should occur at least every two weeks, or at the frequency specified by the professional association to which the counsellor belongs. If this is not manageable, once every three to four weeks can still provide benefits. The length of each session should be agreed to by the participants, but it is suggested that 45–60 minutes is both manageable and sufficient. How long the supervision relationship is to be maintained should be negotiated before it commences. For example, both parties may agree to meet initially for six to eight months. At the end of that time they could decide on a further term or agree to terminate the relationship. Whatever the agreement, both parties should be clear about its terms at the outset. Useful questions to answer at this point include:

- What conditions of supervision did you discuss with your supervisor? How did the supervisor respond?

- What details of venue, time, and frequency of meeting were agreed upon?

How is supervision conducted?

Both counsellors and supervisors must share responsibility for the effective conduct of supervision. Supervisors, for example, should work to ensure that supervision, like counselling, is done in as non-threatening and respectful an atmosphere as possible. It is useful to remember that most counsellors will have doubts about their performance and be anxious about discussing their work. Supervisors need to stress that the general goal of any supervision session should be to increase counsellors' knowledge of themselves and the quality of their interactions with others, that is, their competence as counsellors, and, consequently, the quality of service their clients receive. Over the course of supervision, supervisors can help counsellors become more aware of their specific competencies and weaknesses, and can work with counsellors to enhance or remedy these as the counsellors continue working with their various clients. However, in each particular supervision session it may be useful for supervisors to encourage counsellors to identify specific problems or worries they have about their work, to then generate realistic solutions to those concerns, and, finally, to implement their preferred remedies. The structuring of these sessions parallels the finding-solutions-to-problems approach to counselling. Nevertheless, it should be recognised by both the supervisor and the counsellor that the supervisor may have a different theoretical orientation and background of training and experiences that will influence the structure and nature of the supervision sessions.

Counsellors, too, must ensure that their supervision is productive, well-structured, and goal-directed. By reiterating their professional needs, by clarifying their problems and aims in working with clients, by being prepared for each supervision session beforehand, and by giving supervisors feedback on the conduct and progress of supervision, they can share the responsibility for its successful conduct.

It is important that counsellors and supervisors do not collude to keep the supervision relationship so friendly, polite and ineffectual that important and uncomfortable matters are seldom dealt with. Many such games are possible: 'Let's keep it strictly social'; 'You be nice to me and I will be nice to you'; 'Isn't the system awful?'; 'Sorry, I forgot to review my notes for today's session (again)'.

Supervisors need to be able to identify collusion at the moment it occurs and to discuss it with counsellors directly and openly. One way of doing this is to regularly check that the style and direction of supervision is helpful and relevant to the counsellor's needs and producing new learning and competencies. For their part, counsellors also need to acknowledge such collusion when it happens and not react defensively or feel overly threatened when it is pointed out to them. In addition, counsellors should continually monitor their participation to avoid side-stepping important concerns or minimising their own performance anxieties, such as always blaming the client for difficulties; avoiding difficult questions; pitying oneself for always having such difficult clients; avoiding new ideas and risk-taking.

What follows is a list of suggestions for supervisors conducting supervision. The suggestions are not intended to represent an ideal procedure, but implementing them has been found to result in the delivery of consistently effective supervision. The suggestions may be especially useful as a safe guide and checklist for inexperienced supervisors.

- Begin by asking counsellors what matters they want to address, that is, what is going well and what is not. This should include suggestions regarding what the supervisor should listen for and comment on. Useful starting points are the things that are of most concern to counsellors and those aspects of their work that are rewarding and effective.

- Ask counsellors to give sufficient background information about topics they raise.

- Ask counsellors for a brief, subjective assessment of cases, personal concerns or work situations. Be alert to cultural factors that are affecting counsellor-client relationships.

- At this point, if using video or audio recordings of a counselling session, play a portion of the tape that illustrates the focus of concern. Either the supervisor or the counsellor can stop the tape when wanting to comment. Supervisors should highlight the positive aspects of the counsellor's work, identify those things that need improvement and discuss alternative ways of intervening.

- Help counsellors focus on actual skills they use in counselling, aspects of the relationship in question, the overall trend or direction of counselling, basic issues of trust or understanding, and any personal concerns that have arisen.

- Encourage counsellors to evaluate themselves, to make known their doubts or ask questions about their own behaviour, feelings or work situation.

- Focus on how counsellors handle cases or concerns rather than becoming mired in the details. Is there clear evidence of safe practice and satisfactory progress?

- Encourage counsellors to create their own solutions to the dilemmas present in particular cases. It is not the supervisor's role to solve these problems or act as a distant counsellor to clients. Rather, the supervisor's role is to act as a consultant to counsellors (see *Consultation* in chapter 9).

- At some point during each session, check to make sure that the style and direction of supervision is helpful and relevant to counsellors' needs.

- Terminate each supervision session on a constructive note. Counsellors should be left with a better understanding of their present strengths and assets and clear aims and goals to pursue in their future work.

The above suggestions allow for elements of all five foci of supervision: teaching, personal insight, client review, case management, survival in the job. It is not uncommon to use all five in the course of supervising a single counsellor, and sometimes more than one focus in the same session.

For their part, counsellors should periodically evaluate and review what has occurred in one of their typical supervision sessions. Questions that are useful in this process are:

- What topics were discussed and why?

- How were these topics dealt with?

- How did you evaluate the session?

- How did your supervisor evaluate the session?

Should live supervision or recordings be used?

While neither of these is absolutely essential to effective supervision, they do enable a more objective and careful examination of what has actually occurred and reduce the likelihood of selective remembering. Live supervision is done by having the supervisor present during the counselling session and then, immediately following the session, reviewing what occurred. Live supervision should only be done with the client's prior consent and a clear understanding about what the supervisor's actual role will be during the session. Experience has shown that most clients are willing to have supervisors in attendance and seem to feel supported by their presence.

Audio and video recordings of counselling sessions are another invaluable aid to supervision, and every counsellor should make use of them at regular intervals. It is necessary to obtain a client's prior permission to record all or a portion of any session and to use that recording in supervision. Recordings should not become an end in themselves. On occasion the use of recordings can actually introduce problems rather than circumvent them. For example, it is easy to become overly involved in the details of a case, or to feel restricted to discussing only the contents of a recording, or to feel it necessary to review an entire tape.

How is a supervision relationship terminated?

Both the supervisor and counsellor should discuss the length of their supervisory relationship and schedule periodic reviews of progress before actually beginning. Both participants should feel free to terminate the relationship if the needs of either are no longer being met. Unfortunately, some counsellors feel trapped in a supervision relationship they no longer find beneficial, but they reluctantly continue with a particular supervisor rather than hurt the supervisor's feelings by terminating. Reviewing the relationship at regular intervals can avoid this dilemma by providing a face-saving exit point. Counsellors should remember that supervision is a legitimately selfish endeavour. It is the counsellor's growth and development that is at stake, and competent supervisors should readily accept and understand that fact.

Self-care and managing work stress

For the benefit of themselves and the safety of their clients, counsellors need to look after their own health and emotional well-being. Clients have a right to expect help from mature, healthy counsellors. When their work is compromised by personal difficulties, counsellors have an ethical responsibility to cease practising until they are fit to continue.

Effective supervision may help counsellors to monitor their fitness to practise and reduce their work-related stress. However, the problem of job stress is so common and can be so persistent that a more wide-ranging set of coping strategies may be required. According to Corey and Corey (1989, p. 133) 'work stress is the condition that exists when the environmental demands of work exceed your personal capabilities for effectively coping with the situation'. A person under stress is characterised by physiological tension and persistent choice conflict, and attempts to reduce such tension often can take a maladaptive form such as illness or work absence (Brammer, 1985). For counsellors, such stress can impair their personal and professional functioning. Symptoms may be psychological (cynicism; emotional exhaustion; feelings of helplessness, hopelessness and ineffectiveness), physiological (headaches, muscular aches, high blood pressure, chronic fatigue, frequent colds and 'flu, difficulty in sleeping, digestive problems), or behavioural (absenteeism, social isolation, emotional outbursts, perfectionism, frequent job changes, reduced efficiency).

In dealing with stress, it is important to realise that (a) different individuals can tolerate different amounts of stress, (b) incidents that are stressful to one individual may be merely motivating or challenging to another, and (c) long-lasting periods of stress are generally more harmful than intermittent periods of stress. How an individual perceives a potentially stressful situation is more important than the nature of the situation itself (Druckman and Swets, 1988). Thus, this cognitive nature of stress must be kept in mind when discussing both the effects of stress on counsellors and strategies for reducing or managing it effectively.

Prolonged high stress can result in 'compassion fatigue', a state of disillusionment due to focusing too much on other people's troubles without also caring for oneself, or burnout, an end state of work exhaustion and emotional depletion (see Cherniss, 1980). Since the first stage in this progressive loss of job enthusiasm and interest is stress, it is imperative that counsellors be alert to signs of stress within themselves and be able to effectively manage and reduce their own levels of stress before it becomes overwhelming. Counsellors in private practice need to be alert to the stressful effects of working in isolation, worrying about an income (having sufficient clients, debt collecting, balancing lucrative and lean times) and running a successful business (see *Working in private practice*, page 148).

Most stress management courses focus on strategies to help individuals cope with their own job-related stress, e.g., relaxation, physical exercises, meditation, personal time management, hobbies. By comparison, little attention has been paid to organisational or structural stressors. Factors like excessive case-loads, an unpleasant work environment, autocratic and non-participatory administrative procedures, lack of peer support and peer review, role conflict, role overload and a lack of control over one's conditions of work may contribute at least as much to a counsellor's job-related stress. Following are methods for coping with or reducing stress in the three areas suggested by Edelwich (1980): personal change strategies, job change strategies, organisational change strategies.

1 Personal change strategies

a know yourself, your limitations and strengths;

b like and respect yourself;

c adopt a healthy, positive style of living that suits *you;*

d exercise regularly;

e develop and maintain close family and social relationships;

f indulge yourself by doing things that give you pleasure or relaxation; *do more of what you like and less of what you don't!*

g improve your diet and health – don't cut back on health-promoting routines in an effort to work harder;

h reframe stressful events as something more positive (e.g., a challenge, or a temporary diversion; accept what you cannot change);

i talk to others about how they handle stress;

j identify exceptions to your stressful times – what was different then?

k keep your sense of humour;

l give in and give up once in a while;

m recognise and deal with family and other outside-work stressors.

2 Job change strategies

a learn how to manage your work time to your best advantage;

b have realistic work expectations – keep things in perspective;

c know and accept what the limits of your work responsibilities and your ability to influence others are and what they are not;

d extend your skills and understanding through continuing education;

e set achievable, personal work goals;

f get regular supervision;

g achieve a balance between your work and personal life;

h talk about your successes as well as your failures;

i promote good working relationships with others.

3 Organisational change strategies

a try to have case loads (and work generally) reduced;

b seek to improve the working climate of the agency;

c enhance the physical environment;

d work to have administrative procedures made more democratic;

e establish a peer support group;

f ensure that there is regular in-service training available;

g try to ensure that all staff have clear job specifications and know how the organisation works;

h rotate jobs and responsibilities.

Additional professional activities

A clear understanding of one's work

Professional counsellors are those who can describe their services in clear, understandable language, including their aims, expectations, practices, and limitations. Each counsellor should be able to outline the procedures he/she employs for client intake and orientation, record-keeping, referral and termination. Being able to specify and detail the procedures that are being used is usually an indicator of good counselling practice generally.

Note-taking

Note-taking and record-keeping are increasingly important professional competencies for counsellors. Arguments in favour of systematic record-keeping include:

Benefits to clients: Clear, concise records enable counsellors to chart the progress of particular clients over time and to alter their interventions accordingly. They also provide for continuity of care if and when clients need to be seen by another counsellor or health provider.

Counsellor self-learning: Accumulating and summarising client records over time allows counsellors to identify trends and to reflect on, monitor and review their work so that appropriate changes can be made when necessary.

Claiming payments for services: Detailed records verifying all sessions conducted and the specific services delivered may be necessary when submitting payment claims to third-party payers such as insurance companies or government agencies. In most instances, third-party payers require careful documentation of services delivered and supply their own recording form for that purpose.

Counsellor protection from professional liability: Records can save counsellors time and money in the event of a complaint being made against them. Carefully written records of all client contacts can provide evidence that counselling was professionally and ethically conducted. Even the quality of the records themselves is important. For example, messy and incomplete records may create an impression of inadequate, unprofessional practices.

Generally speaking, records should be kept as succinct as possible. The information in them should be factual, descriptive and objective. Subjective or speculative material should be left out. It is useful to include the following information in client records:

- Identifying data. Counsellors may want to use a coding system so that clients cannot be identified by anyone else. Whether a code is used is usually a question of security and may depend on whether counsellors work in an agency or alone in private practice.

- The dates of all contacts with the client. This should include phone calls and written correspondence as well as actual counselling sessions.

- Details of any contracts or agreements regarding services, including the number and frequency of sessions, fees paid, assessment of presenting problem, and goals for counselling.

- Copies of any written information given to clients prior to or during counselling.

- Regular updates of goals and progress made.

- Copies of any specialist reports or details of contacts with other professionals, including supervision sessions, having to do with a particular client.

- Copies of all release-of-information forms or agreements regarding referrals and recording sessions.

- Client reactions to counselling and progress being made. It is useful to record verbatim client statements regarding dissatisfactions and criticisms, as well as expressions of satisfaction and gratitude.

The original information in client records should not be altered, but it can be added to, even at a later date, simply by adding the relevant information and signing and dating the entry.

Records are confidential to the counsellor and client and should be kept in a safe, secure place. Clients should be informed that notes will be made, that records are kept, and that they can have access to them on request. Also, if clients ask for a copy, a photocopy should be provided. However, the original record should stay with the counsellor. The more open and straightforward the counsellor is about the topic of note-taking and records, the less curiosity and/ or suspicion clients will have about the process. In fact, it is often useful to have clients read the notes at the end of each session and amend them or add any information they think might be important for the counsellor to know.

Counsellors frequently want to know how long client records should be kept. Although it is impossible to give a single answer that applies to every situation, it is important for counsellors and agencies to retain client records for several years. This is because clients may lodge a complaint about the service they received even several years after the end of their counselling relationship. Therefore, it is important that counsellors seek guidance on this matter from one or more sources: their code of ethics, professional association, and/or legal adviser.

When it is clear that records are outdated and are no longer needed, they should be destroyed in a way that ensures client anonymity and confidentiality, e.g., by shredding.

Working in private practice

With the growth of the enterprise culture (Cummins & Hoggett, 1995) and the counselling market (Miller, 1994) in many Western countries, large numbers of counsellors have set up in private practice, either through personal choice or as the result of losing their jobs with publicly-funded health and social service agencies. For many counsellors the image of private practice suggests success, freedom, status and increased income. In fact, the experiences of some counsellors who have gone from salaried work to private practice indicate that along with the benefits are numerous difficulties and worries (see, for example, the *Australian and New Zealand Journal of Family Therapy*, 1987, p. 99–103; Manthei et al., 1994; Paton, 1990). The following discussion summarises the advantages and disadvantages of private practice and gives several suggestions for counsellors who are deciding whether or not to enter private practice.

Advantages: Counsellors often cite greater personal and professional autonomy, the freedom to make their own business decisions, schedule their own work commitments and avoid agency rules and requirements as benefits of working in private practice. For many, entering private practice resulted in a more positive attitude toward their work, a boost in their self-confidence, less work-related stress and a rise in income level.

Disadvantages: Private practice can also have negative aspects. For many counsellors who enter private practice, the hours they work increase, either because they need the extra income or they cannot find time-efficient ways of organising the dual responsibilities of counselling and running a small business. Another area of counsellors' lives that can be affected adversely is the organisation of family life. Paperwork, long hours and concerns about the viability of the business, especially in the early years of setting up, could have negative effects on family and marital relationships. The opportunity for continuing professional education can also be severely restricted. Time away from actual counselling reduces income, and training experiences are often prohibitively expensive.

Suggestions: For counsellors thinking of going into private practice there are a number of things to consider and steps to take to better prepare themselves to succeed.

- Counsellors need to be realistic about working in private practice. For example, the public does not always fully understand and respect the terms *counselling* and *counsellor*. With increasing numbers of counsellors in private practice (including others doing counselling, e.g., psychiatrists, psychologists, social workers), the competition for clients is considerable, and is increasing. Income may not be as high as hoped: clients sometimes fail to arrive for appointments, third-party payers often pay less than the counsellor's base rate, overheads and administrative costs are usually borne solely by the counsellor.

- Counsellors should talk to others already working in private practice before making their own decision. Comments and advice from such people can be invaluable in planning if, how and when to begin a private practice.

- Ideally, the decision to enter private practice should be delayed until a counsellor has had several years of supervised experience in an agency or group practice. This helps to build competence, confidence and a network of workers and services that can be utilised once the counsellor is in private practice.

- Counsellors need to have a plan for marketing themselves and advertising their services. Establishing good working relationships with referring sources (e.g., doctors, community agencies, schools and clergy) is essential.

- Training in business management practices and basic accounting skills before setting up in private practice can save time and trouble in the long run.

- Counsellors going into private practice should consider buying liability insurance. They should talk to others, get the advice of their professional association, and/or their own legal adviser.

- Counsellors in private practice need to find ways of continuing their professional development and maintaining contact with peers and professional colleagues. It is all too easy to become professionally isolated, especially during the early years of getting established.

- Personal safety can be a worry, especially if counsellors are working alone and/or from an office in their home. Thought needs to be given to this matter and adequate safety procedures put in place.

- Counsellors should find ways to broaden their services. These can include things like consultation services, training others, conducting contract research, supervising others. Performing a variety of tasks will help to keep work interesting, rewarding and challenging.

- Finally, counsellors will need to make provision for their own self-care. Since there will be no paid holidays, sick leave or funded training days, it will be up to individual counsellors to provide for these important things themselves.

Advertising one's services

How individual counsellors and group practices market themselves and advertise their services is an important professional issue. It is relatively common for those trained as counsellors, and who are often members of a professional *counselling* association, to alter their professional identity by referring to themselves on their business cards or in the Yellow Pages as a therapist, psychotherapist, or life-planning consultant. Since such terms are not legally restricted or protected, using them may not be blatantly wrong or unethical. However, it is easy to conclude that counsellors' motivations for using these alternative titles involves nothing more than trying to market themselves in ways that will be most lucrative. One social worker practising as a counsellor revealed that she chose various titles according to whom she was working with and what approach she was using to convey varying impressions of herself and her work. This strategy of 'targeting services' by the flexible use of title may be perfectly acceptable, as long as it does not in any way misrepresent the counsellor's qualifications, competence or the services provided.

Most professional counselling associations' codes of ethics address the topic of advertising by stating that such public statements must be accurate and factual in regard to services offered, the counsellor's qualifications, experience, and professional associations. Therefore, before advertising, counsellors should check first with their professional association and its code of ethics for suggestions, guidelines, and limitations (see, for example, the codes in appendices A and B).

Related counselling roles and activities

 ne-to-one counselling is limited in its scope to the problems and concerns of an individual. However, through consultation and related activities, counsellors can reach more people, use more culturally appropriate ways of intervening with clients, contribute to institutional change and assume more active preventative roles.

Related roles

It has long been recognised that a multifaceted approach to helping may be more effective and more culturally responsive than relying on face-to-face counselling alone. Since clients' problems are often complex and beyond the resources of one helper or agency, counselling may of necessity include much more than face-to-face work with individuals, couples or families. And, even if strictly speaking those activities are not counselling, such skills and procedures should be familiar to counsellors. Working in multiple ways will enable counsellors to be more effective with a wider range of clients within a wider range of cultures, organisations and systems. These activities involve roles that go beyond the dynamics and restrictions of the usual one-to-one relationship. They usually require counsellors to be more active, directive, environmentally focused, responsible, present in the community and prevention oriented (Sue et al., 1996).

These activities are usually used when the problem presented by the client is due to external causes (sexism, racism, unemployment), when the client is relatively unfamiliar with the system or culture within which the problem exists (new immigrants having insufficient language skills to apply for available housing, health or educational benefits), and when the aim or goal is prevention of an abuse or injustice rather than remediation of a personal concern, worry or deficit. These alternative helping roles can be part of what is called the ecological approach, an approach that is multilevel, multidisciplinary and focuses on clients in their contexts, including their social interactions, cultures, communities, and total environments (Fried, 1995). These additional roles can include the following activities.

Advocacy

This is a highly active role in which counsellors attempt to encourage or persuade someone else to do something that will benefit clients or client groups who lack the power or resources to do it themselves. For example, counsellors may advocate on behalf of a person with a disability for better access to a building or they may argue for an increased housing benefit for an unemployed labourer.

In order to be successful in the role of advocate, counsellors must be knowledgeable about the topic, agency and procedures involved; they must be clear, direct and forceful in presenting their case; they must be committed to the cause and have the courage to face possible defeat, criticism and animosity.

Clients should be consulted before counsellors take on the role of advocate since the outcome – whether positive or negative – will affect them as well.

Commanding/directing

There are times when counsellors may need to exercise their authority, to act decisively because of their expert knowledge, insight or previous experience (Egan, 1985). For example, in times of crisis it may be necessary to act quickly and authoritatively to ensure that certain courses of action are taken. A suicide in a school may make it necessary for a counsellor to step in in order to organise a coordinated response so that the teaching staff, students and their families, the community, and the media are dealt with effectively (Thompson, 1995). This role may involve giving orders, managing the media, conducting a school-wide response, and/or directing a crisis team.

Coordination

When there are several people or services involved in a particular case or activity, there is often a need for someone to oversee and coordinate the work of everyone involved. Coordination means making sure each contribution is timely, enhances the work of others, and is known to and understood by everyone else. The role involves informing, directing, enabling, clarifying and recording. If the parts work in harmony to accomplish an agreed-upon goal, coordinators have done their jobs well.

An example would be coordinating the services provided to a destitute family with multiple needs, e.g., housing, counselling, legal aid, emergency financial help.

Conflict management

There are times when conflict between individuals or groups is inevitable. It is a normal outcome of people's living and working together. But conflict can inhibit constructive growth and progress and therefore it may be necessary for counsellors to play the role of conflict mediator or to facilitate a compromise. For successful conflict management to occur, the parties involved must be flexible and willing to resolve their dispute. The role of conflict manager requires diplomacy, patience, the skill to diagnose the nature of the *real* conflict, and an ability to persuade both parties to change so that their differences can be settled. An example might be resolving a dispute between newly separated parents over access arrangements to the children, or resolving differences in expectations about household chores between a teenage son and his parents.

Facilitation

When one person takes responsibility for structuring, leading and guiding groups to make a decision or to discharge their responsibilities, that person is performing a leadership role. Facilitation is a particular kind of leadership that involves fostering and utilising the strengths and resources of all the group members (Auvine et al., 1978). The facilitator's role is to foster sharing, cooperation and egalitarianism among members in accomplishing their purpose. Counsellors function as facilitators when they help a community group plan for more effective recreational programmes for their children, or when they facilitate a social welfare agency's discussion of a five-year development plan.

Giving feedback/assessing

There may be times when counsellors are called on to give feedback on the progress, state, or success of a programme, agency or intervention. Feedback can be both confirmatory (what has been accomplished or successful) and corrective (what has not been accomplished or what been unsuccessful) (Egan, 1985). Usually feedback is more effective when it is asked for, specific, constructive, relevant and timely. Counsellors are often asked for feedback from clients, colleagues and groups they may be counselling, working with or facilitating. Providing feedback is a skill with which counsellors need to be at ease and competent to perform.

Information sharing

An essential part of every counsellor's role is to communicate relevant, useful information in an effective manner to those that need it. This may involve speaking accurately and persuasively, writing clearly and succinctly and/or sharing relevant documents (memos, reports and articles) with others who have a need for or an interest in them. Information should be delivered quickly and easily to others who need it: counsellors may circulate up-to-date research reports to interested colleagues; they may write a position paper on the effects of managed mental health care for distribution to a local professional group; they may phone, fax or email key members of relevant groups with information about agency policies or services.

Networking

A common activity among counsellors and other social service workers is networking, that is, establishing direct, person-to-person contacts with others in similar or related areas of work for the purpose of sharing information, skills, and resources. Networking functions most effectively in an atmosphere of openness, trust, and mutual support. In effective networking, hierarchies and formal procedures are set aside in favour of having direct access to the people and/or resources that are required. An example is a counsellor seeking out others at a conference who are currently working with depressed adolescents for the purpose of sharing experiences and learning about innovative new approaches; or a counsellor wishing to set up in private practice contacting others of like mind and those who have already done so.

Professional leadership

Some counsellors, because of their particular training, experience or high level of competence, may become regarded as models of good practice. They may be seen as highly competent and innovative in their work (Egan, 1985). While these should be goals for every counsellor to aspire to, not everyone needs to become a high flyer, or will be accorded that status by colleagues. Professional leadership can be exercised by playing a key role in a counselling organisation, by developing special knowledge or expertise in a particular area of practice. The counselling profession needs competent, dedicated leadership, and talented counsellors should be encouraged to take on key leadership tasks and roles.

Political intervention

Getting caught up in the politics of their work is often anathema to counsellors who prefer to think of themselves as supportive, unbiased, egalitarian and nurturing. Counsellors often view political struggles for power, resources and decision-making capabilities as crass, distasteful and unpleasant. However, counsellors who work in agencies, organisations and communities – in short, all counsellors – need to become politically informed, astute and skilled. Counsellors can accomplish this without sacrificing their own values and personal integrity. Increasingly, decisions about mental health services and resources are contestable and made in an environment of limited resources and personnel. For ethical reasons as well as selfish ones, counsellors ought not to leave such decisions to others who are less informed.

Counsellors will need to learn how to lead others, how to form and work with coalitions, how to influence others, how to frame and present political arguments. To opt out of these tasks merely leaves them to be done by others, and creates the risk that both counsellors and their clients will be disadvantaged by the decisions handed down.

An example of political intervention is a counsellor who works in a large government agency and decides to form a coalition of co-workers to oppose a plan to cut back counselling services provided by the agency so that the agency's computerised records system can be upgraded.

Team building

A popular activity in mental health and social service agencies is team building. This involves fostering and enhancing an atmosphere of cooperation, support and collegiality among those who work together for the purpose of increasing job clarity, performance, efficiency and, ultimately, service effectiveness. Efforts to foster a sense of togetherness usually aim to increase harmony in relationships, effectiveness in communications, clarity of roles and tasks, and the overall quality of life within the organisation.

Typically, team building involves group work, usually led by a competent outsider, that focuses on identified areas of conflict or weaknesses within the organisation. Counsellors have a central part to play in helping agencies which are in need of team building among their staff.

Consultation

Many of the above-mentioned activities can be part of a more general process called consultation, which has been defined as an indirect method of problem-solving in which one professional (the consultant) assists another party, often another professional (the consultee), to solve or remedy the problem experienced by a third party (the client) (Dougherty, 1990). Because of the educational nature of the process, it is not uncommon for both the consultee and the client to be helped in some way (Dougherty, 1990).

Consultation is a helping process whereby the counsellor-consultant and those consulted – an individual, group or organisation – work together to solve a problem or institute change. For example, the consultant may work with the key personnel in an organisation to advise them on how to help particular clients or how to change their procedures in ways which will help individual members in the organisation itself.

Through their training and their self-development, counsellors have skills in communication and interpersonal relationships which equip them to act as effective consultants and to deal with the feelings and difficulties that arise when changes are instituted. Effective counsellor-consultants should be open-minded, skilled in relating to others and able to share power in a relationship of equality and mutual respect. They should be knowledgeable about the consultation process, the change process, and the nature of organisations, in particular the one in which they will be working.

Consulting requires skill in assessment, problem-solving, solution-finding, decision-making, negotiation, planning, evaluation, and the effective use of resources. An example of consultation would be a school principal calling on a school counsellor to diagnose a pupil's problem and advise the teacher on how to deal with it. In this situation it is essential that the counsellor-consultant obtain accurate and full information from as many sources as possible. This could involve directly observing the pupil (client) in the setting of concern or arranging for some third person to systematically record teacher-pupil interactions.

It is essential that the consultant communicate clearly with the principal and teacher so that they understand the consultant's role and their roles, how the consultant assesses the problem, what actions are seen as feasible and what outcomes can be expected. It is also most important to check on progress and evaluate the final outcome.

Through the consultation process, the counsellor-consultant shares his/her expertise by modelling, and involving the teacher in, the processes of problem definition, generation of solutions, and evaluation of results. The consultant 'treats' the individual client (the pupil) only indirectly. The teacher is in direct control of the helping process and selects the methods thought to be the most appropriate from those suggested, determines the best timing, carries out the treatment, and decides when the intervention has been successful.

Types of consultation

Providing an expert service

Consultants and consultees together gather information and define the problem but consultants, because of their expertise and experience, assume responsibility for carrying out the selected intervention. This may involve training others. For example, a factory manager may feel that the production supervisors lack skill in communicating with the workers for whom they are responsible. A school principal may want to appoint deans within a pastoral care network but may feel that the teachers selected need some training before undertaking their new role. In both situations a counsellor-consultant could provide training in communication skills. Such training is in demand in education groups, commercial, industrial, and retailing firms and voluntary social agencies as well as in the professional helping services.

Prescribing a remedy

The consultant acts as a resource person, assisting in fact-finding and/or diagnosis and then suggesting a remedy or course of action for the consultee to implement. For example, a parent may consult a counsellor about a disobedient teenager, a wife about how to help her alcoholic husband or an employee may seek assistance on how to help workmates cope with a domineering supervisor. In each case the counsellor-consultant may gather more information, analyse it and suggest a course of action which could be anything from family counselling in the first case to mediation in the third case.

Mediating

This role involves settling a dispute by engaging the two (or more) parties in a joint, structured, open process of problem solving. The consultant acts as a facilitator, catalyst and/or motivator in order to keep the process moving and to keep the disputants fully involved in both the process and the eventual outcome. Essentially, the process of mediation involves clarifying each side's position in the dispute, what each wants from the other and what each will agree to as a compromise position.

A university student counsellor could assume this role in a dispute between a group of students and their lecturer about the classroom atmosphere. For example, if both sides expressed anger about the disrespectful, critical way in which they felt they were being treated, but each side was willing to enter mediation to resolve the matter, the counsellor could guide the parties through the mediation process to a resolution acceptable to both.

Collaborating

This role involves working cooperatively with a client or client group to achieve a common goal. It is less confrontational than advocacy and depends for its success on a pooling of resources, information and skills. Each party contributes skills, ideas and time, and each works jointly to achieve the desired result. Although it may be time-consuming and at times cumbersome, decisions or goals reached through collaboration are usually long-lasting because each party has had a major role in achieving them.

Examples include a counsellor and a teacher collaborating to assess a child's behavioural difficulties in the classroom, or a counsellor and a small welfare agency deciding how to write a funding application for a new violence prevention programme.

The consultation process

As illustrated in the diagram in figure 9.1, there can be up to eleven stages in the consultation process. While it is helpful to set them out in this way, the stages may occur out of sequence or be repeated. For example, the consultant may be required to establish relationships with new people at several points in the process, and information may need to be gathered to help in the diagnosis stage, in choosing a solution, and in evaluating success.

If the first task is to raise awareness, the consultant will be adopting an advocacy or information-sharing role. If training is to be provided as one of the solutions, the consultant will be delivering an expert service.

What is involved in each stage is elaborated below. The sections on preparation and making contact fit into the third stage, *Establishment of a cooperative relationship*.

Elaboration of the consultation process

Preparation

To be effective, consultants need to begin by assuring themselves that they have adequate interpersonal skills, knowledge of the organisation in which they will be working, and the skills and resources necessary to perform the required consultancy role.

- Know yourself:
  What are your strengths, skills, knowledge?

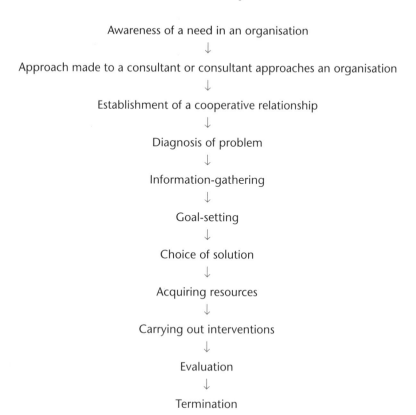

The consultation process

Awareness of a need in an organisation
↓
Approach made to a consultant or consultant approaches an organisation
↓
Establishment of a cooperative relationship
↓
Diagnosis of problem
↓
Information-gathering
↓
Goal-setting
↓
Choice of solution
↓
Acquiring resources
↓
Carrying out interventions
↓
Evaluation
↓
Termination

Figure 9.1

What are your limitations?

In initial contacts how do you come across to strangers?

What are your needs, values, and assumptions?

• Know the organisation you are entering and its personnel:

What are the organisation's goals, beliefs, norms, and values – in short, its culture?

Who are the clients in any proposed change?

Who are the power brokers in the organisation?

Who are the innovators?

Who are the resisters?

Can you analyse the situation from the point of view of the resisters?

(**Note:** Much of your knowledge of the organisation will be obtained during the phases of making contact, diagnosing problems, and information-gathering.)

- Know the area of concern: what skills, resources and expert knowledge are available to you?

  What is the nature of the problem?

  What experience do you have in this area?

  What has been tried before?

  What small successes have been noted?

  What changes might be necessary in the organisation?

  What methods could be used to achieve them?

  What resources are available?

  Are there successful models already in operation?

Making contact

Consultants should make sure that most people in the organisation know that using an outside consultant is proposed. Several methods should be used when making early contact (e.g., letters, telephone calls, visits, discussions). Consultants will need to consider whether initial face-to-face contact should take place at their choice of venue or the consultee's.

When in direct contact, consultants should try to achieve a balance between supportive listening and asking questions that help to identify the need and clarify the commitment to change. The following four questions are useful in determining the need for consultation (Bell & Nadler, 1985):

1   Why are you here? (What is the problem or concern? Can you be of help?)

2   What roles are you to play? (What are you to do and what will be your responsibilities?)

3   What is likely to happen? (What is the goal and how will it be accomplished?)

4   What will be the result? (How will the result be evaluated? Will it be worth the effort?)

Consultants should establish their credibility by outlining their qualifications and experience without either over-emphasising their expertise or devaluing their skills. Consultants should define their role and stay in it, resisting the temptation to become a co-conspirator with the consultee or to offer to solve all the problems themselves. The consultancy relationship is reciprocal, and knowledge and expertise will be shared. Consultants know the field in general; consultees know the particular setting.

Finally, consultants should obtain an initial statement of the problem which focuses on issues and sets some boundaries. The following questions will assist in doing this:

- What is the aim of any intervention?

- What specific responsibilities will the consultant assume?
- Who else will be involved?
- What will be their responsibilities? Will all this be specified in writing?
- What time-span is anticipated?
- What fee will be paid and who will pay any other costs involved?
- How will the work be monitored and reviewed?
- How will the results be reported and to whom?
- To what extent should proceedings be confidential?

Diagnosing problems

Diagnosis involves identifying the problem, its location, and how its effects are experienced in the system. Consultants need to be aware that the presenting and underlying problems may be different. For example, a supervisor may consult a counsellor on the best way to discuss with a male employee who has a disability that his work is deficient and his social behaviour is irritating. Further investigation may reveal that the job specification is inadequate and that the employee has not been given feedback by those with whom he works that his chatter interrupts their concentration. They may have been unable to give such feedback because their feelings of guilt or discomfort in relation to people with disabilities prevent them from being honest.

Consultants can identify problems, strengths, key people and opportunities in the organisation through questioning consultees. Realistic goals are established and any possible constraints on achieving them considered. If more information is required, the problem may need to be redefined and/or refined.

Gathering information

Gather information about what is not working, what does work and what has been tried previously. Identify exceptions, that is, those times when things worked well. What was different then? Explore these aspects of the problem with several members of the organisation or system. The information obtained may provide a basis for action.

The required information may already be available. If not, define the purposes for which new information may be required. Is it needed to convince people, to define a need, or to provide baseline data against which to evaluate progress?

Methods of obtaining information include:

- Listening to the consultee and other people in the organisation.
- Direct observation.
- Questionnaires. These must be appropriate for the target group. Issues such as the possibility of reading difficulties need to be considered.

- Structured interviews.

- Group meetings. One method of gathering information in this setting is outlined:
  a A key question is asked.
  b Participants write down their ideas.
  c The ideas are pooled but not discussed.
  d There is then open discussion of the ideas.
  e Participants privately rank the ideas.
  f The overall ranking is collated and considered.

When gathering information other considerations include the possibility of bias, ownership of the data, and methods of presenting it.

Setting goals and objectives

Consultees should be helped to specify what is to be achieved; how it is to be achieved and the time-span involved. Identifying exceptions to the problem is useful here and usually helps to keep the goals realistic and achievable. *Goals* are general statements of intent, for example, to achieve effective coordination of guidance, careers, and school-to-work activities at Meadow High School.

Objectives are statements specifying meaningful, obtainable, measurable outcomes, e.g., appoint a guidance co-ordinator.

Consider whether the goals and objectives are clear and specific and whether they have been obtained by consensus. Does everyone understand them and what they imply?

Testing for consensus

- Can everyone paraphrase the goals?

- Has everyone had a chance to express their thoughts and feelings about the goals and objectives?

- Are those who disagree willing to state publicly that they will accept a majority decision and give the proposal a fair trial?

Consideration should also be given to whether the organisation has the resources, skills, and money to implement the goals, whether the goals are flexible enough to be changed if circumstances change and whether there are ways of rewarding people who achieve them.

Choosing a solution

Once a goal or goals have been identified, it is useful to explore possible ways of achieving them. Asking several people the question 'What is the first step necessary to achieve that goal?' is often productive. Solutions can also be generated by brainstorming (note: preclude criticism of any ideas raised at this stage).

- Evaluate each solution in relation to the objectives.

- Evaluate each in relation to its practicality and widespread benefits.

- Does the organisation have the necessary people and financial resources?

- Do the staff have the requisite skills or will they need training?

- Will others in the organisation benefit from the implementation of these solutions?

Acquiring resources

Resources need to be readily accessible, relevant, and affordable. Standardised tests, questionnaires, checklists, and structured interviews may be used in diagnosis. Policy statements, reading lists, and guest speakers may be used to raise awareness. It may be possible to try out some resources in a pilot study or to obtain feedback about their value from previous users.

Carrying out interventions

Knowing the strengths of an organisation can help when trying to choose a successful plan for implementing the solution. Consultants should use what has worked before, or what is already working to satisfaction; they should also be prepared to change the plan if it does not work or if it meets with strong resistance. In deciding on a plan it is helpful for consultants to consider the following questions:

- How will change be implemented?

- Who will be responsible for each aspect of the plan?

- Within what time-span will change have to be achieved?

- What methods will be used? Possibilities include:
  role-playing
  simulation exercises
  modelling
  observation
  interaction in pairs, threes, or small groups
  skill-learning and practice (on video, in the actual situation, in simulations)
  feedback from participants
  research exercises
  workshops
  films or videos
  outside speakers
  worksheets
  planning exercises
  case studies
  background reading

lectures
resource-sharing visits
discussion

- Is there a clear understanding of job specifications?
- Is there an adequate division of labour?
- Are the various aspects of the change process adequately co-ordinated?

Evaluating

It is at this stage that the effectiveness of the plan should be assessed. Consultants should go back to the objectives and consider whether they will evaluate formally through the use of questionnaires, checklists, structured interviews or by observation. Evaluation may also be done through informal discussion with staff and management personnel.

- Which of the objectives have been met?
- What has not worked? Why not?
- Is it necessary to redefine the problem(s)?
- Should a new strategy be tried?
- Should there be formal reporting back?
- If yes, to whom and in what form?

Terminating

The conditions under which termination is to occur should be specified in the initial contract so that once the goals have been met the process of disengagement can commence. Terminating a consultancy relationship may involve a gradual withdrawal of support so that there is reduced contact, some form of formal follow-up and, finally, when there is evidence that goals have been met and that the organisation is able to carry on without further support, termination of contact (Dougherty, 1990).

Dealing with resistance

Reluctance to participate in the consultation process can arise at any stage (Dougherty, 1990). People can easily feel threatened, become upset or confused and refuse to cooperate any longer. Resistance is a common phenomenon and must be dealt with successfully if a positive result is to occur. Being open and honest about the consultation process from the start is one way of minimising resistance. Dealing with resistance directly and openly when it arises is another. When it occurs, it is useful to try to understand the reluctance from the resister's point of view; this may help the consultant to understand the resistance more fully and to see its meaning in relation to the process of change that has been proposed.

Resistance may also be lessened if participants are able to see the proposed changes as reducing rather than increasing their stress and if what is proposed fits with their values and ideals. Participants who are involved in the diagnosis and definition of the problem are less likely to feel that their autonomy and security are threatened. Also, the chance to take part in an interesting new experience can act as an incentive.

As change takes place, resistance will be reduced if the feelings of participants are acknowledged and opposing viewpoints are heard and respected. Relationships based on acceptance, trust, support, and where appropriate, confidentiality, contribute to the lessening of resistance.

The programme for change and the organisers of that programme need to be flexible and open to feedback. Where agreement is reached by consensus there is more chance of commitment to change.

Effectiveness of consultation

Achievement of the specified outcomes is not the only criterion for judging the effectiveness of consultation. Other valid outcomes of consultation include the provision of accurate, up-to-date information to an organisation and unmasking aspects of it that may have been denied or hidden. In addition, experiencing a reciprocal relationship can benefit both consultees and consultants. Consultees learn new skills in defining problems, making decisions, planning and communication, and have the satisfaction that comes from being fully involved in the consultation process.

Choosing a consultant

Consultants may come from inside or outside the organisation. Insiders will be familiar with the system but may not be able to achieve enough independence, objectivity, and status to be acceptable and effective. Outsiders, while not knowing the organisation intimately, can bring with them a fresh perspective, objectivity, and independence of the power structure. Answering the following questions can be helpful in determining who would be the most appropriate consultant.

- Why are the services of a consultant required?
- What is it possible to achieve within the limitations imposed by the organisational structure?
- Would it be better to have a neutral chairperson or referee from outside the organisation?
- What is needed most, someone with particular expertise to act as a catalyst, or an analyst?
- Is the consultant needed to assist with the formalising of a system?
- Is someone needed to teach the organisation's personnel new skills?

- What resources does the organisation need to supply to the consultant? (e.g., organisational policy, production goals, list of personnel)
- What preparation does the organisation need to do?
- What should happen after the consultation has ended?
- What evaluation and follow-up should take place?

The counsellor-consultant as trainer

An important consultancy role for counsellors is that of trainer/educator. Teaching clients and other helpers is a relatively common role for counsellors and most often takes the form of a workshop, seminar or short course taught over several weeks. In order for it to be most effective and the outcome long-lasting, such teaching needs careful pre-planning and careful structuring.

For example, a counsellor could well adopt a training/consultant role by teaching a communication skills course for members of an organisation contemplating major changes to its communication system.

Clarity of aims and objectives

It is vital that teaching aims and objectives be clearly specified as a means of structuring and directing a course. For example, teaching communication skills to the staff of a large organisation demands a high level of leader and participant involvement and is much more difficult than imparting information in a lecture situation. In some situations, such training can become a form of group counselling for the participants on the training course. Participants have personal goals in entering into training and they have the opportunity for open sharing of feelings and for honest feedback. They can grow in self-awareness and in understanding of others through the relationships established during the training.

It is also very easy to lose or confuse participants. Clearly stated aims and objectives help to provide a sense of security, direction, purpose, and progress, all of which encourage involvement.

The first step in the training/educator consultancy process is for those desiring training to state their needs clearly and precisely. They may need help to do this. Even though it may take time to get people to identify their training aims, the process itself may provide the trainer with valuable information about their stage of development. The following questions may be useful at this initial stage:

- When, and for how long, are sessions to be held?
- How many people will be involved?
- What facilities are available?
- What sort of training have participants been involved in before, if any?
- What is the spread of ages, experience and education?

- What will each participant learn?
- What overall effect is sought for the organisation?
- What sort of follow-up, if any, is planned?

It must be emphasised that the structure of the course, the explanations, and the selection of practical exercises should all serve to further the specified aims and objectives. Otherwise activities may be nothing more than time-fillers. Participants may be asked to prepare for the course by reading selected material, completing questionnaires or engaging in some form of self-analysis. Finally, when the course is under way, participants are entitled to know the aims of the whole course and the expected learnings from each exercise. Also, they should have the opportunity to provide feedback on the extent to which the aims and objectives have been achieved. In skills training, the emphasis should be on practical exercises with a maximum of participant involvement. However, it is also important that the theoretical and contextual background of the course content be explained, illustrated by the exercises and summarised by the leader afterwards.

Size and composition of groups

Various factors need to be considered when deciding on group size. The amount of space available may limit the number of participants. If physical arrangements are adequate, a group of 20–24 can be handled comfortably by one leader provided the group can subdivide into smaller units where appropriate. Experience suggests a group membership of four to eight is most appropriate for discussions or small group interactions.

When the composition of a group is considered, differences in culture, sex, age, educational level, ability to verbalise, and personality may be significant. Drawing attention to issues or problems that may result from these differences can provide effective teaching points. If, for example, group members are threatened by the presence of a highly qualified member, this issue should be aired. Their feelings may be similar to those clients experience when meeting a counsellor. This parallel can be pointed out to the group.

There seems to be no optimum combination of characteristics. Diversity in the group provides varying points of view. In the end the significant features of the group members usually turn out to be their degree of commitment to the training course, willingness to share openly and to change, and their ability to accept and deal with their own experiences in the group and those of others.

Voluntary or involuntary membership

This issue in relation to counselling clients has already been examined in chapter 5. Voluntary membership is usually preferable. The negative feelings or defensiveness of an involuntary group member may have a dampening effect on others. If the situation is particularly threatening to involuntary members, they may even set out deliberately to sabotage proceedings. Involuntary members may also convey their negative feelings to outsiders and thus prejudice them against such forms of training.

Besides the risk to the group, there are also potential hazards for involuntary members. Some people who appear to function well in ordinary life may really be hiding behind a mask. Open sharing in a group may strip them of their masks and leave them without the help and support needed to deal with their feelings of being exposed.

As with the involuntary client in individual counselling, it is important to discuss the issue of compulsory participation. Ideally, a person with strong negative feelings towards training should be allowed to withdraw. But, if at the outset the consultant/educator suggests to an organisation that voluntary participation is preferred, the issue need not arise. Once the course begins, however, even voluntary participants may find themselves reacting adversely because of the unexpected extent to which the activities are challenging or threatening. Such negative feelings should be dealt with as they arise and not be minimised or ignored.

The physical setting

The physical setting should be as comfortable and relaxing as possible. The room temperature needs to be high enough for comfort but not so high that it puts everyone to sleep. There should be minimal outside interference in the form of extraneous noise or interruptions. A carpeted room, comfortable chairs, plenty of space and working areas for small groups are all conducive to a good course atmosphere. If possible, participants should be free from all other calls on their time during the course. It is helpful if tea and coffee-making facilities are available so that during breaks course members can relax, socialise and shed some of the tensions that may have arisen and/or share their enthusiasm about new learning.

Timing and length of course

Experience suggests that courses lasting two to three days have more impact than those consisting of short sessions spread over a number of weeks. There is enough time for rapport to be developed between the leader and participants and among the participants themselves. This timing also gives the course an impetus that could be lost if there were a week's break between sessions. Participants tend to be fresher and more ready to learn if a course is held in the daytime rather than in the evenings, tacked on to the end of a full day's work. During a full day, breaks every one to one-and-a-half hours are needed.

It may not be possible to obtain ideal course conditions. If the course is spread over a number of weeks, one-and-a-half to two-hour sessions are probably long enough, especially if the sessions are held in the evenings. Another aspect of timing to be considered is placement of the course among the other commitments and stresses in participants' lives. If course members are withdrawn from their work settings at a time of seasonal pressure, both they and their fellow-workers may react negatively. Similarly, leaders should try to avoid a time when everyone is tired.

Materials

The choice of materials will be determined by the aims of the course, the selection of activities to promote those aims, the amount of money available and the ease of access to facilities for filming or printing. There might be a temptation to use audio-visual aids to appear up-to-date or novel rather than because they suit the course aims. The key considerations in deciding to use audio-visual aids are:

- What would best suit the course aims?

- How available are these materials?

- Is the trainer competent to use them and/or is technical assistance readily available?

Video and audio recordings are powerful aids in the teaching of counselling skills but they can be a distraction and cause annoyance if the operator is unfamiliar with the equipment or it has not been checked to see if it is working. Sometimes, too, the effort required to obtain and operate this equipment is too great to be warranted. The use of audio-visual aids actually increases rather than diminishes preparation time. Careful planning is required, otherwise the audio-visual aids will be mere gimmicks or time-wasters. As a rule, recordings should be stopped every 10–12 minutes for structured discussion and/or group interaction. Playing a lengthy audio or video tape to a group without any pauses can have a negative effect on the participants' interest and attention levels.

It is helpful to have copies of exercises printed beforehand but they can also be presented on overhead projector transparencies, on large sheets of newsprint or on a whiteboard. Participants should be asked to bring pens and paper but it is always wise to provide some for those who forget. Finally, directed exercises or reading material can be given to group members to complete prior to the course.

Leaders of training courses and workshops

A high level of maturity and interpersonal competence is required in those who lead training groups. On the personal level it is desirable that leaders be warm, open, self-accepting, and able to self-disclose appropriately. They should be able to refrain from dominating and allow participants to take the initiative. It is important that they be flexible and able to change the programme when this is required. Leaders need to be trained adequately, experienced, and proficient in a wide range of skills. It is highly desirable that they begin work as a consultant-trainer as a sort of apprentice to an experienced leader.

The setting and the composition of the group need to be considered when choosing a leader. Someone who is excellent in an academic setting may not be effective in communicating to a group of unemployed people. A high-powered personality may be threatening to those beginning to experience human relationships training for the first time. The leader needs to be someone the group can readily trust and with whom they can feel secure.

Undertaking to train others requires a considerable commitment of preparation time, energy and involvement. Those who acquire reputations as good leaders need to beware of over-extending themselves by accepting too many invitations.

Leaders may come from within an organisation or may be brought in from outside. Outside leaders may not be as threatening in that they do not have to be faced every day after the course is over. Also, outsiders are not already involved in the complexities of colleague relationships with the participants and do not have to worry about facing them afterwards. Inside leaders, on the other hand, will be aware of participants' characteristics prior to the course; they may have a more accurate assessment of participants' levels of functioning and their specific needs, and they are more readily available for follow-up, particularly if the training has provoked strong reactions in any group members. All of these points need to be considered by the organisation when choosing a leader.

exercise **9.1***

You have been asked to run a course for voluntary social workers on Basic Helping Skills. State your overall aim(s).

exercise **9.2***

In the course you have chosen to use the following exercises. What would be your reasons for using each? In other words, what skills would you expect participants to understand and be able to use after practice?

a   An exercise in using open and closed questions. (See p. 79.)

b   An exercise in finding exceptions to problems. (See p. 99.)

c   An exercise in thinking aloud. (See *Answers to exercises*, p. 86.)

Leading groups

The following rules can serve as useful guidelines for group trainers.

• Instructions for all exercises and activities should be clearly stated, repeated and then illustrated.

• Leaders should resist dominating or talking more than necessary. If instructions and explanations are clear and concise, a maximum amount of time can be spent on having participants practise the skills and discuss their effects afterwards.

- Everyone should be encouraged to participate, especially in the small working groups. These suggestions may help them to do so:

  a Before beginning, emphasise that everyone will gain more from the course by participating fully.

  b As often as possible, subdivide the larger group into pairs or threes. This encourages the participation of all members.

  c Help silent members to participate by occasionally inviting them to answer questions or give their opinion. Be aware of non-verbal reactions and allow members to decide when they are ready to speak.

  d Beware of people who want to use the group for their own needs, e.g., as an audience. Avoid lengthy monologues or dialogues between one member and the leader by:

     i Suggesting that a private issue be discussed at another time, e.g., 'As it is a personal matter, I suggest that we discuss this over lunch'.

     ii Reminding the group of its purpose for meeting, e.g., 'That's interesting and we may be able to come back to that later, but at present we are practising scaling questions'.

     iii Inviting others to participate, e.g., 'Let's check with Mary now' or, 'What's your reaction to that point, Mark?'.

- Suggest that people try to speak for themselves and not for others (unless acting as spokesperson), e.g., participants should try to say, 'I' rather than 'we' or 'they'.

- Make it clear that participants are responsible for the consequences of their own actions within the group, but at the same time try to develop an atmosphere of tolerance and support for others in the group.

- As far as possible, be aware of each person in the group, not just the current speaker. When leading, gauge the reactions of group members other than the speaker.

- When people keep directing statements to the leader, redirect the comments to the larger group, e.g., 'What do the rest of you think?' or 'That's a point others might want to respond to'.

- Be aware of physical movements and postures. They may indicate boredom, frustration, lack of understanding or tension.

- Accept all reactions without imputing rightness or wrongness to them.

- Be aware that leaders are seen as models. As far as possible, demonstrate openness, interest, warmth, trust, and a sense of humour.

- When sub-groups are working on exercises, check with each group to answer questions that arise and to ensure that members are keeping to the task.

- When leaders cannot answer a question, they should simply say so.

- Allow the group to decide whether they want the proceedings to be confidential and what that will actually mean in practice.

Follow-up

To strengthen the impact of a course and stimulate on-going learning, it is valuable to have some form of follow-up. New learnings can be reinforced by subsequent practical work and structured discussions. Without some form of planned follow-up, the effects of a course may last for only a few weeks even though the enthusiasm generated might remain much longer.

Follow-up may take the form of one or a series of short meetings. During these sessions, participants may share experiences in using the skills learned, seek support or further direction, or request help in extending their skills. Because some courses may include participants from distant places, follow-up via a newsletter, further directed reading, or having local contacts available to answer queries may be helpful. The effectiveness of the course could be assessed by attempting to survey its influence on the subsequent fieldwork of participants. Another form of follow-up is for participants to report back to their colleagues or, once they have the experience and confidence, to teach others in their organisations. Finally, course members can be encouraged to attend other, more extensive, training courses in their area.

10 Developing competence

 ounsellors have a continuing ethical responsibility to develop their competence by integrating new learning into their practice, by developing the ability to assess progress with clients and by using effective means to evaluate their overall effectiveness.

Integrating the skills

In progressing through this book you may have felt that it was increasingly difficult to remember and apply everything that has been presented. In addition, you may now feel somewhat unnatural and awkward as you try to implement the model and use specific skills. It may be reassuring to know that others who have practised these skills in a **finding-solutions-to-problems** approach have reported that, at first, training actually seemed to hinder rather than help them and that they too felt less natural and spontaneous in their counselling. However, they have also reported that these feelings diminished as they gained experience in using the skills and the model. In other words, as you practise the various skills in real or role-played counselling situations, you will begin using them with greater confidence and will not be so conscious of your performance. In time, you will begin to develop a personal style that is comfortable, skills-based, coherent and solution-oriented.

Trying to focus complete attention on the client is one way of aiding this process. Counsellors should listen more to clients and to their own inner reactions to clients, and less to their own anxieties and self-consciousness about their performance. In so doing, counsellors will be more helpful to clients and increase the likelihood of using skills appropriately. If counsellors can do these things, they will be putting more of their energy into the real purpose of counselling – finding out about, understanding, and helping clients find solutions to their problems.

It may also be helpful to counsellors to have in front of them a list of stages, questions and possible interventions to which they can refer as they work with clients. Other trainees have reported that such a list gives them greater confidence, and allows them to worry less about remembering what to do next and to focus more on the client's needs. Whenever it might be appropriate to do so, the list could be shown to and discussed with the client, thereby clarifying the process of counselling and demystifying it at the same time.

Another way to aid this process of developing a comfortable, coherent style of counselling is for counsellors to identify times when they were able to focus their attention in a seemingly effortless and effective way. What was happening then that allowed this to occur? Can the critical elements or behaviours be identified and repeated with other clients? In other words, can they do more of the same?

The process of integrating new learning into a smooth and effective style can be greatly aided by the use of audio or video recordings of counselling sessions. Regularly reviewing sessions in this way can reveal insights into what works well, what doesn't and where to focus efforts to change and improve.

Estimating progress

An essential part of counselling is for counsellors to be able to assess where they are in the process of **finding solutions to problems** at any given moment. Counselling, after all, is a purposeful activity that usually follows a predictable sequence of stages. It is important for both counsellor and client to know what progress has been made and what still needs to be done, if only in very general terms. In this book, the process of identifying and implementing solutions to problems has been divided into seven stages:

- pre-counselling considerations;

- getting started;

- exploring the client's situation: what is working and what is not;

- setting desired goals for solving the problem and increasing the times when the problem is absent;

- deciding how to achieve those goals;

- implementing a strategy to achieve the goals;

- evaluating the success of the entire process.

By noting the skills they are using, the types of statements clients are making and by asking themselves certain questions, counsellors can determine at which stage they and their clients are in the counselling process. The skills discussed in chapters 5, 6 and 7 have been introduced at the stage of counselling where their use is generally most appropriate and effective. Thus, if counsellors find themselves using mainly exploration and clarifying skills and they judge their use to be appropriate at that time, they and their clients are probably at the third stage, that is, helping the client explore and clarify problems and/or solutions.

Counsellors can also use the client's statements as a guide to progress. For example, client statements of a general, somewhat vague nature ('I'm not really sure – all I know is that I wanted to talk to someone', and 'Well, what do you think – why was I sent here?') indicate that the process is still at the getting-started stage and that the clients may not yet be willing, committed customers for counselling. Client statements that identify exceptions to the problem or demonstrate efforts to clarify or specify what they would rather have happen indicate that the process has advanced to the goal-setting stage (e.g., 'I just want my parents to trust me enough to let me stay out later on weekends.', or 'When I can say what I mean without becoming so nervous and hesitant, they seem to listen to me').

Clients can be asked for their estimate of how they are progressing, how much work they have left to do, or how long they see counselling continuing. One quick and useful way of gauging answers to these questions is by use of a scale (e.g., 'On a scale of 1 to 10 where 1 is "just beginning" and 10 is "finished, the problem is solved", where would you say you are now? Where do you need to get to for you to be satisfied?'). Another way is to ask a question about what things will be like when counselling is no longer needed (e.g., 'How will you know when you no longer need to see me? How long do think that will take?'). This sort of 'termination talk' can be started as early in counselling as the first session (Berg, 1994) since it helps orient clients to a successful, not-too-distant finish rather than a lengthy, indeterminate process.

Counsellors can also determine the present stage of counselling by asking themselves specific questions. Positive answers to the following indicate that the main task of the stage in question has been accomplished. Negative answers mean that there is probably still work to be done at that stage before progressing to the next.

Getting started

- Do we have a good working relationship?
- Does the client trust me?
- Is the client willing to be here?
- Have I informed the client about his/her rights and what to expect?
- What sort of first impressions do we have of one another?

Exploration of problems or solutions

- Has the problem changed at all in the last two to three weeks? Any improvements?
- Has a problem been identified? How severe is it? What does it involve?
- How has the client managed to cope thus far?
- What is the client's emotional state?
- What are the client's strengths and abilities?
- What solutions have been tried already?

Goal-setting

- Can the client identify times and/or conditions when the problem was not a problem?
- Does the client recognise what part he/she played in making those times happen? That is, that she/he had control over what occurred?
- Does the client know what she/he would like to do that cannot be done now?
- Is the client clear about what changes to make? How things would be better?

Strategy selection

- Does the client have realistic ideas about what might accomplish a chosen goal?
- Does the client know how to choose an appropriate goal?
- Have priorities been established and alternatives evaluated?
- Does the client need encouragement? Information?

Implementation of strategy

- Does the client understand the reasons for implementing a particular strategy?
- Are the implications of the chosen goal and strategy clear?
- Does the client have the support, resources, confidence and motivation to carry out the strategy?

Evaluating success

- Has the original problem been resolved in the desired manner?
- Is the client satisfied with the results of the strategy?
- Is the client able to apply what has been learnt in this instance to future problems?

Evaluating effectiveness

To be fully effective, it is essential for counsellors to be able to assess the overall impact of their interactions with clients. This includes being aware of their style of counselling and its effect on clients, understanding specific skills and how those skills are best used, and being able to demonstrate their success in helping clients find solutions to their problems. It is necessary for counsellors to make systematic use of a number of sources besides themselves in accomplishing these important tasks.

- Counsellors can use a counsellor self-check inventory to assess their own performance. By thinking carefully about what they did and said, they will become more aware of their style and its effect on others.

- Counsellors can ask their clients to complete an interview or counsellor rating scale in which they comment both on the interview as a whole and the counsellor's specific behaviours. Over time, a summary of these reports will provide counsellors with feedback on what their clients found useful, inhibiting, challenging or supporting. Developmental trends or themes may become evident over time as well.

- Other counsellors could occasionally observe by sitting in during an interview or by listening to an audio or video recording of the session. Their comments and observations can be an invaluable source of helpful information.

- Counsellors could join a counsellors' organisation and participate in the business and concerns of that group. By doing so they would become acquainted with other counsellors doing similar work, share ideas with them, and, as a result, be prompted to think about their own work in the context of larger issues facing the helping professions.

exercise **10.1**

1   Using video or audio tape, record two consecutive sessions with a client. Make sure, of course, that the client understands what you want to do with the recordings and why, and he/she gives his/her consent. Review the tapes, paying attention to your use of skills, the progression of counselling from one interview to another, how sessions are begun and ended. What aspects of your performance need changing? What aspects are effective?

2   Keep a cumulative summary of all of your counselling contacts over a period of 6–12 months. Record such information as client sex, age, cultural background, presenting problem, problem severity, number of sessions, outcome, and any other information you would find interesting or useful to you. At the end of the period of 6–12 months, summarise the data in some useful way (e.g., tables or graphs). What does it tell you about your current practice? Future training needs?

3   Go back to the 'personal theory' exercise in chapter 1 (exercise 1.2). Write another version of your theory of helping. What changes have you made? Why?

4 Have your work reviewed by another counsellor or supervisor. The review should go beyond a typical supervision session to include all aspects of your work, such as your working knowledge of your theory or model, your work practices/routines, your methods of inducting clients into the role. Make a list of the procedures/factors you want your 'auditor' to comment on. What did you learn about your work from this activity? What changes to your practices are needed?

Re-reading and reviewing

Now that you have completed this book, you may wish to return to various parts of it to review particular skills or think more carefully about the ideas presented. It is hoped that you will do this often and that the process of reading and re-reading sections of the book will contribute substantially to your continuing education and the development of your confidence and competence as a counsellor.

References

Ahia, E. (1991). Enhanced therapeutic skills: Family and ethnic dynamics, part I. Cited in A. E. Ivey, M. Bradford Ivey & L. Simek-Morgan (1993). *Counseling and psychotherapy: A multicultural perspective* (3rd ed.). Boston: Allyn and Bacon.

Amatea, E. S. (1991). *Brief strategic intervention for school behavior problems.* San Francisco: Jossey-Bass.

Australian and New Zealand Journal of Family Therapy, (1987). *8,* pp. 99–103.

Auvine, R., Densmore, B., Extrom, M., Poole, S. & Shanklin, M. (1978). *A manual for group facilitators.* Madison, WI: The Center for Conflict Resolution.

Ballou, M. (1995). Bibliotherapy. In M. Ballou (Ed.). *Psychological Interventions: A guide to strategies,* pp. 55–65. London: Praeger.

Bell, C. R. & Nadler, L. (Eds). (1985). *Clients and consultants: Meeting and exceeding expectations.* (2nd ed.). Houston: Gulf Publishing.

Berg, I. K. (1994). *Family based services.* New York: W. W. Norton.

Berg, I. K. & Miller, S. D. (1992). *Working with the problem drinker.* New York: W. W. Norton.

Berg, I. K. & De Jong, P. (1996). Solution-building conversations: Co-constructing a sense of competence with clients. *Families in Society, 77,* pp. 376–391.

Bergin, A. E. & Garfield, S. L. (Eds). (1994). *Handbook of psychotherapy and behaviour change.* New York: Wiley.

Binder, J. L. (1993). Is it time to improve psychotherapy training? *Clinical Psychology Review, 13,* pp. 301–318.

Bloom, B. L. (1992). Planned short-term psychotherapy: Current status and future challenges. *Applied and Preventive Psychology, 1,* pp. 157–164.

Brammer, L. (1985). *The helping relationship: process and skills* (3rd ed.). Englewood Cliffs, NJ: Prentice-Hall.

Cherniss, C. (1980). *Staff burnout.* London: Sage.

Coles, D. (1995). A pilot use of letters to clients before the initial session. *Australian and New Zealand Journal of Family Therapy, 16,* pp. 209–213.

Corey, G., Corey, M. & Callanan, P. (1988). *Issues and ethics in the helping professions* (3rd ed.). Pacific Grove, CA: Brooks/Cole.

Corey, M. S. & Corey, G. (1989). *Becoming a helper.* Pacific Grove, CA: Brooks/Cole.

Cummings, N. A. (1990). Brief intermittent psychotherapy throughout the life cycle. In J. K. Zeig & S. G. Gilligan (Eds). *Brief therapy: Myths, methods, and metaphors,* pp. 169–184. New York: Brunner/Mazel.

Cummins, A-M. & Hoggett, P. (1995). Counselling in the enterprise culture. *British Journal of Guidance and Counselling, 23,* pp. 301–312.

Davies, S., Elkington, A. & Winslade, J. (1993). Putangitangi: A model for understanding the implications of Maori intra-cultural differences for helping strategies. *New Zealand Association of Counsellors Journal, 15,* pp. 2–6.

de Bono, E. (1971). *The use of lateral thinking.* Harmondsworth: Penguin.

de Bono, E. (1994). *Parallel thinking from Socratic thinking to de Bono thinking.* London: Viking.

de Shazer, S. (1985). *Keys to solutions in brief therapy.* New York: W. W. Norton.

de Shazer, S. (1988). *Clues: Investigating solutions in brief therapy.* New York: W. W. Norton.

de Shazer, S. (1991). *Putting difference to work*. New York: W. W. Norton.

Dixon, D.N. & Glover, J.A. (1984). *Counseling: A problem-solving approach*. New York: Wiley.

Dougherty, A. M. (1990). *Consultation: Practice and perspectives*. Pacific Grove, CA: Brooks/Cole.

Druckman, D. & Swets, J. A. (Eds). (1988). *Enhancing human performance*. Washington, D.C.: National Academy Press.

Dryden, W. (1993). *Reflections on counselling*. London: Whurr Publishing.

Eckert, P. A. (1993). Acceleration of change: Catalysts in brief therapy. *Clinical Psychology Review, 13*, pp. 241–253.

Edelwich, J. (1980). *Burnout*. New York: Human Sciences Press.

Egan, G. (1985). *Change agent skills in helping and human service settings*. Monterey, CA: Brooks/Cole.

Fraser, J. Scott. (1995). Process, problems, and solutions in brief therapy. *Journal of Marital and Family Therapy, 21*, pp. 265–279.

Fried, J. (1995). Ecological strategies. In M. Ballou (Ed.). *Psychological Interventions: A guide to strategies*, pp. 175–193. London: Praeger.

Friedman, S. (1994). Staying simple, staying focused: Time effective consultations with children and families. In M. F. Hoyt (Ed.). *Constructive therapies*. New York: Guilford Press.

Friedman, S. & Fanger, M. Taylor (1991). *Expanding therapeutic possibilities: Getting results in brief psychotherapy*. Toronto: Lexington Books.

Fukuyama, M. (1990). Taking a universal approach to multicultural counseling. *Counselor Education and Supervision, 30*, pp. 6–17.

Furman, B. & Ahola, T. (1992). *Solution talk*. New York: W. W. Norton.

Gentner, D. S. (1991). A brief strategic model for mental health counseling. *Journal of Mental Health Counseling, 13*, pp. 58–68.

Gudykunst, W. B. & Kim, Y. Y. (1984). *Communicating with strangers: An approach to intercultural communication*. London: Addison-Wesley.

Guterman, J. T. (1994). A social constructionist position for mental health counseling. *Journal of Mental Health Counseling, 13*, pp. 58–68.

Hoyt, M. F. (1991). Teaching and Learning short-term psychotherapy within an HMO. In C. Austand & W. H. Berman, (Eds). *Psychotherapy in managed health care: The optimal use of time and resources*. Washington, D.C.: American Psychological Association.

Ivey, A. E. (1994). *Intentional interviewing and counseling* (3rd ed.). Pacific Grove, CA: Brooks/Cole.

Ivey, A. E., Ivey, M. B. & Simek-Downing, L. (1987). *Counseling and psychotherapy: a multicultural perspective* (2nd ed.). Boston: Allyn and Bacon.

Ivey, A. E., Ivey, M. B. & Simek-Morgan, L. (1993). *Counseling and psychotherapy: Integrating skills, theory, and practice* (3rd ed.). Englewood Cliffs: Prentice-Hall.

Johnson, L. D. & Miller, S. D. (1994). Modification of depression risk factors: a solution-focused approach. *Psychotherapy, 31*, pp. 244–253.

Karasu, T. B. (1986). The specificity versus nonspecificity dilemma: toward identifying therapeutic change agents. *American Journal of Psychiatry, 143*, pp. 687–695.

Kerwin, A. (1994). Ignorance is strength. *Lingua Franca*. March/April, 7.

Kiser, D. J., Piercy, F. P. & Lipchik, E. (1993). The integration of emotion in solution-focused therapy. *Journal of Marital and Family Therapy, 19*, pp. 233–242.

Kocet, M. (1994). Student focus: The counselor as client – a personal perspective. *ACA: Counseling Today, 37*, p. 52.

Lambert, M. J. & Cattani-Thompson, K. (1996). Current findings regarding the effectiveness of counseling: Implications for practice. *Journal of Counseling and Development, 74*, pp. 601–608.

Lawson, D. (1994). Identifying pretreatment change. *Journal of Counseling and Development, 72*, pp. 244–248.

Lee, C. C. (1996). MCT theory and implications for indigenous healing. In D. W. Sue, A. E. Ivey & Pedersen, P. B. *A theory of multicultural counseling & therapy*. Pacific Grove, CA: Brooks/Cole.

Leong, F. T. L. & Kim. H. H. W. (1991). Going beyond cultural sensitivity on the road to multiculturalism: Using the intercultural sensitizer, as a counselor training tool. *Journal of Counseling & Development, 70*, pp. 112–118.

Lipchik, E. (1994). The rush to be brief. *Networker*, March/April, pp. 35–39.

Locke, D. (1990). A not so provincial view of multicultural counseling. *Counselor Education and Supervision, 30*, pp. 18–25.

Manthei, M. (1981). *Positively me* (rev. ed.). Auckland: Methuen.

Manthei, M. (1990). *Decisively me*. Auckland: Heineman Reed.

Manthei, R., Rich, P., Agee, M., Monk, G., Miller, J., Bunce. J., Webb, S. & Hermansson, G. (1994). 'Being in control': A survey of counsellors who have moved into private practice. *New Zealand Journal of Counselling, 16*, pp. 14–31.

McConnaughy, E. A. (1987). The person of the therapist in psychotherapeutic practice. *Psychotherapy, 24*, pp. 303–314.

McFadden, J. (Ed.) (1993). *Transcultural counseling: Bilateral and international perspectives*. Alexandria, VA: American Counseling Association.

McFadden J. (1996). A transcultural perspective: Reaction to C. H. Patterson's "Multicultural counseling: From diversity to universality". *Journal of Counseling & Development, 74*, pp. 232–235.

Miller, J. H. (1994). Professionalisation in counselling: Are we in danger of losing our way? *New Zealand Journal of Counselling, 16*, pp. 7–13.

Molnar, A. & de Shazer, S. (1987). Solution-focused therapy: Toward the identification of therapeutic tasks. *Journal of Marital and Family Therapy, 13*, pp. 349–358.

Munro, A., Manthei, B. & Small, J. (1988). *Counselling: The skills of problem-solving*. London: Routledge.

Nelson, M. L. & Nuefeldt, S. A. (1996). Building on an empirical foundation: Strategies to enhance good practice. *Journal of Counseling & Development, 74*, pp. 609–615.

Norcross, J. C. & Grencavage, L. M. (1989). Eclecticism and integration in counselling and psychotherapy: Major themes and obstacles. *British Journal of Guidance and Counselling, 17*, pp. 227–247.

Nuttall, E. V., Sanchez, W. & Webber, J. J. (1996). MCT theory and implications for training. In D. W. Sue, A. E. Ivey & P. B. Pedersen. *A theory of multicultural counseling & therapy*. Pacific Grove, CA: Brooks/Cole.

Paton, I. (1990). Perils and pleasures of private practice. In J. Small & T. Ambrose (Eds). *Counselling and guidance towards the nineties.* Massey University, Palmerston North: New Zealand Association of Counsellors.

Patterson, C. H. (1996). Multicultural counseling: from diversity to universality. *Journal of Counseling and Development, 74,* pp. 227–231.

Pawlovich, W. (1994). Establishing and maintaining competence: An ethical responsibility. In W.E. Schulz (Ed.) *Counselling ethics casebook: Case studies in professional behaviour.* Ottawa, Canada: Canadian Guidance and Counselling Association.

Peavy, R. V. (1996). Counselling as a culture of healing. *British Journal of Guidance and Counselling, 24,* pp. 141–150.

Pedersen, P. B. (1976). The field of intercultural counseling. In P. Pedersen, W. J. Lonner & J. G. Draguns (Eds). *Counseling across cultures.* Honolulu, Hawaii: University Press of Hawaii.

Pedersen, P. B. (1990). The multicultural perspective as a fourth force in counseling. *Journal of Mental Health Counseling, 12,* pp. 93–95.

Pedersen, P. B. (1991). Multiculturalism as a generic approach to counseling. *Journal of Counseling and Development, 70,* pp. 6–12.

Pedersen, P. (1993). The multicultural dilemma of White cross-cultural researchers. *Counseling Psychologist, 21,* pp. 229–232.

Pedersen, P. (1996). The importance of both similarities and differences in multicultural counseling: Reaction to C. H. Patterson. *Journal of Counseling & Development, 74,* pp. 236–237.

Pedersen, P. B. & Ivey, A. (1993). *Culture-centered counseling and interviewing skills.* London: Praeger.

Ponterotto, J. (1988). Racial consciousness development among White counselor trainees. *Journal of Multicultural Counseling and Development, 16,* pp. 146–156.

Ramondo, N. (1991). Cultural issues in therapy: On the fringe. *Australian and New Zealand Journal of Family Therapy, 12,* pp. 69–78.

Richardson, T. Q. & Molinaro, K. L. (1996). White counselor self-awareness: A prerequisite for developing multicultural competence. *Journal of Counseling & Development, 74,* 238-242.

Rogers, C. R. (1957). A note on "The Nature of Man". *Journal of Counseling Psychology, 4,* pp. 199–203.

Schulz, W. E. (1994). *Counselling ethics casebook.* Ottawa, Canada: Canadian Guidance and Counselling Association.

Seligman, M. E. P. (1996). The effectiveness of psychotherapy. *American Psychologist, 50,* pp. 965–974.

Sexton, T. L. (1996). The relevance of counseling outcome research: Current trends and practical implications. *Journal of Counseling & Development, 74,* pp. 590–600.

Sexton, T. L. & Whiston, S. C. (1996). Integrating counseling research and practice. *Journal of Counseling & Development, 74,* pp. 588–589.

Sheppard, G. W. (1994). Boundary violations in counsellor-client relationships. In W. E. Schulz (Ed.) *Counselling ethics casebook.* Ottawa, Canada: Canadian Guidance and Counselling Association.

Smith, L. T. (1989). On being culturally sensitive: The art of gathering and eating kina without pricking yourself on the finger. Keynote address to the New Zealand Psychological Society Conference, Auckland University, New Zealand. Typed manuscript.

Speight, S. L., Meyers, L. J., Cox, C. I. & Highlen, P. S. (1991). A redefinition of multicultural counseling. *Journal of Counseling & Development*, 70, pp. 29–36.

Spruill, D. A. & Benshoff, J. M. (1996). The future is now: Promoting professionalism among counselors in training. *Journal of Counseling and Development*, 74, pp. 468–471.

Steenbarger, B. N. (1992). Toward science-practice integration in brief counselling and therapy. *The Counseling Psychologist*, 20, pp. 403–450.

Sue, D. W. (1981). *Counseling the culturally different: theory and practice*. New York: Wiley.

Sue, D. W., Ivey, A. E. & Pedersen, P. B. (1996). *A theory of multicultural counseling & therapy*. Pacific Grove, CA: Brooks/Cole.

Sue, S. (1983). Ethnic minorities in psychology: a reexamination. *American Psychologist*, 38, pp. 583–592.

Sue, S. & Zane, N. (1987). The role of culture and cultural techniques in psychotherapy. *American Psychologist*, 42, pp. 37–45.

Talmon, M. (1990). *Single session therapy*. San Francisco: Jossey-Bass.

Thompson, R. (1995). Being prepared for suicide or sudden death in schools: strategies to restore equilibrium. *Journal of Mental Health Counselling*, 17, pp. 264–277.

Tyler, L. (1969). *The work of the counselor* (3rd ed.). New York: Appleton-Century-Crofts.

Vontress, C. E. (1979). Cross-cultural counseling: An existential approach. *The Personnel and Guidance Journal*, 58, pp. 117–122.

Waldegrave, C. T. (1990). Just therapy. *Dulwich Centre Newsletter*, 1, pp. 5–46.

Wall, M. D., Kleckner, T., Amendt, J. H. & duRee Bryant, R. (1989). Therapeutic compliments: Setting the stage for successful therapy. *Journal of Marital and Family Therapy*, 15, pp. 159–167.

Weiner-Davis, M. (1992). *Divorce busting*. New York: Simon & Schuster.

Weiner-Davis, M., de Shazer, S. & Gingerich, W. (1987). Building on pre-treatment change to construct the therapeutic solution: An exploratory study. *Journal of Marital and Family Therapy*, 13, pp. 359–365.

Weinrach, S. G. & Thomas, K. R. (1996). The counseling profession's commitment to diversity-sensitive counseling: A critical reassessment. *Journal of Counseling & Development*, 74, pp. 472–477.

Winslade, J. (1996). An interview with Tim Bond. *New Zealand Association of Counsellors Newsletter*, 16:5, pp. 42–44.

Answers to exercises

Chapter 5

Exercise 5.2

2a Physical conditions

  i Usually clients will feel most comfortable in position 2.

  ii Clients will often perceive a desk as a barrier between themselves and the counsellor, but some clients may welcome this distancing. Generally, the most welcoming positions are where both client and counsellor are alongside of or in front of the desk, positions two and three.

2b Eye contact

  Generally, position **ii** is the most comfortable for clients.

2c Movement, gestures, posture, stance

  Positions **i–iii** are usually intimidating; position **iv** is usually seen as welcoming.

Exercise 5.3

These situations may be threatening, irritating or anxiety-provoking to counsellors. In each case counsellors first will need to acknowledge and explore the feelings being expressed by the client.

Exercise 5.5

a (Solution focus) What improvements have you noticed in the last week or two?

  (Problem focus) You seem very upset. Would you like to tell me about it?

b (Solution focus) What have you been doing to cope with this situation?

  (Problem focus) I understand you've been made redundant. Should we talk about where this leaves you?

c (Solution focus) What useful things have you already thought of?

  (General, open inquiry) What would you like to talk about? or, How can I help you?

Exercise 5.7

1 b and c are open-ended.

2 a What was your reaction to completing the job inventory?

  b Why did you decide to leave school?

  c What possibilities are there for getting home?

  d What could have prevented the argument?

Exercise 5.8

1 Do their reactions suggest something else you could be doing differently?

2 What do you have to do to convince them of that?

3 Any ideas about things you might try?

Chapter 6

Exercise 6.3

1 a S; b G; c G; d S; e G; f G; g S; h S; i G; j G; k S; l S.

Chapter 7

Exercise 7.10

Sample Transcript Analysis:

Statement	Skill	Analysis
1 Wife: The problem is this: I have to do most of the housework and hold down a full-time job. I'm doing my best, but I can go only do so much! And on top of this I have to be this sexy, available lover! He just doesn't understand how much there is to do and how tired I am!		(Four issues seem to be emerging: being exhausted, not having enough time to do everything, feeling unappreciated, and being angry about her partner's demands and lack of understanding.)
1 Counsellor: You've mentioned several things at once, including not feeling appreciated for any of them. Which one should we talk about first?	Reflection of feeling plus sorting issues.	To affirm and recognise her anger, and to allow her to choose the direction the interview takes.
2 Wife: Yes, well it does anger me that he seems to expect so much. What I would really like to be able to do is make him understand just how hard I work!		(Client agrees with the reflection and chooses to focus on increasing her husband's understanding of her situation and getting some recognition for all she does.)
2 Counsellor: Has there ever been a time in your relationship when you have been able to do that with him?	Exception question.	Focuses on the positive by asking for examples of times when she did feel understood and appreciated, that is, times when the problem she described was not a problem.

Chapter 9

Exercise 9.1

Overall aims:

   a To develop in participants an understanding of the helping process and the skills necessary to engage with their clients as people, not problems;

   b To be able to identify client skills, strengths and desired outcomes;

   c To convey trust and hope to clients;

   d To compliment their successes and to identify realistic solutions to their concerns.

Exercise 9.2

   a *Open versus closed questions*: To enable participants to distinguish between open and closed questions and to use each type of question appropriately.

   b *Finding exceptions to problems:* To teach participants how to ask exception questions and how to identify and highlight those exceptions to problems that are client-initiated and controlled.

   c *Thinking aloud*: To teach participants to use the skill of thinking aloud and to identify times when its use is appropriate in helping others.

Appendix A

British Association for Counselling
Code of Ethics & Practice, May 1996[#]

For Counsellors

1 Status of this code

1.1 In response to the experience of members of BAC, this code is a revision of the 1992 code.

2. Introduction

2.1 The purpose of this code is to establish and maintain standards for counsellors who are members of BAC, and to inform and protect members of the public seeking and using their services.

2.2 All members of this Association are required to abide by existing codes appropriate to them. They thereby accept a common frame of reference within which to manage their responsibilities to clients, colleagues, members of this Association and the wider community. Whilst this code cannot resolve all ethical and practice related issues, it aims to provide a framework for addressing ethical issues and to encourage optimum levels of practice. Counsellors will need to judge which parts of this code apply to particular situations. They may have to decide between conflicting responsibilities.

2.3 This Association has a Complaints Procedure which can lead to the expulsion of members for breaches of its Codes of Ethics & Practice.

3 The Nature of Counselling

3.1 The overall aim of counselling is to provide an opportunity for the client to work towards living in a more satisfying and resourceful way. The term 'counselling' includes work with individuals, pairs or groups of people often, but not always, referred to as 'clients'. The objectives of particular counselling relationships will vary according to the client's needs. Counselling may be concerned with developmental issues, addressing and resolving specific problems, making decisions, coping with crisis, developing personal insight and knowledge, working through feelings of inner conflict or improving relationships with others. The counsellor's role is to facilitate the client's work in ways which respect the client's values, personal resources and capacity for self-determination.

3.2 Only when both the user and the recipient explicitly agree to enter into a counselling relationship does it become 'counselling' rather than the use of 'counselling skills'.

3.3 It is not possible to make a generally accepted distinction between counselling and psychotherapy. There are well founded traditions which use the terms interchangeably and others which distinguish them. Regardless of the theoretical approaches preferred by individual counsellors, there are ethical issues which are common to all counselling situations.

4. The Structure of this Code

This code has been divided into two parts. The Code of Ethics outlines the fundamental values of counselling and a number of general principles arising from these. The Code of Practice applies these principles to the counselling situation.

A.   CODE OF ETHICS

A.I   Counselling is a non-exploitative activity. Its basic values are integrity, impartiality, and respect. Counsellors should take the same degree of care to work ethically whether the counselling is paid or voluntary.

A.2 Client Safety:

All reasonable steps should be taken to ensure the client's safety during counselling.

A.3 Clear Contracts:

The terms on which counselling is being offered should be made clear to clients before counselling commences. Subsequent revisions of these terms should be agreed in advance of any change.

A.4 Competence:

Counsellors shall take all reasonable steps to monitor and develop their own competence and to work within the limits of that competence. This includes having appropriate and ongoing counselling supervision/consultative support.

B.   CODE OF PRACTICE

B.1 Introduction:

This code applies these values and ethical principles to more specific situations which may arise in the practice of counselling.

B.2 Issues of Responsibility:

B.2.1 The counsellor-client relationship is the foremost ethical concern, but it does not exist in social isolation. For this reason, the counsellor's responsibilities to the client, to themselves, colleagues, other members of the Association and members of the wider community are listed under separate headings.

B.2.2 To the Client:

Client Safety

2.2.1   Counsellors should take all reasonable steps to ensure that the client suffers neither physical nor psychological harm during counselling.

2.2.2   Counsellors do not normally give advice.

Client Autonomy

2.2.3   Counsellors are responsible for working in ways which promote the client's control over his/her own life, and respect the client's ability to make decisions and change in the light of his/her own beliefs and values.

2.2.4   Counsellors do not normally act on behalf of their clients. If they do, it will be only at the express request of the client, or else in the exceptional circumstances detailed in B.4.

2.2.5   Counsellors are responsible for setting and monitoring boundaries between the counselling relationship and any other kind of relationship, and making this explicit to the client.

2.2.6   Counsellors must not exploit their clients financially, sexually, emotionally, or in any other way. Engaging in sexual activity with the client is unethical.

2.2.7   Clients should be offered privacy for counselling sessions. The client should not be observed by anyone other than their counsellor(s) without having given his/her informed consent. This also applies to audio/video taping of counselling sessions.

Pre-Counselling Information

2.2.8   Any publicity material and all written and oral information should reflect accurately the nature of the service on offer, and the training, qualifications and relevant experience of the counsellor (see also B.6).

2.2.9   Counsellors should take all reasonable steps to honour undertakings offered in their pre-counselling information.

Contracting

2.2.10 Clear contracting enhances and shows respect for the client's autonomy.

2.2.11 Counsellors are responsible for communicating the terms on which counselling is being offered, including availability, the degree of confidentiality offered, and their expectations of clients regarding fees, cancelled appointments and any other significant matters. The communication of terms and any negotiations over these should be concluded before the client incurs any financial liability.

2.2.12 It is the client's choice whether or not to participate in counselling. Reasonable steps should be taken in the course of the counselling relationship to ensure that the client is given an opportunity to review the terms on which counselling is being offered and the methods of counselling being used.

2.2.13 Counsellors should avoid unnecessary conflicts of interest and are expected to make explicit to the client any relevant conflicts of interest.

2.2.14 If records of counselling sessions are kept, clients should be made aware of this. At the client's request information should be given about access to these records, their availability to other people, and the degree of security with which they are kept (see B.4).

2.2.15 Counsellors have a responsibility to establish with clients what other therapeutic or helping relationships are current. Counsellors should gain the client's permission before conferring with other professional workers.

2.2.16 Counsellors should be aware that computer-based records are subject to statutory regulations under the Data Protection Act 1984. From time to time the government introduces changes in the regulations concerning the client's right of access to his/her own records. Current regulations have implications for counsellors working in social service and health care settings.

Counsellor Competence

2.2.17 Counsellors should monitor actively the limitations of their own competence through counselling supervision/consultative support, and by seeking the views of their clients and other counsellors. Counsellors should work within their own known limits.

2.2.18 Counsellors should not counsel when their functioning is impaired due to personal or emotional difficulties, illness, disability, alcohol, drugs or for any other reason.

2.2.19. It is an indication of the competence of counsellors when they recognise their inability to counsel a client or clients and make appropriate referrals.

B.2.3 To Former Clients:

2.3.1 Counsellors remain accountable for relationships with former clients and must exercise caution over entering into friendships, business relationships, sexual relationships, training and other relationships. Any changes in relationship must be discussed in counselling supervision. The decision about any change(s) in relationship with former clients should take into account whether the issues and power dynamics present during the counselling relationship have been resolved and properly ended.

2.3.2 Counsellors who belong to organisations which prohibit sex with all former clients are bound by that commitment.

B.2.4 To Self as Counsellor:

2.4.1 Counsellors have a responsibility to themselves and their clients to maintain their own effectiveness, resilience and ability to help clients. They are expected to monitor their own personal functioning and to seek help and/or withdraw from counselling, whether temporarily or permanently, when their personal resources are sufficiently depleted to require this (see also B.3).

2.4.2   Counsellors should have received adequate basic training before comm-encing counselling, and should maintain ongoing professional development.

2.4.3   Counsellors are encouraged to review periodically their need for professional indemnity insurance and to take out such a policy when appropriate.

2.4.4   Counsellors should take all reasonable steps to ensure their own physical safety.

B.2.5 To other Counsellors:

2.5.1   Counsellors should not conduct themselves in their counselling-related activities in ways which undermine public confidence in either their role as a counsellor or in the work of other counsellors.

2.5.2   If a counsellor suspects misconduct by another counsellor which cannot be resolved or remedied after discussion with the counsellor concerned, they should implement the Complaints Procedure, doing so without breaches of confidentiality other than those necessary for investigating the complaint (see B.9).

B.2.6 To Colleagues and Members of the Caring Professions:

2.6.1   Counsellors should be accountable for their services to colleagues, employers and funding bodies as appropriate. The means of achieving this should be consistent with respecting the needs of the client outlined in B.2.2.7, B.2.2.13 and B.4.

2.6.2   Counsellors are encouraged to increase their colleagues' understanding of the counselling role. No colleague or significant member of the caring professions should be led to believe that a service is being offered by the counsellor which is not, as this may deprive the client of the offer of such a service from elsewhere.

2.6.3   Counsellors should accept their part in exploring and resolving conflicts of interest between themselves and their agencies, especially where this has implications for the client (see also B.2.2.13).

B.2.7 To the Wider Community:

Law

2.7.1   Counsellors should work within the law.

2.7.2   Counsellors should take all reasonable steps to be aware of current law affecting the work of the counsellor. A counsellor's ignorance of the law is no defence against legal liability or penalty including inciting or 'counselling', which has a specific legal sense, the commission of offences by clients.

Social Context

2.7.3   Counsellors will take all reasonable steps to take account of the client's social context.

B.3 Counselling Supervision/Consultative Support:

B.3.1 It is a breach of the ethical requirement for counsellors to practise without regular counselling supervision/consultative support.

B.3.2 Counselling supervision/consultative support refers to a formal arrangement which enables counsellors to discuss their counselling regularly with one or more people who have an understanding of counselling and counselling supervision/consultative support. Its purpose is to ensure the efficacy of the counsellor-client relationship. It is a confidential relationship (see also B.4).

B.3.3 Counsellors who have line managers owe them appropriate managerial accountability for their work. The counselling supervisor role should be independent of the line manager role. However where the counselling supervisor is also the line manager, the counsellor should also have access to independent consultative support.

B.3.4 The volume of supervision should be in proportion to the volume of counselling work undertaken and the experience of the counsellor.

B.3.5 Whenever possible, the discussion of cases within supervision/consultative support should take place without revealing the personal identity of the client.

B.3.6 The ethics and practice of counselling supervision/consultative support are outlined further in their own specific code: the Code of Ethics & Practice for the Supervision of Counsellors (see also B.9).

B.4 Confidentiality: Clients, Colleagues and Others:

B.4.1 Confidentiality is a means of providing the client with safety and privacy. For this reason any limitation on the degree of confidentiality offered is likely to diminish the usefulness of counselling.

B.4.2 Counsellors treat with confidence personal information about clients, whether obtained directly or indirectly or by inference. Such information includes name, address, biographical details, and other descriptions of the client's life and circumstances which might result in identification of the client.

B.4.3 Counsellors should work within the current agreement with their client about confidentiality.

B.4.4 Exceptional circumstances may arise which give the counsellor good grounds for believing that the client will cause serious physical harm to others or themselves, or have harm caused to him/her. In such circumstances the client's consent to a change in the agreement about confidentiality should be sought whenever possible unless there are also good grounds for believing the client is no longer able to take responsibility for his/her own actions. Whenever possible, the decision to break confidentiality agreed between a counsellor and client should be made only after consultation with a counselling supervisor or an experienced counsellor.

B.4.5   Any breaking of confidentiality should be minimised both by restricting the information conveyed to that which is pertinent to the immediate situation and to those persons who can provide the help required by the client. The ethical considerations involve balancing between acting in the best interests of the client and in ways which enable clients to resume taking responsibility for their actions, a very high priority for counsellors, and the counsellor's responsibilities to the wider community (see B.2.7 and B.4.4).

B.4.6   Counsellors should take all reasonable steps to communicate clearly the extent of the confidentiality they are offering to clients. This should normally be made clear in the pre-counselling information or initial contracting.

B.4.7   If counsellors include consultations with colleagues and others within the confidential relationship, this should be stated to the client at the beginning of counselling.

B.4.8   Care must be taken to ensure that personally identifiable information is not transmitted through overlapping networks of confidential relationships. For this reason, it is good practice to avoid identifying specific clients during counselling supervision/consultative support and other consultations, unless there are sound reasons for doing so (see also B.2.2.14 and B.4.2).

B.4.9   Any agreement between the counsellor and client about confidentiality may be reviewed and changed by joint negotiations.

B.4.10 Agreements about confidentiality continue after the client's death unless there are overriding legal or ethical considerations.

B.4.11 Counsellors hold different views about whether or not a client expressing serious suicidal intentions forms sufficient grounds for breaking confidentiality. Counsellors should consider their own views and practice and communicate them to clients and any significant others where appropriate (see also B.2.6.2).

B.4.12 Special care is required when writing about specific counselling situations for case studies, reports or publication. It is important that the author either has the client's informed consent, or effectively disguises the client's identity.

B.4.13 Any discussion between the counsellor and others should be purposeful and not trivialising.

B.5   Confidentiality in the Legal Process:

B.5.1   Generally speaking, there is no legal duty to give information spontaneously or on request until instructed to do so by a court. Refusal to answer police questions is not an offence, although lying could be. In general terms, the only circumstances in which the police can require an answer about a client, and when refusal to answer would be an offence, relate to the prevention of terrorism. It is good practice to ask police personnel to clarify their legal right to an answer before refusing to give one.

B.5.2   Withholding information about a crime that one knows has been committed or is about to be committed is not an offence, save exceptionally. Anyone hearing of terrorist activities should immediately take legal advice.

B.5.3   There is no legal obligation to answer a solicitor's enquiry or to make a statement for the purpose of legal proceedings, unless ordered to do so by a court.

B.5.4   There is no legal obligation to attend court at the request of parties involved in a case, or at the request of their lawyers, until a witness summons or subpoena is issued to require attendance to answer questions or produce documents.

B.5.5   Once in the witness box, there is a duty to answer questions when instructed to do so by the court. Refusal to answer could be punished as contempt of court unless there are legal grounds for not doing so. (It has been held that communications between the counsellor and client during an attempt at 'reconciliation' in matrimonial cases are privileged and thus do not require disclosure unless the client waives this privilege. This does not seem to apply to other kinds of cases).

B.5.6   The police have powers to seize confidential files if they have obtained a warrant from a circuit judge. Obstructing the police from taking them in these circumstances may be an offence.

B.5.7   Counsellors should seek legal advice and/or contact this Association if they are in any doubt about their legal rights and obligations before acting in ways which conflict with their agreement with clients who are directly affected (see also B.2.7.1).

B.6.   Advertising/Public Statements:

B.6.1   When announcing counselling services, counsellors should limit the information to name, relevant qualifications, address, telephone number, hours available, and a brief listing of the services offered.

B.6.2   All such announcements should be accurate in every particular.

B.6.3   Counsellors should distinguish between membership of this Association and accredited practitioner status in their public statements. In particular, the former should not be used to imply the latter.

B.6.4   Counsellors should not display an affiliation with an organisation in a manner which falsely implies the sponsorship or verification of that organisation.

Directive made by the Management Committee
23 March 1996

Membership of BAC is not allowed to be mentioned by any person or organisation in press advertisements, in telephone directories, on business cards, on letterheads, on brass plates, on plaques, etc. BAC members are encouraged to make oral and written statements to the public and potential clients in letters and pre-counselling leaflets. These statements must include the fact that membership of BAC is not a qualification in counselling but means that the individual, and where appropriate the organisation, abides by the Codes of Ethics & Practice and is subject to the Complaints Procedure of the British Association for Counselling. Copies of these Codes and the Complaints Procedure are available from BAC.

This directive does not apply to BAC Recognised Courses, BAC Accredited Counsellors, Supervisors, Trainers and Fellows who receive separate instruction.

B.7. Research:

B.7.1   The use of personally identifiable material gained from clients or by the observation of counselling should be used only after the client has given consent, usually in writing, and care has been taken to ensure that consent was given freely.

B.7.2   Counsellors conducting research should use their data accurately and restrict their conclusions to those compatible with their methodology.

B.8. Resolving Conflicts between Ethical Priorities:

B.8.1   Counsellors will, from time to time, find themselves caught between conflicting ethical principles. In these circumstances, they are urged to consider the particular situation in which they find themselves and to discuss the situation with their counselling supervisor and/or other experienced counsellors. Even after conscientious consideration of the salient issues, some ethical dilemmas cannot be resolved easily or wholly satisfactorily.

B.8.2   Ethical issues may arise which have not yet been given full consideration. The Standards & Ethics Sub-Committee of this Association is interested in hearing of the ethical difficulties of counsellors, as this helps to inform discussion regarding good practice.

B.9. The Availability of other Codes and Guidelines Relating to Counselling:

B.9.1   The following codes and procedures have been passed by the Annual General Meetings of the British Association for Counselling:

Code of Ethics & Practice for Counselling Skills applies to members who would not regard themselves as counsellors, but who use counselling skills to support other roles.

Code of Ethics & Practice for the Supervision of Counsellors exists to guide members offering supervision to counsellors and to help counsellors seeking supervision.

Code of Ethics & Practice for Trainers in Counselling & Trainers in Counselling Skills exists to guide members offering training and to help members of the public seeking counselling training.

Complaints Procedure exists to guide members of BAC and their clients resolving complaints about breaches of the Codes of Ethics & Practice.

Copies and other guidelines and information sheets relevant to maintaining ethical standards of practice can be obtained from the BAC office, 1 Regent Place, Rugby CV21 2PJ.

Guidelines also available:

Telephone Helplines: Guidelines for Good Practice is intended to establish standards for people working on telephone helplines (sponsored by British Telecom). Single copies available from Telephone Helplines Association, 61 Gray's Inn Road, London WC1X 8LT.

Copyright BAC 1992   Amended AGM September 1993

(Management Committee addition 1 May 1996)

Appendix B

New Zealand Association of Counsellors – Handbook November 1995
Te Ropu Kaiwhiriwhiri o Aotearoa

New Zealand Association of Counsellors Code of Ethics[#]

Introduction

The purpose of this Code of Ethics is to establish and maintain standards for Counsellors and to inform and protect members of the public seeking their services.

Ethical standards comprise such values as integrity, competence, confidentiality, and responsibility. Members of this Association, in assenting to this code, accept their responsibility to clients, colleagues, the Association, their agencies and society. The client's interest is paramount, but where counsellors have a conflict of responsibilities they have to use their considered judgment.

Principles and guidelines

This code of ethics expresses some ethical principles and then lays down some guidelines for the practice of counselling. This code cannot resolve all ethical issues, but it does provide a framework for addressing ethical and practice-related issues.

The nature of counselling

Counselling involves the formation of special relationships characterised by openness and trust. Counsellors seek to assist clients to increase understanding of themselves and their relationships with others and/or to develop more satisfying and resourceful ways of living and/or to bring about a change in their behaviour.

General principles

1. The principle of autonomy

Counsellors shall respect the dignity and worth of every individual, the integrity of families/whanau and the diversity of cultures. This implies respect for people's right to make decisions that affect their own lives, to choose whether or not to consent to anything that is done to them or on their behalf and to maintain their own privacy. Exceptions to the principle

---

#New Zealand Association of Counsellors, c/o James Shepherd (Executive Officer), PO Box 165 Hamilton. Ph: 64 7 8478 974;   Fax: 64 7 8478 974

of autonomy occur when there is clear danger to the client, counsellor or public at large and when the individual's competence to make a decision is clearly limited.

2. The principle of not doing harm

Counsellors shall avoid any diagnostic labels, counselling methods, use of assessment data or other practices which are likely to cause harm to their clients.

3. The principle of beneficence

Counselling is a helping profession which expects counsellors to act in ways that promote the welfare and positive growth of their clients. In situations where there is the possibility of both harm and benefit the responsibility is on counsellors to ensure that their own actions are chosen with a view to bringing about the greatest balance of good.

4. The principle of justice

Counsellors shall be committed to the fair and equitable distribution of counselling services to all individuals and social groups. Counsellors shall also promote social justice through advocacy and empowerment.

5. The principle of fidelity

Counsellors shall be honest and trustworthy in all their professional relationships.

The counselling relationship and client rights

Access

Any person shall have the right of access to appropriate counselling.

However counsellors should not assume that they are the most appropriate person to provide this counselling and should refer clients to another counsellor who might be in a better position to provide it by reason of their gender or culture or for any other reason as indicated by the client's needs.

Consent

Counsellors shall uphold the principle of free and informed consent for clients in counselling; that is to say that clients must be fully informed of what is meant by counselling and must freely consent to participate. Full information implies comprehension, and free consent implies a lack of pressure to comply with proposals. Participation in research should also be based on free and informed consent.

Confidentiality

Communication between counsellor and client shall be confidential and treated as privileged information unless the client gives consent to any particular information being disclosed. Exceptions to this principle occur when, in the professional judgment of the counsellor, there is clear and imminent danger to the client or others. This includes circumstances where the client's competence to make a decision is obviously limited. In these circumstances the counsellor shall take reasonable personal action or inform responsible authorities.

Any records of the counselling relationship are to be considered professional information for use in counselling. They should not be considered the property of the institution or agency by which the counsellor is employed.

When information gained from a counselling relationship is used for purposes such as counsellor training, supervision or research, the counsellor shall protect the client's identity.

Discrimination

Counsellors should recognise the dignity of the person and avoid discrimination against clients on the basis of their race, colour, sex, sexual orientation, social class, age or religious or political beliefs.

Impartiality

When dealing with more than one party counsellors shall offer their service without favouritism or bias either in word or action. Impartiality involves a commitment to aid all participants, in reaching mutually satisfactory agreements. Counsellors shall declare any previous acquaintance with a client which may prejudice their ability to remain neutral.

Group Counselling

In group settings counsellors should make every effort to protect individuals from physical and/or psychological harm resulting from interaction within the group.

Abuse of Power

Counsellors shall not abuse their position by taking advantage of clients for purposes of personal, professional, political, financial or sexual gain. Counsellors are responsible for setting and monitoring the boundaries between a counselling relationship and any other kind of relationship and for making such boundaries as clear as possible to the client.

Sexual Harassment

In the counselling relationship the client shall be free from the possibility of sexual exploitation or sexual harassment. Counsellors shall not engage in sexual activity with their clients.

Fees

Counsellors should, at the outset, clarify with clients, fees if any, and methods of payment. When setting fees the Counsellor should ensure that they are fair, reasonable, commensurate with the service provided and give due regard to the client's ability to pay.

Referral

Counsellors shall refer clients on when they cannot meet their needs. It is the counsellor's responsibility, as far as possible, to verify the competence and integrity of the person to whom they refer a client.

Termination

Counsellors shall work with clients to terminate counselling when the clients have received the help they sought, or when it is apparent that counselling is no longer helping them.

Competence and Professional Development

Counsellors shall not claim competence which they do not possess.

Counsellors shall monitor their counselling work through regular supervision by professionally competent supervisors.

Counsellors shall monitor and work within the limits of both their own competence and their own personal resources.

Counsellors shall seek ways of increasing their professional development.

Counsellors shall be vigilant in monitoring their fitness to practise as counsellors with respect to their emotional, mental, and physical health.

Counsellors shall withdraw from part or all of their counselling practice while their fitness is significantly impaired in any or all of these respects.

Responsibility to the Wider Community

Counsellors should advocate policies and legislation that promote social justice, improved social conditions and a fair sharing of the community's resources.

Counsellors should actively support the principles of partnership as embodied in the Treaty of Waitangi.

Counsellors should act to prevent and eliminate discrimination in the wider community against individuals and groups on the basis of race, colour, sex, sexual orientation, social class, age or religious or political belief.

Counsellors should seek to increase the range of choices and opportunities for all members of the community, with special regard for the disadvantaged.

Responsibility to Colleagues and the Profession

Counsellors should treat colleagues with respect, courtesy, fairness and honesty.

Counsellors should respect professional confidences about the clients of colleagues.

Counsellors should not solicit the clients of other colleagues and should avoid assuming professional responsibility for them without appropriate communication with the counsellor or agency concerned.

Counsellors should take action through appropriate channels against unethical conduct by other members of the profession, especially where it is harmful to clients.

Counsellors should adhere to professional standards in making known the availability of their services.

Counsellors should uphold and foster the values, integrity, knowledge and ethics of the profession.

Relationship with Employing Institutions

Counsellors should adhere to and uphold the ethics of the profession and should avoid compromising them in the face of institutional requirements.

Counsellors should seek to negotiate a clear job description for themselves when working within an organisation and should honour such a document when they have agreed to it. Employers have an obligation to shape their expectations of the roles of counsellors in relation to the ethics of the profession.

Counsellors should contribute to policy development and seek to maintain and improve the quality of service in their work setting.

Counsellors should promote Equal Employment Opportunity policies in their work settings. They should also promote equitable access to the services provided by the organisation in which they work.

It is unethical for counsellors to use their position within an organisation to recruit clients for their own private practice.

Index